# THE HIDDEN PLACES

*of*

*Lancashire*

*and Cheshire*

Written by *Jo Noel-Stevens & Martin Stevens*

Foreword by **ANGELA RIPPON**

# Acknowledgements

This book would not have been compiled without the dedicated help of the following : Zoe - Production, Fleur , Elaine & Michelle - Administration, Sarah - Artist, and last but by no means least, Jo Noel-Stevens and Martin Stevens - Writing & Research.

All have contributed to what we hope is an interesting, useful and enjoyable publication.

## OTHER TITLES IN THIS SERIES

The Hidden Places of North Yorkshire
The Hidden Places of Devon & Cornwall
The Hidden Places of Somerset, Avon & Dorset
The Hidden Places of Southern & Central Scotland
The Hidden Places of Yorkshire South, East and West
The Hidden Places of Nottinghamshire, Derbyshire & Lincolnshire
The Hidden Places of Oxfordshire, Buckinghamshire & Bedfordshire
The Hidden Places of Gloucestershire & Wiltshire
The Hidden Places of Hampshire & Isle of Wight
The Hidden Places of Lancashire & Cheshire
The Hidden Places of Hereford & Worcester
The Hidden Places of Norfolk & Suffolk
The Hidden Places of Cumbria
The Hidden Places of Sussex

ISBN 1-871815-90-8
First Published in 1991
© M & M PUBLISHING LTD
Tryfan House, Warwick Drive, Hale, Altrincham, Cheshire. WA15 9EA

Printed and bound in Great Britain by
The Guernsey Press Co. Ltd, Guernsey, Channel Islands.

# Introduction

THE HIDDEN PLACES is designed to be an easily used book. Taking you in this instance, on a gentle meander through the beautiful countryside of Lancashire & Cheshire: however, our books cover many counties and will eventually encompass the whole of the United Kingdom. We have combined descriptions of the well-known and enduring tourist attractions with those more secluded and as yet little known venues, easy to miss unless you know exactly where you are going.

We include hotels, inns, restaurants, caravan parks and camping sites, historic houses, museums, gardens and general attractions throughout each of these fascinating counties: together with our research onthe local history. For each attraction there is a line drawing and a brief description of the services offered. A map at the back of the book shows you exactly how to get to your destination and indicates the chapter relevant to each area. There is also a reference guide giving you full details of all the hotels, inns, etc., detailed.

We do not include firm prices or award merits. We merely wish to point out *The Hidden Places* that hopefully will improve your holiday or business trip and tempt you to return. Should we succeed in our intent, then please do greet your host or landlord and thank them for our pleasure which inspired us to prompt your visit.

# THE HIDDEN PLACES
## of
# *Lancashire & Cheshire*
## *Contents*

# Foreword

*How many times have you heard someone say "I don't know why we keep going abroad on holiday every year, when we haven't begun to explore or get to know our own country."*

*And it's true, Britain as a whole is full of the most wonderful countryside and coastline, and whether it is in the far west peninsular of Devon and Cornwall or in the Orkneys, we have some of the world's finest natural treasures. But it's the hidden nooks and crannies, the quiet places and the unexpected, that hold much of the true charm of any region.*

*Being a local helps, they have known about such places for generations. But the visitors may pass them by, and so miss many of the real pleasures.*

*So these books are by way of a privilege. Bringing you access to places, county by county, you may never have seen before. So enjoy, and perhaps understand why those of us fortunate enough to have been born here think of it as being God's own Kingdom.*

ANGELA RIPPON

# *Cottonopolis*

## CHAPTER ONE

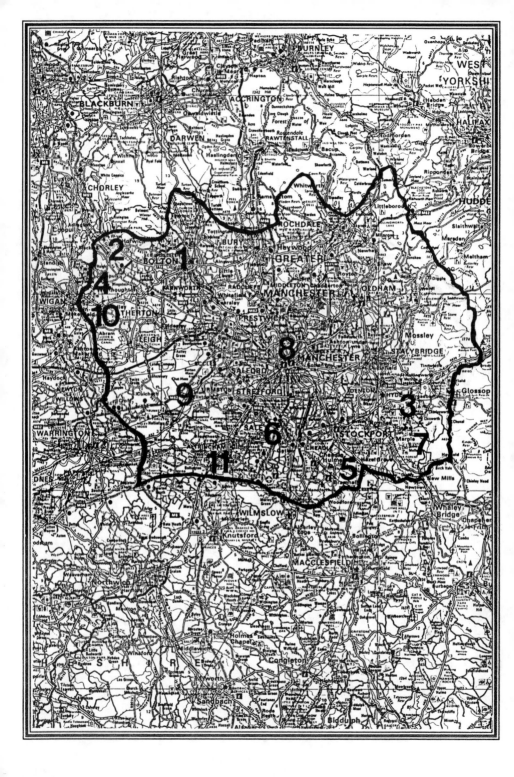

# Chapter One
# Map Reference Guide

*St. Peter's Square, Manchester*

CHAPTER 1

# *Cottonopolis*

Only a very short time ago, if anyone had suggested taking a short holiday in **Manchester,** they would have been regarded, to say the least, as eccentric, however now Manchester has a thriving tourist industry and is a popular destination.

What has changed? To a degree Manchester has. The city is cleaner, brighter than it ever was in the past, with purer air, cleaner buildings, green spaces and parks where once was dereliction. It also has a new regard for its extraordinary civic and industrial heritage, and whilst heritage is an overused word, it reflects the real interests and awareness of a new generation of visitors.

Manchester's history lies in Roman times with a small but important fort on the River Irwell, a tributary of the Mersey, where the road between Chester and York began its long ascent through the Pennine hills.

Roman Manchester is probably as good a starting point as any for a visit to the city. At Castlefields, just behind Deansgate, close to both Deansgate Station and the G-Mex exhibition centre, you'll find a replica fragment of a Roman wall and a small guard house on the actual site of the ancient fort of Mancunium. Manchester's real importance belongs to a later era, to the Industrial Revolution of the late 18th century and one particular product - the spinning and weaving of cotton.

It was Lancashire's mild, moist climate, together with the abundant water of fast flowing Pennine streams that created an ideal environment for the spinning and weaving of cotton. As far back as the 13th century, they were weaving cloth around Manchester - mainly wool. The mechanisation of the industry following the invention of Arkwright's Mule and Crampon's Spinning Jenny in the 18th century led to rapid growth of the industry, not so much in Manchester but in the rapidly growing towns and villages nearby - Bolton, Oldham, Ashton, Bury and Rochdale. Vast imports of raw cotton from the United States which came through the port of Liverpool along the Bridgewater and the Leeds-Liverpool canals were balanced by equally significant exports of brightly printed fabrics to the expanding British Empire.

Manchester became the region's great trading centre, affectionately called Cottonopolis, with its Exchange fixing the price of raw cotton worldwide.

You can still visit the Royal Exchange where much of this trading took place in the late 19th and early 20th century, a vast handsome building between Corporation Street and St. Anne's Square. When it was no longer needed for this purpose, rather than being demolished or altered beyond recognition, it was transformed into a remarkable Theatre and constructed inside the original great hall. The building still keeps its Cottonopolis flavour and character, but is now a leading centre for the arts in the North West.

Manchester's emergence into what historians describe as the world's first industrialised city was not just based on cotton. Good communications and easy access to nearby coalfields enabled it to grow rapidly as a major centre of engineering, initially forging mill engines to service the new mills, followed by steam locomotives, and as the 19th century progressed, a wide variety of heavy engineering equipment and machinery, from power stations and ship engines to aeronautics, much of it for export. Trade was given a considerable boost in 1894 with the opening of the Manchester Ship Canal, turning the city into a great inland port as sea going ships docked close to the city centre and in the adjacent Salford Docks.

Much of Manchester's industrial and engineering past can be understood from a visit to the remarkable Greater Manchester Museum of Science and Technology, also in Castlefields, which occupies a site of national importance - the actual Liverpool Road station of the pioneering Liverpool-Manchester Railway, at whose Rainhill trials of 1826 Stephenson's Rocket achieved immortality.

The little station waiting room has been beautifully restored, with passengers in period dress and the bell to summon them to the train in the style of a stagecoach, prior to departure. Steam train rides with replica or vintage locomotives are often arranged.

You'll also see the great Power House of working machinery, mill engines, power units and locomotives using a variety of fuels, all made within Greater Manchester, including a massive Beyer Garret steam locomotive from South African Railways made at Bayer Peacock's works in Gorton. In addition, you will find the Electricity House which tells the story of power generation, the Air and Space Gallery which emphasises links with the aeronautical industry and space technology, and 'Underground

Manchester' which features a reconstructed sewer of macabre realism through which you can walk. Of particular interest to children in an adjacent former warehouse is Xperiment!, a 'hands-on' science centre. Within easy walking distance of Castlefields is Granada Studios Tour. Granada Television's headquarters are in Water Street, and the company had the brilliant idea of opening part of the studios to the public, so you can visit the set of Coronation Street, sit in a replica House of Commons bench, or discover at 221B Baker Street the residence of Mr Sherlock Holmes.

However, Manchester City Centre is more than these things. You don't have to be in the city long, whether you arrive by train (the city lies in the centre of excellent network rail services, both Inter-City and suburban, now known as Network Northwest) or by car (there is an excellent system of well signed off-street car parking) before you begin to appreciate that you really are in a great European city. A superb heritage of late Victorian and early Edwardian warehouses and office blocks, some of them richly decorated and of monumental proportions, gives the narrow streets of the city centre a sense of wealth and importance which later sky-scraper office blocks can't match.

Albert Square is an inevitable focal point. The city's magnificent Gothic Town Hall, designed by Alfred Waterhouse and built between 1871 - 1877 at a cost of a million pounds, overlooks this now pedestrianised Square, with its memorial to the Consort and statues of freetrader John Bright and social refomer Oliver Heywood. The Town Hall's richly decorated interior includes wall paintings by the Pre-Raphaelite artist Ford Madox Brown, illustrating various aspects of the history of the city. The City's Tourist Information Centre is in the Town Hall extension, the St Peters Square side of the Town Hall.

Close by is another architectural masterpiece, the circular Central Library by the American architect Frank Lloyd Wright, built in the 1930s of white Portland stone. The Free Trade Hall in Peter's Street is the City's main concert hall where the world famous Halle Orchestra founded in 1857 by Sir Charles Halle performs. It stands on a site which had a tragic association with the 1819 Peterloo massacre, where a crowd of 60,000 meeting to debate Reform in the House of Commons were charged by local soldiery.

Links with this old Manchester can be found in and around the city's 15th century Cathedral, built in Perpendicular Gothic style, and beautifully restored after 1940s war damage with a wealth of delightful carving and unusual 18th century wrought-iron rails. Just across Fennel Street is the astonishing Cheetah's Hospital, built around a 14th century Manorial

7

Hall, and containing one of England's oldest and most remarkable libraries, together with a 'bluecoat' school that still survives in the traditions of its founder Humphrey Chetham, a Rector of Manchester who left a bequest which was used in the 17th century to turn the manor house into a college for poor boys. It is now a school for young musicians. A short walk away is another fragment of old Manchester, the half-timbered Shambles, carefully removed to its present position during 1960s development, but still an atmospheric Elizabethan building and popular city centre pub.

The City has long been a centre of learning and scholarship. Among its great men are John Dalton, the founder of atomic theory, and the physicist James Prescott Joule. Their intellectual inheritance is reflected in the two great Universities - Manchester University itself on Oxford Road, and the newer University of Manchester Institute of Science and Technology, which together with nearby Salford University and two large Polytechnics constitute one of the largest complexes of higher education in Western Europe. The Manchester Museum and the splendid Whitworth Art Gallery form part of the University complex on Oxford Road, the latter with an outstanding collection of watercolours that balances the fine collection of old masters and Pre-Raphaelites in the City Museum on Moseley Street. Beyond the University lies Platt Fields, a pleasant park which also houses the city's Costume Museum.

With such a large student population, it is not surprising that the city is a major cultural centre, with two large Victorian theatres, the Palace and the Opera House which take Opera and touring productions, as well as the Royal Exchange Theatre and the more experimental small scale Contact Theatre in the University. The city also has a variety of jazz and folk clubs and a lively night life, and a wide choice of eating places including Chinese restaurants, behind Piccadilly.

Most great cities throughout the world have a 'China Town', and Manchester is no exception. As one would expect, a thriving oriental pot pourri of restaurants, gift shops, warehouses and banks are to be found in this small area of Manchester. The Chinese influence on the area is signified by the enormous and beautiful pagoda styled archway, which is the symbolic entrance to China Town. However, there are restaurants from all parts of the Orient to be found here, including Japan, Thailand, India, Hong Kong, and all places East!

Food from a completely different part of the world can be enjoyed at a unique establishment in Barton Arcade in Barton Square.

**Ganders Go South,** but you might come from all points of the compass to visit this very special restaurant with the 'New Orleans feel'. There is

8

something very evocative about the words 'Cajun' and 'Creole', and when they are associated with food, you know you are in for a treat. Traditional dishes with an emphasis on fish and chicken conjure up the authentic taste of New Orleans. Gumbo and Jambalaya and Steak Teryaki are featured here, while chef Bruce Gregory will cook just about anything special you may wish for! And to accompany the excellent food, red hot or cool Dixieland jazz is provided by Don Long, the famous trombonist, and his band. Some of the true greats of the jazz world come here to play, and with names like Harry 'Sweets' Edison, Roy Williams and Kenny Baker on the bill, jazz enthusiasts make for this restaurant in droves. Owner Barry Lavin originally operated the wine bar 'Ganders' at Goose Green in Altrincham. The 'Go South' suffix relates to that 'Deep South' feel and atmosphere. Great cooking and live music combine to make this place a rare treat, not only for the customers but for the staff as well!

Lovers of French cuisine will be admirably served at **Brasserie St Pierre** in Princess Street. This highly recommended Brasserie is set in splendid surroundings, and is well worth a visit.

For Italian fare, we would have no hesitation in recommending two separate establishments for you to choose from. Better still, give yourself a treat and try both! The **Sannino Pizza & Pasta Restaurant** in Fountain Street is billed as 'World Famous', and rightly so if its fare is anything to go by. Modestly priced pizza and pasta dishes are there to be enjoyed in typically Italian surroundings and decor. Sannino also has branches in Glasgow and Leeds. The **Terrazza Italian Restaurant** in Dickonson Street is also highly recommended for its excellent Italian cuisine and service. It is located right in the heart of China Town - a really odd site for such a splendid example of Italian fare at its best!

The most popular shopping areas are from Piccadilly down pedestrianised Market Street, where most of the larger chain stores are, into the fashionable pedestrianised streets and courtyards around St. Anne's Square, off Deansgate and along King Street where speciality shops, bookshops and boutiques make this one of the most sophisticated areas of any city in Britain.

As you would expect, Manchester also has a great variety of good quality inns and public houses. We cannot possibly give you a comprehensive list in the space available, but the following places are certainly worth a visit.

On the corner of Fountain Street and Phoenix Street, the charming Tudor style **Chef & Brewer Tavern** stands out amidst the modern architecture surrounding it. The inn provides all the normal pub services and bar food on its ground floor, and has an excellent restaurant area on the floor above.

Situated in Shambles Square, **Sinclairs** stands on the original site of The Punch House, which was started by John Shaw in 1738. However, records indicate that a building has stood on this site since the 14th century. The Punch House housed the first Gentlemen's Club in Manchester, and was occupied by John Shaw until his death in 1796, at the age of 83 years. Around 1845, oysters were introduced to the premises, and alcoholic beverages some 20 years later. Fifteen square yards of the site of the old Punch House is now occupied by the north-west corner of Sinclairs. In 1971, along with the **The Old Wellington Inn,** the building was lifted as part of the City redevelopment, and it was re-opened by Samuel Smith's Old Brewery in 1981.

Also in Shambles Square, The Old Wellington Inn is one of the places where the commerce that made Manchester great began. In it lived some of the men and women who founded the City's first bank and cotton industry, and built its first quay. Also born here was the inventor of Phonetic Shorthand, John Byrom. Other inhabitants helped to found at least one City church and a hospital. The exact date of the building is unknown. A spurious date of 1328 was once displayed in the Inn, but experts now put its construction date at around 1550. Literally, the greatest upheaval the building had ever seen took place in the summer of 1971, when it was 'lifted' four feet nine inches during the construction of the Shambles Square Market Place development.

If you have ever fancied downing a pint of bitter in a library, you can 'quench' this ambition at Tetley's **'The Bank'** public house! It occupies the site of the old Portico Library in Charlotte Street, which is just at the back of Piccadilly and close to the Arndale Shopping Centre. Good pub food is also available in these most unusual surroundings.

For those of you seeking accommodation outside the heart of the city, **The Imperial Hotel** is just one and a quarter miles from Manchester city centre in Hathersage Road. It is a hotel worth staying at if you prefer to be away from the hustle and bustle of city centre life. It has recently been refurbished and extended throughout, and guests are given a very warm and friendly welcome. The hotel has twenty seven bedrooms, twenty of which have en-suite bathrooms. All are fully equipped with the usual amenities such as colour television and tea and coffee making facilities. Fully centrally heated throughout, there is a relaxing lounge bar together with a tastefully decorated dining room. The staff at the hotel are charming, and do their best to make guests feel comfortable during their stay. Ideally situated for both business people and holiday makers alike, the hotel is only a few minutes walk from local transport services. The BBC, Granada TV Studios, Manchester International Airport, the G. Mex Exhibition and Conference Centre are all within easy reach. For guests staying at the hotel with a car, there is ample convenient parking to the rear.

*The Imperial Hotel*

Manchester isn't just city centre, and it is surprisingly easy to escape into fine areas of countryside, for example Heaton Park, reached either by road on the A576 (the link to the M62) or by Bury line trains from the handsome old Victoria Station - soon to be replaced by Britain's first new high speed street "super" trams through the city centre. Acres of superb open countryside, a Regency house and formal gardens, boating lakes, a rare breeds centre and a restored old fashioned tramway system.

Much of this countryside lies within the satellite Metropolitan Boroughs that form the county of Greater Manchester. Including the City of Manchester itself, there are no less than nine constituent Boroughs around the central core, the others being - Salford, Wigan, Bolton, Bury, Rochdale, Oldham, Tameside and Trafford. All have their special qualities and areas of individual interest.

**Salford** is Manchester's twin across the River Irwell. Its art gallery in Peel Park in the Crescent by the River Irwell now contains the Lowry Centre, a tribute to L.S. Lowry, the great Lancashire artist who during the 1920s and 30s meticulously recorded a now vanished scene of industrial poverty and social hardship. The old Salford of Harold Brighouse's 'Hobson's Choice' and Walter Greenwood's 'Love on the Dole' has echoes in Lowry's paintings.

The biggest change in Salford is the emergence of Salford Docks as a major tourist and residential centre. Renamed **Salford Quays**, the waterfronts now provide a backdrop to apartments, pubs and walkways,

11

and are eventually to be served by a planned extension to the Metro. At the other side of the city lies a different kind of waterway heritage, the astonishing Bridgewater Canal basin at Worsley (reached by bus or the A572 road from the City Centre) where, in an area of lovely woodlands, you can see where the Duke of Bridgewater first opened his canal from his Worsely coal mines to the centre of Manchester in the 1760s. This new canal halved the price of steam coal and thus began the Industrial Revolution that helped to change the western world.

**Wigan** is the town that turned a music hall joke on its head. The old canal basin on the Leeds-Liverpool Canal had a coal wharf known as 'Wigan Pier', jokingly referred to by George Formby, and by George Orwell in a documentary book about working-class life in the North in the 1930s. But Wigan has used the complex of old warehouses and mills around the canal basin to create a new Wigan Pier, a major leisure attraction with its own Piermaster. There are canal boat rides, and remarkable exhibitions based on local social history of the "Way We Were", with costumed actors whose activities in the reconstructed schoolroom bring back not always anxiety-free memories of childhood.

Wigan isn't a town living in the past, but has a modern town centre, and it enjoys fine countryside such as the Douglas Valley with its Trail on its doorstep. Even its coal mining past has interesting links with the natural world - Pennington Flash, a large lake caused by mining subsidence, is now a wildlife reserve and country park.

One of Burtonwood Brewery's most popular public houses and restaurants can be found on the A6 between Chorley and Bolton at **Westhoughton.** Known as the **Waggon and Horses,** the building dates back to the 17th century. Visitors cannot fail to notice the  original stained glass windows, as they are constantly the subject of discussion.

*Waggon and Horses, Burtonwood Brewery*

12

Westhoughton is known to have had strong links with Royalty and the landed gentry, and this is depicted in detail by the skill of the craftsmen who originated the ingle windows. These illustrate scenes of various historical incidents which have occurred within the locality.

Substantial renovations took place in September 1990, with the emphasis on retaining the 'Olde Worlde' character of the lounge bar. This hospitable roadside inn and restaurant has now been enlarged to accommodate a 64-seater family restaurant which boasts spectacular, uninterrupted views of the West Pennine Moors and Rivington Hills. The restaurant is open seven days a week from lunchtime until late evening. The menu is impressive and caters for all tastes, including vegetarian. Meals can also be eaten in the lounge bar area.

Upon entering the premises, visitors are immediately impressed by the warmth and friendliness of the place. Above the open fireplace is an impressive hand crafted mural, which relates the story of the famous 'Keawyeds'. Apparently, this is Westhoughton slang for 'cow heads'. The story goes that a cow lodged its head in a five bar gate, and unfortunately the farmer was unable to get it unstuck. Faced with the dilemma of having to break the gate to free it, he chose the less expensive option and chopped the cow's head off!

The Waggon and Horses is well worth a visit when you are in the area. The warm and friendly manner of the staff creates an atmosphere conducive to relaxation, whether you are enjoying either a meal in the restaurant or a drink at the bar.

At **Standish,** on the A49 north of Wigan, you'll find another excellent eating house, the **Langtrees Restaurant.**

Part of the charm of New Langtrees Restaurant is that it is very much a family concern, with Derek and Pat Daniels managing the restaurant and son Steve, the Head Chef. There are at least four separate menus, all offering an amazing range of dishes. At Sunday lunch and high tea - the Langtrees speciality - there is a choice of four starters, eight main course dishes and a selection of sweets and coffee to follow. The imaginative a la carte menu, offering a combination of French and English cuisine in over thirty dishes, reflects Steve's culinary flair and is sure to please gourmets. There are separate menus for snack lunches, buffets and other special occasions as well as a children's menu.

Motorcycle enthusiasts of a previous generation may ponder nostalgically about the time when Langtrees was Lil's Transport Cafe, but they are sure to approve of the conversion. There is a friendly and comfortable air about New Langtrees, enhanced by the fine musical instruments on display.

Derek was once a member of a brass band and has talents that extend to a selection of wind instruments. Derek and Pat also offer limited bed and breakfast accommodation and there is a separate resident's lounge. All meals are served in the main restaurant.

*New Langtrees Restaurant*

**Bolton** is another mill town that defies expectations, its very fine Victorian town hall being the central point in a recently extensively refurbished pedestrianised shopping and leisure area with shopping malls, a restored market hall, a superb leisure centre including a swimming pool, the celebrated Octagon Theatre, and an excellent local museum.

Bolton Festival, at the end of August, is a very popular event. It runs for a whole week and there is a vast range of attractions, which include Morris Dancing and brass bands. The Victorian market is a favourite event, with everyone dressing up in full period costume.

A few minutes walk from the town centre is a most pleasant guest house - **Morden Grange.** It's near enough to enjoy the week at ease, but sufficiently far away to be well clear of any unavoidable noise. Built in 1907, the house is particularly distinguished for the lovely colours of the stained-glass in the windows of the front door, and the well-kept front garden is extremely colourful in spring. Inside the house, visitors are impressed by a large, antique pine staircase, beyond which two more stained-glass windows seem to light up the house.

Pam and Geoff Suter have just come to live here and are already gaining a good reputation, particularly for Pam's marvellous cooking. Her obvious delight in her culinary skills is totally justified, and Geoff is very proud and enthusiastic about her ability. A typical evening meal will be a three-course dinner, with a roast and freshly prepared produce which Pam buys daily. Breakfasts can be light or large, and special diets present no problems.

Pam and Geoff provide a very friendly and welcoming atmosphere. Throughout the house, everything is spotless and bright: the eight bedrooms are very spacious, and although none are en-suite, they are very well equipped with their own wash-basins and tea-making facilities. Satellite television is provided in each room and Geoff has a very good video collection which can be viewed in the bedrooms. There is also television in the lounge-cum-dining-room downstairs.

The town is close to the motorway network, so this is a most useful base in which to stay and explore the surrounding area.

*Morden Grange Guest House*

The Croal-Irwell Valley to the south of Bolton now forms part of one of the great countryside success stories of recent years. From Moses Gate Country Park southwards, a former derelict industrial valley has now been turned into a beautiful green corridor of lakes, streams, woods and walkways, supported by a lively warden and recreation service.

To the north of Bolton lie magnificent moorlands, forming the southern edge of the West Pennine Moors, through which walking opportunities abound, varying from full moorland hikes to gentle strolls. For example, there are lakeside walks in Jumbles Country Park around Jumbles Reservoir, the wide open moors around Winter Hill, and the lovely open parkland around Rivington and Anglezarke Reservoirs, including the Lever Park with its remarkable hanging gardens and medieval Tythe barns.

Further across the main A6 from Horwich, you'll find the village of **Blackrod,** and at Little Scotland, **Gallaghers Restaurant.**

This establishment is situated in such a position that on a clear day, visitors to the pub and restaurant can see the sea. The pub itself has been much improved with modernisation, but the restaurant is an entirely new addition. Built just over two years ago and opened in March of 1990, it has beamed ceilings and polished floorboards, and the tables are attractively laid with fresh flowers and sparkling cutlery and glasses.

The menu has been carefully put together, maximising the use of fresh produce which is locally available. The chef is pleased to prepare special dishes on request as long as 24 hours notice is given. Starters range from homemade soups to duck, smoked salmon, mussels, kidneys and avocado, and all are exquisitely garnished and beautifully presented.

The list of main courses are equally appetizing and accompanied by fresh vegetables or crisp salads. The calves liver cooked until pink and served with a Drambuie sauce and cream sounded particularly appealing, as did the king prawn wrapped in smoked salmon and fillet of lemon sole, lightly battered and deep fried until golden brown. Vegetarians are particularly welcome and a menu has been especially prepared for them.

*Gallaghers Restaurant*

It would be difficult to fault the standards set by Pat and Ann Gallagher, and even more difficult to justify the reasonable cost of £35 to include wine. Definitely worth a visit in our opinion!

A fine Pennine moorland backcloth is shared by **Bury,** a town famous for its black puddings, but like Bolton enjoying an attractively refurbished town centre. One recent fascinating development has been the reopening of the old railway line between Bury, Ramsbottom and Rawtenstall as the East Lancashire Steam Railway. The former Bolton Street Station is now a small museum, with regular steam services through the Upper Irwell valley at weekends and during holiday times.

**Rochdale** has its origins in medieval times. It lies in a shallow valley formed by the little River Roch on the slopes of the Pennines, whose broad summits just above the outskirts of the town are often snow covered in winter. Another once prosperous cotton town, its handsome Town Hall rivals Manchester in style if not in size.

Rochdale was the birthplace of both the 19th century political thinker, John Bright, and the celebrated entertainer Gracie Fields, but perhaps its chief claim to fame is with the birth of the Co-operative movement. In carefully restored Toad Lane to the north of the town centre, you'll find the world's first consumer Co-operative store, the Rochdale Pioneers.

Between Rochdale and **Littleborough** lies Hollingworth Lake, originally built as a supply reservoir for the Rochdale Canal, but for many years a popular area for recreation known colloquially as "The Weavers' Seaport", for cotton workers unable to enjoy a trip to the seaside. It is now part of the Hollingworth Lake Country Park with a fine visitor centre, and you can still enjoy trips on the lake as well as walks around its shores.

It's worth taking the A58 Halifax road from Littleborough to see the famous Blackstone Edge Roman Road, a stone causeway crossing this high Pennine pass. It is walkable from the roadside layby to the medieval cross, the Aigin Stone at its summit, a superb viewpoint over the entire Lancashire plain to the coast.

The great square red mills of **Oldham** still dominate the town, though many have now been put to new uses. The town, soon to be linked to central Manchester by the new MetroLink Supertram, is notable for its lively Coliseum Theatre and for its position close to superb scenery in the South Pennines and the Peak District, most notably the moorland villages of Delph, Denshaw, Dobcross and Uppermill. **Uppermill** lies in the upper reaches of the Tame Valley with lovely canalside walks (boat trips in the summer), a countryside centre at Brownless, local walks and an attractive village centre with millshops. Dovestones Reservoir, just in the Peak District, is a popular sailing and birdwatching centre.

Tameside was a name coined in 1974 to describe the District which includes the towns of **Stalybridge, Ashton, Hyde** and **Denton,** and other communities which fringe onto the Cheshire Pennine border. All have pleasant town centres with much of interest. The Church of St Michael and All Angels at Ashton, for example, is noted for its medieval glass, whilst St. Lawrence's at Denton has the nickname 'Th'owd peg' because reputedly neither nails nor metal were used in its construction, only wooden pegs.

The Tame and Etherow Valleys, both higher tributary valleys of the River Mersey, have been kept as attractive linear green spaces and walkways through otherwise busy urban districts, and contain some lovely areas of unspoiled countryside on the edge of both the Peak District and the South Pennines. The Etherow Valley includes the 200 acres of hilltop and grassy slopes that form Werneth Low Country Park.

For lovers of the rural life, we can think of no better place to stay than at **Needhams Farm** at **Werneth Low**. This is a farmhouse with a difference, and the hospitality shown to guests by proprietors Ian and Charlotte Walsh is exceptional.

Ian and Charlotte run a small working farm as well as providing first class accommodation. The farm is situated outside the boundary of the Peak National Park, and nestles between Werneth Low Country Park and Etherow Country Park. To locate the farm, one has to look first for Werneth Low road and then Uplands road. A courtesy service to and from the airport and Manchester's Piccadilly station is readily available with prior notice. We thought this an excellent idea for holidaymakers who enjoy walking and wish to leave the car behind.

The farmhouse dates from around 1590, and is warm, welcoming and comfortable. The accommodation is to a very high standard and has direct dial telephones, colour television, shaver sockets, clock radio's, hairdryers, and even a shoe cleaning box. As well as two double en-suite rooms, there is an en-suite family room, one double with private toilet, a twin and one single room.

Meals are taken in the cosy intimate dining room, which has a residential license. Ian and Charlotte provide evening meals which are freshly prepared with local produce and offer a choice of starters. These include french onion, lobster, and cream of salmon or pheasant soup. Renowned old favourites are also available and include egg mayonnaise, prawn cocktail with sherry sauce and farmhouse pate with whiskey or brandy. You will surely agree by now that this is definitely a farmhouse with a difference.

The main courses available are also imaginative, and guests may select from steaks, fish, chicken or beef, which are served in delicious sauces. Of course, a traditional farmhouse evening meal is on the menu every day and is equally good. Prices for an evening meal vary from seven pounds upwards and represent extremely good value.

Guests with children will be interested to note that the farm has two highland cows named Honeybucket and Honeybun, who have calves known as Petal, Princess, and Primrose. The atmosphere of the farm is totally relaxed and informal - so much so that guests wishing to drink from the bar are encouraged to help themselves and write down what they have had in a book. The hospitality which Ian and Charlotte afford their guests can only be described as truly British at its best, and we would highly recommend the farm to lovers of the rural life or 'townies' wanting to escape to the tranquility of the countryside.

*Needhams Farm*

The Mersey Valley leads into **Stockport,** a town famed for its 700-year-old market, part of which is in a handsome Victorian market hall. The huge century-old brick archways of the town's main railway viaduct form a striking feature across the town. The outer fringes of Stockport edge onto the green slopes of the Peak District and include towns such as **Marple** in the Goyt Valley, noted for the Peak Forest Canal, part of the 100 mile Cheshire Canal Ring.

The **Springfield Hotel** in Marple is ideally situated for both the tourist and the business person alike. The Peak District with its exciting scenery and magnificent walks is just a short drive away. In Marple itself is the natural canal basin, and this is where the Macclesfield and Peak Forest Canals meet.

Mr and Mrs Bellamy are the owners of The Springfield Hotel and although they have only been resident proprietors for the past two years, they have considerable experience of the hotel and catering industry behind them. Easy to find, the hotel is situated on the A626 road from Marple to Marple Bridge. The interior of the hotel is superbly decorated and extremely comfortable, and everything one could wish for in a small select hotel can be found on the premises.

The seven bedrooms are all en-suite and beautifully furnished. No expense has been spared when it comes to the comfort of the guests. Tastefully decorated with coordinating fabrics and furnishings, the rich mahogany furniture lends an air of elegance and charm to each room. The lounge has a comfortable and welcoming atmosphere, with a lovely open fire and superb views across open parkland. Licensed drinks are dispensed from a wonderful Victorian drinks cabinet in an informal and relaxed manner.

The dining room can best be described as sumptuous, with crisp white linen table cloths and gleaming cutlery and crystal adorning the tables. Breakfast and dinner are served in this exquisite setting, and on colder days and evenings a lovely open fire adds warmth and ambience to the room. Here, guests can enjoy a pleasant dinner in relaxing surroundings whilst selecting from the table d'hote menu. Meals are prepared and served by the owners, as is the carefully selected wine list.

*Springfield Hotel*

Just south of Stockport, you will find a very special place which should feature high on your list of essential places to visit. **Bramall Hall** is considered to be one of England's finest treasures. The building has immense charm and a wealth of character. Its structure has been altered and extended many times, but the classic 'magpie' effect has been retained. The Hall stands in a park which was landscaped by its Victorian owner Charles Nevill after the much loved style of Capability Brown. It affords a grand vista, reaching from the terraces across to the lawns, lakes and the trees beyond.

Bramall Hall is now enjoying one of its most exciting periods, with the assistance of the English Heritage and generous public donations. Stockport MBC has recently renovated the building and conserved the magnificent Tudor wall paintings. Now there is a major programme to restore the Hall's furnishings, the park and the gardens to the splendour of their heyday. The oldest parts of Bramall Hall were built as long ago as 1375, but the building has since seen many alterations, both inside and out. For example, there was once an entire extra floor which was removed in about 1815 because of fears that it was too heavy for the supporting timbers. It was in 1375 that the estate came to John de Davenport through his marriage into the local family. Their coat of arms can be seen in the 15th century stained-glass within the Great Hall.

Originally, the Lord of the Manor had the power to sentence local criminals to death, and at one time this was depicted by two large rather grisly looking busts of felons above the main gates. These have now been removed, and can be found in the Great Hall on either side of the magnificent fireplace. Also to be found in the Hall are unique wall paintings, which were painted in the 16th and 17th century. In the Ballroom, the walls are painted as a tapestry. One scene shows two wild boars attacking a hunter, while the other depicts musicians playing and singing. It is actually possible to read the 400-year-old tune on their music sheet. Bramall Hall's greatest treasure is a heraldic table carpet made around 1565. It is nearly twenty feet long and was used to cover the high table. It bears the Tudor shield, together with shields recording family marriages back to 1397.

*Bramall Hall*

The wealth of 19th century industrialists in this area is shown by the acquisition of the Hall in 1883 by Charles Nevill, owner of the cotton printing mill at Strines. He made many improvements to the house and park, and his influence is reflected in the Victorian furnishings in several of the rooms. The exterior of the Hall is a superb example of black and white Tudor architecture, and is distinctive of England's contribution to world architecture. The Hall stands in nearly 100 acres of fine parkland and is a most attractive place to explore. Throughout the year programmes of events are organised, including regular concerts of both classical and jazz, workshops, exhibitions, and brass rubbing to name but a few. The Stable Cafe offers homemade snacks, lunches and teas, and there are two safe play areas for children to enjoy.

To the north of Stockport lies the Mersey Valley Country Park, which as its name suggests is a linear Park along the river, with walking and riding routes alongside the River Mersey, leading into a series of lagoons and lakes that form Sale Water Park, noted for sailing and birdlife.

Sale Water Park lies in the Borough of Trafford, which takes its name from one of the country's greatest industrial estates, Trafford Park, home of MetroVick and other great industrial giants. In fact, Trafford is also one of the greenest of Greater Manchester's boroughs, taking in the pleasant leafy suburbs of **Altrincham** and **Hale** as well as **Urmston** and **Sale.** Manchester's International Airport is within Trafford, as is Old Trafford Cricket Ground, home of Lancashire Cricket and England Test Matches, and the nearby Manchester United Ground and Football Museum.

**Dunham Massey Hall,** on the B5160 Lymm road out of Altrincham, is one of Cheshire's most outstanding National Trust properties. It was built in 1732 for George Booth, the 2nd Earl of Warrington, who commissioned the then little known architect John Norris. It was John Norris who perceived the idea of encasing an earlier Tudor building. The 2nd Earl was also responsible for laying out the park, and purchasing the 18th century collection of furnishings and Huguenot silver. The house and estate subsequently became the principal home to the 9th Earl of Stamford in 1905. It was he who commissioned another architect by the name of Compton Hall to undertake the alterations to the south and front of the house, which we see today.

The interior of the house and its refurbishment owes much to the sensitivity of Percy Macquoid, who handled the redecoration of the state rooms. He is acknowledged as being one of the finest and most distinguished furniture historians. The house was bequeathed to the National Trust in 1976 by Roger the 10th Earl of Stamford. Many of the paintings, prints and photographs are of the prominent Booth and Grey family, who through their association with Dunham Massey have left their mark for future generations to appreciate.

As visitors wander through the house, they can catch a glimpse of personal possessions such as documents and books which formerly belonged to members of the Booth and Grey families. One cannot fail to be impressed by the craftsmanship, richness and elegance of such a magnificent house with such fine furnishings.

In sympathy with the house, the garden is in the process of being restored by the Trust, and broadly speaking is in the character of the late-Victorian Pleasure Ground. The Trust has managed to retain modified parts of the Edwardian scheme such as the parterre, and the notable remnants of earlier schemes. Organised events such as midsummer music evenings are staged throughout the year. Visitors are encouraged to visit the licensed restaurant for refreshments and the National Trust shop for souvenirs.

*Dunham Massey Hall*

The **Lennox Lea Hotel** in Sale is situated in a quiet tree-lined cul-de-sac. This attractive Victorian building stands in its own grounds and offers ample free car parking. Experienced travellers will know that a hotel is only as good as its staff, and you are certainly assured a warm welcome and friendly attentive service from the proprietor John Wormald and his highly professional team. John's brother Michael takes care of the restaurant and banqueting facilities which the hotel has to offer. From the purchase of fresh market produce through to the preparation of breakfast or a sumptuous Wedding Banquet, Michael ensures that guests receive only the very best.

The Lennox Lea retains the style and elegance of past times whilst providing up to the minute facilities. The interior of the hotel is beautifully appointed and sumptuously furnished. The cocktail bar enables guests to enjoy a friendly and relaxing drink, either in the bar itself or on the garden terrace. The Alexander Suite Restaurant offers a varied and imaginative menu with distinctive cuisine. The ambience of the dining room makes it an ideal venue, whether you are dining for business or for pleasure. Each of the 31 bedrooms are luxuriously furnished and have en-suite bathrooms or shower, with colour TV, movie channel, direct dial telephone, and of course a hospitality tray. The hotel's function rooms cater admirably for special occasions, and have proved to be extremely popular for weddings, banquets and professional dinners.

*The Lennox Lea Hotel*

If you take the A6144 out of Sale, then turn onto the B5158 Urmston road, you will first come to **Flixton.** It was here that we discovered a superb place to dine.

**Harrison's** is a small and cosy family run restaurant where the customer's enjoyment is foremost in the minds of owner Craig Cavanagh and his attentive staff. At Harrison's, the atmosphere is warm and friendly, and the cuisine is of the highest standard. Every dish on the menu is prepared and cooked to order, using only the freshest and finest ingredients. There is a wide selection of dishes on the menu, including many vegetarian dishes and a comprehensive wine list to suit every palate and pocket. Harrison's 7* star table d' hote menu is an exceptional value four course meal, plus your favourite choice of liqueur.

*Harrison's*

The cuisine is French and English, and the menu comprises over 20 starters and 40 main courses, plus a wide selection of sweets, all made to order. Open Tuesday to Saturday evening from 7 pm until 10.30 pm, and Sunday lunchtime from 12 pm until 4 pm, Harrison's is closed on Sunday and Monday evenings. Whether you are looking for a quiet dinner for two or a great evening out with friends, Harrison's has to be close to the top of the list. Craig Cavanagh, who is also head chef, has worked in such places as The Royal Oak Hotel (Egon Ronay Restaurant of the Year), and the Savoy Hotel on the coast.

*Hall i' th' Wood, Bolton*

# *East Lancashire*

## CHAPTER TWO

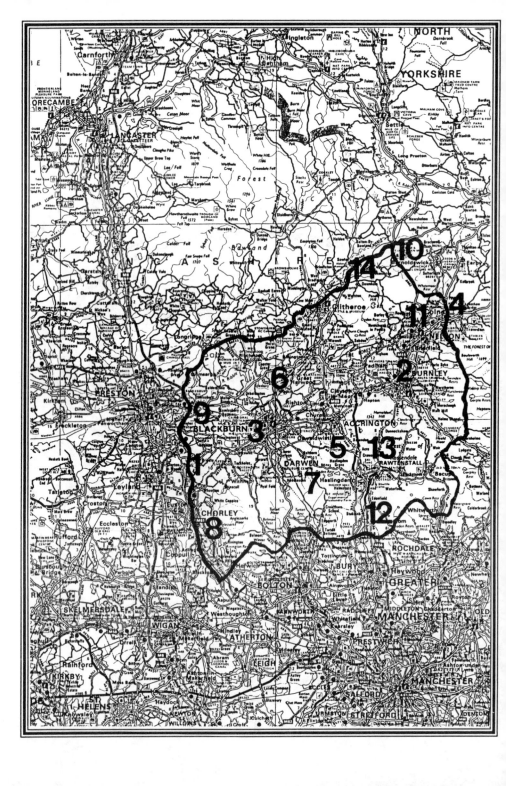

# Chapter Two
# Map Reference Guide

| Name | Map Ref No |
|------|-----------|
| Astley Hall. | 8 |
| Cavendish Arms | 1 |
| Crown Hotel | 11 |
| Doug Moore Boatbuilders | 10 |
| Fernbank Guest House | 8 |
| Gaghills House Hotel | 12 |
| Genevieve | 10 |
| Herders Inn | 11 |
| Hole In The Wall | 4 |
| Malt Shovel | 2 |
| May House Restaurant | 3 |
| Monks House | 10 |
| Moon's Mill | 9 |
| Mytton Fold Farm | 6 |
| Old Rosin's Inn | 7 |
| Valley Aquatics | 5 |
| Weavers Cottage | 13 |
| Wytha Farm | 14 |

*Pendle Heritage Centre, Banonford*

CHAPTER 2

# *East Lancashire*

If Manchester is Cottonopolis, East Lancashire is the Cotton Capital's hinterland, a series of densely populated towns crowding into the Pennine valleys, each with its own special character and close to open moorland landscape of desolate grandeur.

Pendle Hill, that great whaleback of a mountain, dominates the northern part of this region. It is a constant feature on the skyline, giving its name to the District which includes the towns and villages on its eastern flank.

This is an area rich in legend and history - nothing is more evocative than the tragic story of the Pendle Witches who, in the early 17th century, in an atmosphere of superstition and prejudice, were brought to trial at Lancaster Castle and either imprisoned or executed on the flimsiest of evidence. Among these were a notable gentlewoman, Mistress Alice Nutter of Roughlee, near Barley, and two old, half crazed women, Mothers Demdike and Chattox, on whose wild confessions Alice Nutter met her fate.

Something of that old, dark tragedy still broods around Pendle, made much of in Harison Ainsworth's romantic novel, 'The Lancashire Witches'.

For all that, this is countryside of intimate beauty. You can take a choice of routes north of Burnley or Nelson into Barrowford and on to Barley, where there is a car park and a small Visitor's Centre, and from where there is a popular, well marked path to the summit of Pendle Hill. This is a steep climb, but affords a magnificent viewpoint across to the coast, and on clear days, Yorkshire's Three Peaks and the Lakeland mountains beyond. There are delightful walks along the little valley formed by Pendle Water, perhaps to White Hough and Mistress Nutter's home - now a farmhouse - in Rough Lee, or around the nearby reservoirs of Lower and Upper Black Moss, the brooding outline of Pendle Hill always a presence.

A town on the edge of Pendle that few visitors wish to miss is **Whalley,** with its grey ruined Cistercian Abbey, founded in 1296, and rich in historic and architectural interest. The grounds are open to the public. The town of

31

Whalley itself has great character and charm, and lanes link it to the village of Sabden, from where a steep and scenic pass crosses Nick o' Pendle, a notable viewpoint and hair raising descent towards Pendleton, Clitheroe and the Ribble Valley.

Just south of Whalley lies the village of **Langho.** Guests staying at **Mytton Fold Farm Hotel** in Langho are assured of a warm Lancashire welcome from the proprietors, Mr and Mrs Hargreaves. Frank and Lillian Hargreaves are the third generation to own this 100 acre farm, which has been tastefully extended and modernised over the years. Mytton Fold Farm is set in the beautiful Ribble Valley and boasts splendid views of Pendle Hill and the surrounding Ribble countryside.

Once a traditional farmhouse dating back to 1702, it has now been transformed. Originally a four bedroomed house, in just eight years it now boasts 27 en-suite bedrooms and two bridal suites with four poster beds. Each of the rooms are named after local birds and trees, and provide all the usual facilities one would expect from a first class hotel.

Prior to dining in the restaurant, guests are encouraged to relax in the lounge bar, which has an original cast iron fireplace dating back 130 years. The lounge bar and restaurant are open to the public, but there is also a resident's lounge for anyone wishing to sit quietly. The restaurant is renowned for the standard of the food it serves, and specialises in home cooked food using fresh local produce wherever possible.

Family run, the Mytton Fold Farm Hotel really does provide a first class service, in a tranquil and peaceful setting. Little can be faulted, if anything, and the friendliness of the management and staff is assured.

*Mytton Fold Farm Hotel*

**Barrowford,** to the north-east of Pendle Hill, is an interesting village to explore, most especially the fascinating Pendle Heritage Centre at Park

Hill. This is a group of 17th and 18th century farm buildings built by a local family, the Banisters, and now containing a fascinating exhibition area telling the story of Pendle, and an audio-visual display on the facts known about the Lancashire Witches.

It's only a short way from Barrowford along the Leeds-Liverpool canal to **Foulridge.** A stroll or boat trip along the canal almost inevitably includes dropping in to the **Hole in the Wall Inn** for a refreshing pint of real ale and a sustaining bar snack. Bed and breakfast accommodation is also available in four rooms which have lovely views.

Sandra and John Stather have a reputation for their warm hospitality and homemade food. The menu is simple and selective because everything is freshly prepared daily and served individually to order. Sandra's home-made pies are a favourite and the traditional Sunday lunch is always well attended.

The darts board and pool room are among the Inn's other attractions, and musical guests are encouraged to share their talent on a rather fine organ. Pictures adorning the walls include one of a local by-gone celebrity - 'Buttercup' the cow. The story goes that when this hapless animal fell into the canal, she was to swim a mile before finally being rescued near the inn and successfully revived with a tot of whiskey! Anglers will be pleased to know that there is also the opportunity to catch fish!

*Hole In The Wall Inn*

North of Foulridge on the B6251 is the old town of **Barnoldswick.** The Leeds-Liverpool Canal passes from Lancashire into Yorkshire on the outskirts of town. In Gillians Lane, off the Colne Road, you'll find the Bancroft Mill Engine, the last of 13 mills to be built in the town. The mill closed down in 1978, but the engine has been fully restored and is now in perfect working order. This is in fact a complete working museum, and on Steaming Days you will be able to see how the mill operated in its heyday.

**Monks House** is run by a super couple who are friendly, warm and hospitable. Catering for overnight bed and breakfast, Monks House is both comfortable and inexpensive. The house is nicely situated in the centre of the town, close to the Mill Engine Museum. A listed building, it was originally a farm and dates back to the 18th century. In addition to bed and breakfast, an evening meal is provided if required. The traditional English breakfast is large and really sets guests up for the day.

If you are looking for a day or a week on the water, then we can thoroughly recommend the luxury narrow boat hire centre at **Doug Moore (Boatbuilders) Ltd.** This is run by Doug and Marie Moore from the Lower Park Marina on the B6383 Kelbrook Road. They also operate a working boatyard, and its situation on the summit pound of the Leeds-Liverpool Canal is lovely. Here, the waterway climbs out of the industrial backcloth of the Lancashire mill towns and enters into the soaring Pennine hills and dales.

There are three types of hire available: daily, short-term, or weekly - the choice is yours. The boats are fully equipped with excellent facilities, and on arrival you are given every assistance and full instructions in handling the craft. This will include accompanied help as you tackle the first locks (not applicable for daily hire) and you will soon gain confidence to negotiate these yourself. The boats are both easy to handle and very quiet to operate, making this a pleasurable and gentle way to see the best of the surrounding countryside.

*Doug Moore Boatbuilders*

The shop is stocked with unusual ideas for gifts - many with a nautical theme, like painted ware, brassware, books and maps. To be sure of having the appropriate map or guide so you can do your homework before you arrive, you can always give Doug and Marie a call and order them beforehand! The telephone number is (0282) 815883.

Touring can be an exhausting business, no matter how enjoyable it might be. If you are feeling hungry after your visit to Barnoldswick, we would strongly urge you to stop off at **The Genevieve Restaurant,** just opposite the Civic Hall in Station Road. Carole and Gerry Stone are the proprietors of this super little restaurant. Carole is the chef and Gerry is her willing helper. Gerry hails from County Kildare where he once worked on a stud farm, and he is very interesting to talk to if you happen to be a horse racing enthusiast! The Genevieve is renowned for its excellent English home cooking, and it has become so popular with the local older generation that Carole also provides a 'meals-on-wheels' service. As well as serving reasonably priced daily specials, you can also obtain an excellent Sunday Lunch here.

These days, we find that more and more people tend to opt for farmhouse holidays rather than the conventional bed and breakfast, or guest house accommodation. Frances and Brian Oliver who run **Wytha Farm** are two such people. Originally from the North East, Frances and Brian have lived on Wytha Farm since 1973. A warm and friendly couple, Frances looks after the farmhouse and Brian is kept busy tending the farm.

Brian's knowledge of the area is substantial, and he will happily spend the evening helping guests to plan their daily outings. Frances provides guests with a superb English farmhouse breakfast and evening meal, and likes to add the personal touch by using home-grown produce. Packed lunches can be ordered in advance, and cots are available for young children on request. The standard of service and accommodation is excellent and represents good value for money.

*Wytha Farm*

35

The farmhouse is situated between Gisburn and Colne at **Rimington,** just a few miles east of Sawley Abbey. The views from Wytha Farm are outstanding, and guests can be shown around the farmyard and enjoy the use of the garden. The tendency for holidaymakers to take their pets with them has increased considerably during the last few years, and Brian and Frances are quite happy to accommodate them if they are well behaved.

**Colne** is another mill and market town, with lines of sloping grey roofs stretching along a gentle hillside above the valley formed by Colne Water. Here you'll find a monument on the main road near the War Memorial to one Wallace Hartley, who had the misfortune to be bandmaster on the Titanic in 1912. He heroically stayed at his post, conducting the band in 'Nearer my God to Thee' as the doomed liner was sinking beneath the icy Atlantic.

Ray and Derinda Britton are the publicans of **The Crown Hotel** in Colne, and they are experienced publicans who always provide customers with a warm and friendly welcome. The hotel is situated on Albert Road, which is the main A56 connecting Colne with Nelson and Burnley. The hotel has six bedrooms, all with en-suite facilities. A private snooker room with full size table is one of the hotel's features and is popular with guests. The restaurant has a full a la carte menu as well as the chef's specials of the day. Bar snacks and meals can also be ordered from the bar.

To the east of Colne, the moorlands rise to the bleak summits of the Pennines, but one particular hamlet is of special interest - **Wycoller,** reached either from the main A6068 Keighley road at Laneshaw Bridge or via the mill village of Trawden.

This almost deserted Pennine village was once a thriving handbook weavers' settlement that lost most of its inhabitants when new factories took trade away. Wycoller Hall, now a ruin, was the inspiration for the setting of Ferndean Manor in Charlotte Bronte's 'Jane Eyre'. The Brontes, keen walkers, would often have walked over here from Haworth. Much remains of interest in the village - a lovely old hump-backed packhorse bridge crossing Colne Water, and above the village, a single slab gritstone bridge, Clam Bridge, thought to be Iron Age in origin.

The settlement now forms part of Wycoller Country Park, and you must leave a car in the car park to walk a few hundred yards down the hill into the village. At Hall Barn Information Centre there are displays about village history and local natural history, and a choice of easy walking trails in and around the Country Park are available.

**The Herders Inn** is a beautiful Freehouse Inn dating back over 300 years. It is situated on the main road between Colne, Wycoller and

Haworth. A large detached stone-built building, the Inn has glorious views across the Lancashire Moors and Bolsworth Hill. Penny and Allan Hutchinson have been in residence at The Herders Inn for eight years now and have built up an enviable following of locals. Customers travel from far and wide to sample their warm hospitality and excellent service. Traditional Ales are a strong feature of the Inn and have proved to be extremely popular with visitors and locals alike. Whilst Allan is in charge of the cellar, Penny takes great pride in the catering side of the business. Bar snacks are always available, and the Inn has become renowned for its traditional, speciality Sunday Lunches. However, if you decide to call in for lunch on a Sunday we would strongly recommend that you arrive early to avoid disappointment. An interesting feature in the bar is a wall plaque relating the history of the Inn over the last 300 years. We cannot speak highly enough of this well kept and superbly run inn, and definitely recommend a visit if you are in the area.

*The Herders Inn*

**Burnley** is another East Lancashire cotton town rich in history. The Weavers Triangle, on the Manchester road, is a remarkable collection of cottages and workshops around the canal basin, and Queen Street Mill, which was the last working steam powered cotton mill in Lancashire, is now a heritage centre.

The name **Malt Shovel Hotel** seems to conjure up expectations of real ale and a traditional English pub atmosphere, and visitors will not be disappointed. Derek and Christine Allen run this locally popular family pub, where Lancashire-brewed beer is on tap and good bar snacks and light meals are available throughout the day. The varied menu includes one or two house specialities such as chilli-con-carne and steak-pie cooked in ale. Children's portions are available on request and there is plenty on the menu to appeal to their tastes. In the large, well-tended beer garden, there is a children's play area for families who may enjoy sitting outside in the warmer summer months. Indoors, there is also a games room for the convenience of guests.

Only half a mile from the M65, the Malt Shovel Hotel is not only a good base from which to tour, but also a convenient place to break a journey. Members of the English Tourist Board, Derek and Chris offer accommodation in four large, well-equipped bedrooms. There is a residential dining room and a separate television lounge for residents only.

*Malt Shovel Hotel*

Townley Hall and Park, on the A671 Todmorden road to the east of the town, is a fine area of parkland with a grand, neo-Gothic country house. It was formerly the home of the Townley family and is now Burnley's main art gallery and museum, with outstanding collections of furniture, paintings, ceramics, archaeology and local history, as well as frequently changing temporary exhibitions.

About two miles to the west of Burnley on the A671 near Padiham lies Gawthorpe Hall, a beautiful early Jacobean house first built between 1600 and 1605 and restored in the 1850s by Sir Charles Barry. It was the home of the Kay-Shuttleworth family, social reformers, until 1972, and now belongs to the National Trust. It houses the Rachel Kay-Shuttleworth textile collection as well as part of the National Portrait Gallery collection. There are craft workshops, attractive gardens and a cafeteria.

Moorland roads south from Burnley lead over and into Rossendale, a District which includes the towns of **Bacup** and **Rawtenstall.**

Bacup, like Manchester, lies on the River Irwell, here little more than a stream. It is a compact community, whilst Rawtenstall has one of the region's most popular dry ski slopes, Ski Rossendale. It is now the terminus of the East Lancashire Steam Railway, and has one of the most delightful

38

of Victorian museums, Rossendale Museum, in the grounds of Whitaker Park.

**The Weavers Cottage** at Rawtenstall is one of the finest remaining examples of its period. The increased production of woollen thread due to Hargreaves' invention of the Spinning Jenny led to similar 'loomshops' being built throughout the mid-Pennine area in the late 1700s, as enterprising weavers employed their families and neighbours to increase business. Wool weaves best when dry and warm, hence the south-facing facade of the Cottage with its many windows.

A working handloom and spinning wheel can be seen on the top floor, and the Cottage also has an early Victorian Kitchen and a Clogger's workshop as well as a wealth of local history displayed in the form of pictures and maps. It is situated on Bacup Road, on the A681 opposite Rawtenstall Cricket Field, and is open summer weekends and Bank Holiday Mondays from 2 to 5 pm.

*The Weavers Cottage*

Another museum definitely worth a visit is the **Whitworth Museum** in North Street, **Whitworth.** The display room here is crammed with exhibits and photographs which explore the history and people of the town and surrounding district. Run by the Whitworth Historical Society, the Museum is entirely dependent on local support and would be glad of your interest. The Museum is open on Tuesdays from 7.30 - 9.30 pm, and Wednesdays and Saturdays from 2 - 4 pm.

The A681 from Rawtenstall will take you east to **Waterfoot,** and here you will find accommodation in a house of great character. **Gaghills House Hotel** is a splendid old mill house, built in 1868. This excellent example of 19th century architecture is set in its own mature gardens, and the location of Waterfoot in the heart of the Rossendale Valley has much to offer in the way of historic and scenic interest. In fact, the house itself was for many years the home of Sir H.W. Trickett, one of the pioneers of the footwear industry in Rossendale. On entering the reception area, the oak panelled hall and staircase are an immediate attraction. The resident's lounge and dining room both retain the original stained glass windows and minster stone fireplaces. The fully licensed dining room with its moulded ceiling adds to the atmosphere and original character of the house. All of the bedrooms are en-suite, with colour television, coffee and tea making facilities, direct dial telephone and radio. Hair dryers are available on request. The area has an abundance of leisure activities, including tennis, squash, snooker, fishing, golf, bowling, badminton, swimming and skiing. There are also plenty of nature parks and rambles for walkers.

*Gaghills House*

At **Helmshore,** just south of the main road between Rawtenstall and Haslingden, and best reached along the B6214 from Haslingden, you will find the Helmshore Textile Museums. These include the 18th century Higher Mill with its 18 foot diameter rim-geared waterwheel and fulling stocks still in working order, as well as early textile carding and spinning machines, including an early Hargreaves Spinning Jenny. The Museum of the Lancashire Textile Industry is situated in an adjacent three storey mill, where cotton spinning is demonstrated together with exhibitions of bobbins and weaving.

A passing interest in fish could easily turn into a serious hobby after a visit to **Valley Aquatics,** on Flip Road in **Haslingden.** Barry and Linda Price are specialists in 'Nishiki Goi', more commonly known as Japanese Koi Carp, with the largest stocks in Britain. There is also a large selection of other cold-water and tropical varieties and never less than 25,000 fish on view, ranging from specimens which are three-inches to eight times that in length! The larger species include 'Pacu' - a vegetarian Piranha - catfish and lungfish. On the extensive landscaped site there are two large ponds, a covered stock-pond, a showroom with Koi tanks and forty tropical tanks. There is also a seating and refreshment area and an enormous lake stocked with thousands of superb fish. Barry and Linda buy in the fish when they are small and rear them at the centre, and there is the opportunity to see the quarantined growing area through special viewing windows.

In addition to fish stocks, snapper turtles, terrapins and fancy ducks, Valley Aquatics provides a complete service for the fish-keeper, whether an amateur setting up a first aquarium or a specialist requiring the fixtures, fittings and plants for a complex pond. This is a great place to take the family for a fascinating day out.

*Valley Aquatics*

**Blackburn** is the largest town in East Lancashire, notable for its modern shopping malls, its Market Hall, its celebrated three day market, its modern Cathedral incorporating the nave of the 1826 building, and Thwaite's Brewery, one of the largest independent brewers of real ale in the North. The Lewis Textile Museum is devoted to the cotton industry and explores the development of cotton spinning and weaving from cottage looms to modern factories. The Museum and Art Gallery in Museum Street has among its many treasures eight paintings by Turner, the Hart collection of medieval manuscripts, an outstanding collection of Japanese prints and antiques, and the finest collection of Eastern European Icons in Britain.

In Blackburn in 1888, John Stringer, a machinist and mill furnisher, built May House, an imposing building which reflected his considerable standing in the area. It is assumed that he named the house after one of his daughters, but it was more probably named after Mary, his wife.

41

The decoration in the house is unique and splendid. 'May' is featured over the mahogany fireplace, and May dancers, in soft colours, encircle the lounge ceiling in a marvellous frieze by Italian craftsmen. There is mahogany panelling, and delicate stained glass (frequently used in this house) depicts the signs of the zodiac. Some parts of the house are still being meticulously renovated and restored to their former splendour.

**May House Restaurant** is now in the capable hands of partners Shirley Archibald and Mark and Carole Broadbent. Their combined experience in the hotel and catering business is obvious from the moment you enter this superb building. It is rare indeed to find such elegance hand in hand with the warmth and friendliness which is much in evidence here. You are made to feel most welcome - every attention is given to your needs, enabling you to relax and enjoy the delicious food, which is skilfully prepared and served in the professionally unrushed manner to which you would like to become accustomed.

Mark is a highly qualified chef with a wealth of experience, both in this country and also in Austria. He creates his own individual style of cuisine with great flair, using interesting combinations of fresh local and exotic produce. His imaginative menus, which are changed weekly, include a variety of tempting dishes for vegetarians.

*May House Restaurant*

May House is conveniently placed for people touring the area. Just five minutes walk from the restaurant is Witton Park, a popular family outing with its sports facilities, including athletics track, surrounded by some 480 acres of woodland and rolling farmland with waymarked walks. A short drive northwards from May House will, within ten minutes or so, bring you to medieval Salmesbury Hall, where there are frequent antique fairs as well as art and craft exhibitions featuring the work of local artists and craftsmen. Alternatively, within the same amount of time you could be approaching the breathtaking scenery of the Trough of Bowland.

Eanam Wharf, on the Leeds-Liverpool Canal in Blackburn, is a restored area of huge canal warehouses now superbly transformed into attractive craft workshops, offices and waterside bars.

About five miles west of Blackburn, off the A675 road towards Preston, lies Houghton Tower, a fortified Tudor mansion defensively positioned on a hilltop overlooking the River Darwen. This was the ancestral home of the de Houghton family, and it was in the Banqueting Hall in 1617 that the loin of beef being enjoyed by His Majesty King James I so delighted the monarch that he knighted it, and it has been known as 'Sirloin' ever since. The house is open to the public, and the King's bedchamber, audience chamber, ballroom and other fine rooms are in a superb state of preservation. There are also exhibitions of historic documents, dolls and Chinese teapots, and a fine rose garden.

Just before the A675 crosses the M6 and leads into Preston, you will come to **Higher Walton.** Definitely worthy of a visit when you are in the vicinity is **Moon's Mill Craft Museum and Gallery.** Not only is the gallery of particular interest to craftsmen and women, but the building itself has a chequered history of different uses. Originally built in 1883, this quaint timber fronted building was once known as the Reading Room. Situated on the corner of Kittlingborne Brow, it provided refuge as a leisure centre for mill workers. Upstairs, the men could play billiards, downstairs there was a reading room, and after a hard day's work, visitors were able to enjoy the luxury of a bath.

*Moon's Mill Craft Museum & Gallery*

A far cry from days gone by, Moon's Mill now houses some of the finest craft work to be found in Lancashire. The walls are adorned with various types of crafts, including proprietor Dorothy Horsfall's own unique collection of Swiss straw lace, corn dollies and other straw-work. Admired by many local craftsmen and women, she has become well known in the area for her own particular forte - every third weekend she teaches straw-work to enthusiastic students.

Other craft work on view ranges from jewellery, woodwork, embroidery and quilting, to canalware, pottery and pyrography. One corner of the museum is devoted to a picture history of Higher Walton. Downstairs, the museum combines a sales area with a tea room serving homemade food.

At **Brindle,** on the B5256, you'll find the **Cavendish Arms.** The summer of 1990 was an especially busy time for Peter Bowling and his fiancee, Alison, who run the pub. This pretty village was celebrating the eight hundredth anniversary of its church, which is immediately next door. Week-end events featuring Field Days, Sheepdog Trials, and Craft Fayres went on well into December to mark the occasion.

Set at right angles to each other, the church and the pub look as pretty as a picture, as the saying goes. Their pasts are closely linked - indeed, there has been a pub on this site since the church was first built. But behind this picturesque scene there are memories of bloody and historic events.

In 1530, the Gerard Arms stood here. The present building, named after the Cavendish family who lived at Holker Hall, dates from the 17th century, and the history of the pub and the area are depicted in pictures hanging in the private function room upstairs. But the really distinguishing features here are the stained-glass windows, which tell the story of the momentous Battle of Brunanburgh. It took place nearby in the year 937 AD, and united England under one king for the first time. One of the scenes shows King Athelstan receiving a new sword to replace his broken one. In another, some surviving Vikings stop in their flight to bury a chest of treasure. This Cuerdale treasure was not re-discovered until 1840.

The framed account of the full story of the battle hangs in the bar. Here, there are many more features to admire - beams and brasses, open fires and low ceilings, and a 'duck or grouse' doorway to one of the rooms. The taproom contains a glass case displaying a stuffed hare. From the days before blood sports became controversial, the quaint inscription celebrates this valiant quarry, who eluded the hounds for 37 minutes on 3rd November 1875.

Picturesque, historical, a garden for good weather - and good food, too! Trained as a chef, Peter offers attractively presented homemade bar food in the pub.

*Cavendish Arms*

South of Blackburn lies **Darwen,** another town dominated by cotton mills and moorlands. The West Pennine Moors surround the town and offer wonderful opportunities for the walker, the naturalist or the fisherman. There are Information Centres at Roddlesworth to the west of the town above Sunnyhurst Wood, and at Clough Head above Haslingden Grane. A favourite local walk is to Darwen Tower, a distinctive moorland monument and landmark, built in 1897 to celebrate Queen Victoria's Diamond Jubilee and the opening of Darwen Moors to the public. Inside are 80 spiral steps to the viewpoint at the top. Another popular area is around Entwistle (served by the scenic West Pennine Railway line between Blackburn and Bolton) and Turnon Bottoms, leading down to Jumble Country Park or past Edgworth to Peel Tower above Holcombe. The Tower was built in 1851 in appreciation of Sir Robert Peel, founder of the modern police force, who was born in nearby Bury.

Just outside of Darwen is **Hoddlesden,** and here, in exceptionally pleasant surroundings, **The Old Rosin's Inn** offers a comprehensive list of facilities for the most discerning of clients and customers. These facilities range from a simple bar meal to banqueting requirements. Whether you stay for a day or a week, or simply visit for a meal or a drink, you are assured the hospitality of the resident proprietors Bryan Hankinson and Brenda Fletcher, who will do their very best to make your visit an enjoyable one.

A recent publication entitled 'What's Inn a Name' invited its readers to amplify the account of how The Old Rosin's acquired its name. According to the local butcher, John Cox, Rosin was his grandfather and John was actually born in the pub. Legend goes that in the good old days a local band would often rehearse in the rooms above the pub, and John's grandfather, correctly named John Townshend, would conduct them. When he wanted the band to emphasise something he would tap his baton and shout 'Come on Lads, give it some ROSIN'. This subsequently became the nickname by which the pub is officially referred to today.

Due to the acquisition of adjoining cottages, the pub has also become a hotel of considerable size and standing. The Old Rosin's now affords high class accommodation, an excellent restaurant and the kind of hospitality rarely found these days.

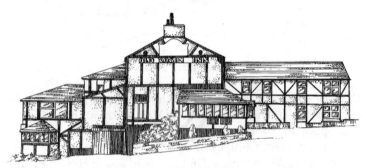

*The Old Rosin's Inn*

Further west lies Rivington Pike, a moorland summit capped by a tower which rises up to 1,191 feet above sea level with spectacular views over the Lancashire plain. The Pike now forms part of an attractive Country Park which includes Lever Park with its gardens and Tythe barns, and the immense length of Rivington and Anglezarke Reservoirs which supply the city of Liverpool with fresh water. This partly explains why a scale model of the long vanished Liverpool Castle was built in Lever Park by Lord Leverhulme.

William Hesketh Lever, later Lord Leverhulme, founded Port Sunlight in 1888, and built his soap and detergent empire into what became the huge Unilever Corporation. He bought a large estate in Rivington and built a country house now demolished, but the gardens and parkland remain, a gift by Lord Leverhulme to the town and people of Bolton. It is now a delightful Country Park, with refreshments available at the two restored Tythe Barns.

If Lever Park is associated with soap, the nearby town of **Chorley** is linked with sugar, being the birthplace of Henry Tate in 1819. He was the founder of Tate and Lyle sugar refiners, and benefactor of the London art gallery that still bears his name - the **Tate Gallery**.

46

Chorley town dates back to an ancient settlement which existed here in Roman times, but Borough status was probably given in 1250, and the town has had a market since at least 1498. The covered market still takes place on Tuesdays, Fridays and Saturdays, with an open air or 'Flat Iron' market on Tuesdays. St Laurence dates back to 1360, but was restored in the early 19th century, and its parish register reputedly once contained the birth of Myles Standish, the Captain of the New England Puritans who sailed from Plymouth in the Mayflower in 1620.

But the jewel of Chorley is **Astley Hall,** situated in 105 acres of beautiful wooded parkland. Visiting the hall is like a voyage into the past, to the time of late Tudor and early Stuart England. The structure reflects the grand building styles and elegant and lavish interior decoration of several periods. During its history, Astley Hall has been tenanted successively by five affluent families, and each has imprinted their own taste on the external and internal restoration, influenced by the various fashions and magnificent treasures of that glorious age.

In 1922, the last heir, Reginald Arthur Tatton, made a gift of the country house, many of its contents and adjacent surrounding acres, to the Chorley Corporation. About the same time, the park was purchased by the War Memorial Committee in memory of those lost in the First World War, and it was donated to the town two years later.

*Astley Hall*

There are some splendid views in the landscaped park, where the floral features are a riot of colour. Wooded walkways with footbridges cross the River Chor and a large lake contains a carpet of waterlilies in summer. Adjacent to the house are bowling and putting greens, tennis courts, a cafe,

47

and a picnic area. A childrens' play-area is equipped with swings, roundabouts, climbing frames and paddling pool, and a pets corner accommodates a variety of birds and animals. For those interested in the local wildlife, a nature trail has been established through the wooded area of the park.

Fernbank, at Bolton Road in Chorley brought us to the **Fernbank Guest House.** This establishment is run by Catherine Blanchfield and her two daughters. New to the business of running a guest house, Catherine is sure to succeed as she has lots of enthusiasm, confidence and charm.

If you are in the area, it would be as well to bear in mind that not only do they offer bed and breakfast facilities here, but during the summer months, afternoon teas as well. Overnight car parking is not a problem, which makes the guest house ideal for touring the West Pennine Moors and the Rivington Country Park.

*Turton Tower, Chapeltown, Blackburn*

# Lancaster and the Forest of Bowland

CHAPTER THREE

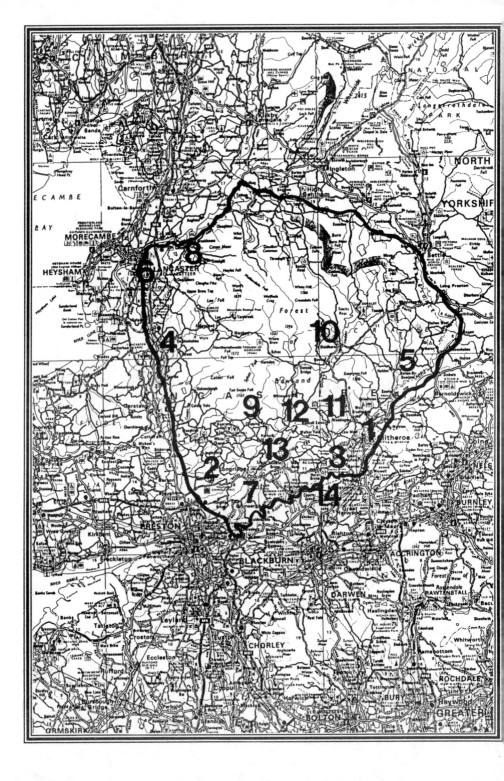

# Chapter Three
# Map Reference Guide

| Name | Map Ref No |
|------|:----------:|
| Baygate Farm | 5 |
| Brickhouse Hotel | 9 |
| Brooklyn Guest House | 1 |
| Charnley House | 7 |
| Corporation Arms | 2 |
| Elliots | 6 |
| Farmers Arms Hotel | 6 |
| Greenbank Farmhouse | 4 |
| Harrop Fold Country Hotel | 5 |
| Hodder Bridge Hotel | 12 |
| Hough Clough Farmhouse | 9 |
| Meadow Side | 13 |
| Mitton Green Barn | 3 |
| Mitton Hall | 3 |
| Moorcock Inn. | 11 |
| Old Post House | 1 |
| Pages Farm | 10 |
| Parrock  Head Farmhouse Hotel Hotel | 10 |
| Red Rose Cottages | 1 |
| Royal Kings Arms Hotel | 6 |
| Scarthwaite Country Hotel | 8 |
| Brown Leaves Hotel | 14 |

*Stoneyhurst College*

CHAPTER 3

# Lancaster and the Forest of Bowland

The ancient city of **Lancaster** on the River Lune proudly boasts of its 'Legacy', which extends back many centuries. Unlike York, which has long been internationally known as a tourist attraction, its Red Rose cousin has taken longer to be discovered.

In fact, Lancaster has an equally important place in English history, and there is much for the serious visitor to explore. It's also a surprisingly compact city, easily reached either by road, just off the M6, or by rail from a centrally positioned station where most Inter-City trains call.

Within yards of the railway station you'll find Lancaster Castle, a great medieval fortress, founded by the Normans to keep out Scottish invaders, and strengthened by John of Gaunt, Duke of Lancaster, in the 15th century. Its huge, square keep dates back to 1200, and was raised in height and impregnability at the time of The Armada. Astonishingly, perhaps, most of the building still functions as a prison, but certain sections are open to the public, including the 18th century Shire Hall, the cells, the Crown Court, Hadrian's Tower and, a touch of the macabre, the Drop Room where prisoners were prepared for the gallows.

Close by is a building with less grim associations - the lovely Priory Church of St. Mary, which once served a Benedictine Priory established here in 1094. Most of the present church dates from the 14th and 15th centuries, and particularly interesting things to see are fragments of Anglo-Saxon crosses, magnificent medieval choir stalls, and some very fine needlework. Nearby is a link with Roman Lancaster - the remains of a bath house which also served soldiers as an inn.

A short walk from the Castle leads into the largely pedestrianised city centre, for shops, the market and much besides. The City Museum, in the Market Place, occupies the Old Town Hall, built between 1781-3 by Major

55

Jarrett and Thomas Harrison. As well as the city's art collection and an area of changing exhibitions, you'll find displays and collections of material illustrating aspects of the city's industrial and social history. Also here is the Museum of the King's Own Royal Regiment, a regiment which was based in Lancaster from 1880 onwards.

In Church Street is the Judges' Lodging, a beautifully proportioned building dating from the 1620s when it was built as a private house for Thomas Covell, but later used for judges during the Lancaster Assizes. It now houses two separate museums, the Museum of Childhood containing the Barry Elder doll collection, and a Furniture Museum containing many examples of the workmanship of Gills, the famous Lancaster cabinetmakers.

Around the corner in Sun Street is the Music Room, an exquisite early Georgian building originally designed as a pavilion in the long vanished garden of Oliver Marton. It is notable for some superb decorative plasterwork.

If you are staying in Lancaster for either business or pleasure why not try the unsurpassed levels of luxury and service that **The Royal Kings Arms Hotel** has to offer. OVernight accommodation at this hotel will indeed make your stay in Lancaster a memorable one. The hotel is ideally situated for easy access to the city centre and attractions that Lancaster has to offer. The elegance of the unique Priory Restaurant, provides a perfect setting for perhaps enjoying afternoon tea seated beneath the Minstrels Gallery. The variety of the Royal Kings Arms presents both guests and visitors with delicious new and exciting standards in cuisine. It is indeed a pleasure to unwind in the mellow corners of the hotel's lounge bar, or enjoy a relaxing drink in the popular 'Kings' bar.

*Royal Kings Arms Hotel*

For bunisess travellers, the hotel offers the city a central conference facility, and the venue is perfect for delegates who wish to get down to business and utilise the extensive facilities and services available. The bedrooms are light, airy and unashamedly luxurious. All of the rooms throughout welcome. No expense has been spared in providing home from home considerations. Those of course include en-suite with in-house videos, direct dial telephones, writing desks, hairdryer, trouser press and a welcome refreshment tray. The staff are caring and considerate in a way that will make you feel absolutely at home during your stay.

Market Street is where you will find one of Lancaster's finest eating establishments. 'Elliots' eating house is run by Michael Diver and is renowned for its 'ample portions', graphically illustrated by customers who rarely leave without expressing a hearty 'phew!' Close to the museums and Castle, the building dates back to the 1830s, and is situated on two floors. The ground floor is devoted to the restaurant and the upper floor doubles up as a coffee and drinks lounge. The seating arrangements can accommodate up to 55 diners, most of whom return time and time again in order to enjoy the excellent choices available on the menu.

*'Elliots'*

Michael and his family have many year's experience behind them, most of this having been gained the hotel and restaurant trade. The menu is essentially international, but is enhanced by speciality sauces produced from personal recipes of Michael's. The American Surf and Turf sounded particularly interesting with its Mexicana sauce and butterfly prawns, but if this is not to your taste, then why not try the Roast rack of lamb with herbs, accompanied by a rich gravy. For vegetarians, the choice is just as interesting and includes Bulghur wheat and walnut casserole, Spinach crepe almondine, Vegetarian lasagne, or Mung beans and mushroom biriani.

If it is a simple coffee and light snack you require, then a short walk away is another establishment owned by the Diver family. This is an elegant Georgian coffee house which can be found at 28 Sun Street, where light snacks are available from 9 am until 4 pm.

Down by St. George's Quay, along the riverside, is the Maritime Museum, occupying the former 18th century Customs House. This Museum gives an insight into another part of Lancaster's history - its significance as a great port. This dwells largely on the port's links with the West Indies and the slave trade, but there are also exhibitions about the local fishing industry, the Lancaster Canal and the Morecambe Bay Gas field.

Ideally situated for access to the main shopping centre and local attractions, the **Farmers Arms Hotel** is to be found on Penny Street, which forms part of the busy one-way traffic system. Run by Lynne and Tony Williams, it has a very friendly family atmosphere. This can be attributed to the hospitality extended by the proprietors to their guests. Most of the 21 bedrooms have en-suite facilities and are more than comfortably furnished. The hotel is situated alongside the canal, and this makes an ideal setting during the summer months for outdoor barbecues. Children are more than welcome and a games room is available for their use.

*The Farmers Arms Hotel*

The restaurant provides seating for up to 32 diners, and the emphasis is on traditional English food interspersed with a few of Tony's well-loved Canadian delicacies. Bar snacks are available and the standard of these are reflected by an Egon Ronay award recommending them. The restaurant is open seven days a week from 12 until 2 pm, and evenings from 7 until 9.30 pm. Lynne and Tony proudly boast that nobody is ever turned away, whatever the hour. Guests and diners will be pleased to know that parking is available at the rear of the property.

When in Lancaster, it's worth travelling via East Road and Wyresdale Road on the eastern edge of the town to Williamson Park. Here you can see the thrilling Ashton Memorial - a great green copper domed building, a kind of miniature St. Paul's, standing on a hilltop in the centre of a delightful Edwardian park. It forms a landmark seen for miles around, and gives a magnificent viewpoint across Morecambe Bay, the Lakeland Hills and the Forest of Bowland. It now houses exhibitions and multi-screen presentations about the Life and Times of Lancaster's Lord Ashton and The Edwardians. There is a Tropical Butterfly House in the former conservatory.

The beautiful range of hills that lie to the east of Lancaster across to the Ribble Valley form the Forest of Bowland. 'Forest' is a bit of a misnomer, but is used in the sense of a medieval hunting 'forest' or reserve. Most of this Area of Outstanding Natural Beauty is in fact open moorland and fell country, heather grouse moor, rough grazing and water catchment. There are some areas of mainly coniferous forest, most notably Gisburn Forest to the east of Stocks Reservoir, but mostly this is an area of wild, open space, crossed by a number of roads which provide drives of great beauty.

Quiet lanes to the south-east of Lancaster will lead you to **Dolphinholme,** in the upper Wyre Valley. Dolphinholme is a quiet, sleepy village set in the midst of beautiful farmland and countryside. There are many attractive walks near here, not just in the well-known Trough of Bowland and Wyresdale, but also along canal banks. And, of course, the sea is not far away.

For those who are prepared to spend a bit of time seeking out the good things in life, there is a marvellous opportunity to stay in a rather special farmhouse nearby at **Over Wyresdale.**

**Greenbank Farmhouse** is the home of Jean Smith and her husband, Stan, who, with the help of their daughter, Jenny, have opened it for bed and breakfast guests. On entering this 17th century house, the oak panelling and an impressive staircase set expectations for the rest of the interior. There are no disappointments! The galleried landing leads to three tastefully furnished bedrooms which all have good views. Downstairs, the Resident's Lounge is superb, with an original stone inglenook fireplace, old beams and a collection of copper. In the cosy dining room, furnished in period style, guests are served a large farmhouse breakfast. Evening meals are by arrangement and can range from a simple lasagne to a full four course dinner.

No longer a working farm, Greenbank Farmhouse stands today in two acres of land with a pretty, well-kept garden. However, the building was originally the local dairy, and records still exist showing the milk output and number of cheeses made each day.

*Greenbank Farmhouse*

Perhaps the most celebrated of the many scenic routes across the Forest of Bowland is the minor road from Lancaster to Clitheroe which crosses the Abbeydale Moors and the Trough of Bowland before descending into the the lovely Hodder Valley around Dunsop Bridge. This is a popular road in summer months, with most lay-bys and parking places filled as people enjoy a pause to take in magnificent scenery and often breathtaking moorland views.

Almost equally as fine for the driver or the cyclist, as grand and desolate in their way as any moorland pass in the Scottish Highlands, are the roads which go from Slaidburn over to Bentham via Cross of Greet - medieval wayside cross - or going east from Slaidburn on the B6478 before turning north via Stocks Reservoir and Gisburn Forest (where there are picnic places and car parks in the forest and by the reservoir) to Clapham over Bowland Knotts.

You can return to Lancaster along the beautiful Lune Valley that forms the northern fringe of Bowland, perhaps tracing a route along quiet roads via Wray and Claughton, perhaps taking in **Caton,** which has the remains of an ancient cross, and its twin village **Brookhouse.** Brookhouse has a fine church with a 15th century tower, together with a richly carved

Norman doorway whose decoration includes the figures of Adam and Eve under a tree.

**The Scarthwaite Country Hotel** in Caton is situated in the heart of the Lune Valley, close to the river famous for its salmon fishing. It is an ideal place to stay, particularly if angling is one of your hobbies. The setting is exceptional and proves an excellent choice for wedding receptions, conferences or training programmes.

Easy to find, it is located just one and a half miles from the M6 at exit 34 towards Kirby Lonsdale. Open to non-residents, the hotel has wide ranging facilities and prides itself on being able to cater for a variety of special occasions. The Scarthwaite Hotel has 10 en-suite bedrooms, all with colour television, direct dial telephones and the usual tray of complimentary tea and coffee.

The hotel is ideally situated for visitors wishing to visit the historic city of Lancaster or the seaside resorts of Morecambe and Heysham.

*The Scarthwaite Country Hotel*

The Hodder valley is somewhere to linger in - an intimate beauty that contrasts with the wild moorland of the hilltops. You'll find here a series of lovely villages such as Whitewell (Bowland's 'Little Switzerland' in a deep, wooded valley), Dunsop Bridge and Newton in Bowland.

**Slaidburn** is a jewel, a compact village with a fine 15th century church, notable for its great three-decker pulpit and unusual Jacobean chancel screen. The village has rows of cottages that indicate its links with weaving, and a famous pub, the Hark to Bounty, with an upstairs room which housed the ancient Moot Courtroom of the Forest of Bowland and is said to have been used by Oliver Cromwell when he was in the area.

**Pages Farm** can be found in Woodhouse Lane, just on the outskirts of Slaidburn. Close to the Stocks Reservoir and near the Trough of Bowland, it is a 17th century farmhouse which has retained its lovely oak beams and exudes atmosphere and character. Accommodation is in the form of two double bedrooms and one twin room, all with en-suite facilities. Owned and run by Mary and Peter Cowking, this lovely couple always do their best to provide guests with a warm and friendly welcome and first class service.

Just one mile from the village is the **Parrock Head Farmhouse Hotel.** Nestling in a hidden corner of Fell and Valley, this is a 17th century 'long' farmhouse which has been tastefully restored, whilst keeping many of its original features. This work has been carried out with great skill, creating a warm atmosphere.

Guests are welcomed in the cosy low-timbered bar reception area, and it is from here that access is obtained for anyone wishing to take advantage of the garden terrace. Both the bedrooms in the farmhouse and the garden rooms have been elegantly furnished and are wonderfully light, airy and spacious. All of the rooms have bathrooms and showers en-suite, and facilities include telephone, television and tea and coffee making equipment.

An imaginatively converted hay loft has been transformed into a lounge and timbered library, also elegantly furnished with antiques, sofas and armchairs. Fresh flowers are always in evidence here. The views from this room are magnificent and enhance the sense of tranquility. The former farm milking parlour has been converted into an elegant restaurant, which is under the personal supervsion of Vicky Umbers. Food is cooked to the highest of English standards and comes to the table beautifully presented. The dinner menu changes daily using the freshest of produce, including an assortment of herbs from the kitchen garden. To complement the dinner menu, the wine list is moderately priced and includes wines from all over the world.

*Parrock Head Farmhouse Hotel*

Breakfast choices can vary from simple coffee and toast to huge English breakfasts, including black pudding and potato cakes. Light lunches are always available, and picnics can be prepared on request. A prior reservation should be made for Sunday Lunches.

Slaidburn has a welcoming car park, and is a good centre for country walks. A network of beautiful, little visited lanes, hardly wide enough to get a small car along, radiate westwards into the high fell country or eastwards into the main Ribble valley to the charming village of **Bolton-by-Bowland.** Here you'll find a village green complete with stocks and a stone cross. The medieval church has rich carvings and a tomb dating from 1500 carved with the heraldic shields of many famous local families. Nearby Rainber Scar, which overlooks the river, is known as Pudsey's Leap. Here, a local rogue called William Pudsey, accused of minting his own coins, is said to have escaped from pursuing soldiers by leaping on horseback across the river. The story also suggests that Pudsey was later pardoned by his own Godmother, Queen Elizabeth I.

**Baygate Farm Guest House** is situated in the village of **Holden,** just outside Bolton By Bowland and close to Gisburn and Clitheroe. An especially friendly welcome awaits guests all year round from Mr and Mrs Townson, who have been in residence here for over 20 years. The farmhouse is ideally situated for touring the Fells and Dales. Three twin bedded rooms with tea and coffee making facilities make up the accommodation, and you can tuck into a splendid full English breakfast after a good night's sleep. Baygate Farm is incredibly good value for visitors who enjoy farmhouse holidays.

About three miles west of Bolton by Bowland, nestling in a secluded valley, is the hamlet called **Harrop,** meaning 'Valley of Hares'. It has three farms, all of them called Harrop Fold! Victoria and Peter Wood's farm is situated on top of the bracken-covered Harrop Fell, which rises to 900 feet. Their son, Daniel, manages the farm, enabling them to concentrate (with his brother and sister-in-law) on a very special 'hidden place' - Peter and Victoria's 17th century long house. It may be 'hidden', but secret it is not. Now known as **The Harrop Fold Country Farmhouse Hotel,** many notable recommendations testify to its excellence.

Victoria revels in cosseting her guests. A welcoming glass of wine, fine cutlery, crystal glasses, and a profusion of fresh flowers only hint at what to expect. Country antiques, Victorian button-back chairs, oak beams and lovely views create a peaceful ambience of relaxation and warmth. The same atmosphere prevails during the cosy Christmas and New Year breaks.

Sunday breakfast includes a Bucks Fizz Starter. Afternoon tea is a small buffet by the fire-side in winter, or in the beautiful garden (where peacocks roam) in the summer. Peter and Victoria can supply local details for guests wishing to tour or picnic. Alternatively, 'happily tired guests' can be collected at the end of a walk. Nearer to hand, a driving tee is specially provided for golfers, and those feeling less active can contemplate the extensive views from the upstairs reading lounge, which also houses the Maritime Collection, dedicated to Victoria's seafaring forbears.

Victoria, together with her son Andrew (a talented chef), prepares superb and enticing country cooking for the evenings, when non-residents (by prior appointment) can join house-guests. One particular meal is produced from Victoria's great-grandma's recipe - 'Sarah-Ellen's beefsteak, kidney and oyster pie'. They also have their own label house-wines and an excellent 'connoisseur' wine list.

'...and so to bed'. Romantic touches adorn each of the seven bedrooms, but perhaps one of the smaller ones best embodies the spirit of Harrop. It has the luxury of an en-suite bathroom, the charm of a verandah, and the thoughtful provision of a door to the garden for walkers and early risers. Typically, it is romantically named 'Saetrgarden', after the old dwelling places of Norse shepherdesses.

Less suited to children, this luxurious retreat is ideal for couples and business people.

*Harrop Fold Country Farmhouse Hotel*

Three miles south of Bolton by Bowland lie the ruins of Sawley Abbey, a Cistercian monastery founded in 1147 by William de Percy. The first monks came here from Fountains Abbey in Yorkshire to help establish a sister foundation by the Ribble.

The old stone town of **Clitheroe** is the capital of the Forest of Bowland. Like Lancaster, it too is dominated by an 800-year-old castle on the hill, set on a limestone crag high above the little town. Little more than a ruin in a small park, when you stand inside the keep hidden voices relate aspects of the castle's history with suitable sound effects. The Castle Museum has collections of local geology and history, including a cloggers' workshop, a printer's shop and a lead mine.

Clitheroe's narrow, winding streets are full of character. You'll find old pubs and shops, narrow alleyways and steps, an excellent Tourist Information Centre, and the old Grammar School. An unusual feature is the Civic Hall Cinema, an unspoiled 1920s cinema lined in plush velvet, which still has the grand piano used to accompany silent movies. It is still in use as the town cinema.

It doesn't take long to discover that there is no shortage of good accommodation in the town. You could, for example, enjoy a comfortable and relaxing break at the **Old Post House Hotel.** Dating back to 1873, it is one of the finest personally run residential hotels in the area, situated in the very heart of Clitheroe. The proud crest on the front of the hotel bears witness to the fact that, until 1928, the building was the area's main Post Office and Sorting Office. Once inside, guests will discover a modern hotel which, with its Victorian decor, provides an air of Dickensian charm. All of this, combined with the breathtaking scenery of the magnificent Trough of Bowland, makes a stay at the Old Post House Hotel a never to be forgotten experience.

The cotton industry and local land owners formed the basis of Clitheroe's wealth in the 19th century, and this is evident in many interesting Victorian properties. **Brooklyn House** is one of these, and in many ways it is more like a country house in Grasmere than a 'Victorian Town House within a few minutes stroll of the centre', which is how Colin and Elizabeth Underwood describe their Guest House.

A very high standard has been maintained in the house thanks, no doubt, to Colin's other occupation which is in building. Across the road, another house, also dating from the 1880s, is used as an annexe and is equally well appointed. In both houses most of the bedrooms are en-suite, and there is an elegantly furnished resident's lounge to relax in.

The dining room - all dark wood and olde worlde - is in the main house, and there is a choice of continental or 'hearty' English breakfast. Colin and Elizabeth are extremely helpful and friendly hosts, and will fit in with special diets if required. Although evening meals can be arranged, it is well worth exploring the many pretty local villages to discover some of the excellent eating houses nearby.

*Brooklyn House*

It could be that you prefer the independence of a self-catering holiday, and if so, we discovered a lady who will certainly be able to help you. Mrs Elizabeth Parkinson is the proprietor of **Red Rose Cottages,** a specialist agency for self-catering accommodation in Lancashire, principally near Preston and Clitheroe. Currently, the agency has 30 cottages on its books, all regularly inspected and approved by the English Tourist Board.

*Red Rose Cottages*

The properties are furnished and equipped to a very high standard, and the varying sizes cater for from two to eleven people. All sorts of permutations are possible: isolated farmhouses, village cottages, Victorian terraced houses, cottages for dog owners, cottages for non-smokers, cottages for families with cots and high chairs provided, cottages with log-burning stoves or full central heating. All the properties have colour television and nearly all have laundry facilities. Some are suitable for disabled persons, many have gardens, patios and barbecue areas, and most have car-parking space.

The agency is happy to advise prospective guests on specific requirements regarding suitability, location and so forth, and each property is amply supplied with tourist information and helpful notes on local shops, pubs, restaurants and medical facilities, etc.

It is obvious from even the most cursory inspection that Red Rose Cottages have been chosen with immense care and are immaculately maintained - whatever the style of holiday required, there will be accommodation to suit.

Clitheroe is an excellent centre for exploring Bowland. You can go eastwards to discover Pendle Hill and the villages in and around its western slopes, including **Downham,** one of the most lovely villages of all in a region of exceptionally fine villages. It has a superb 15th century church, and links with the Assheton family who feature in Harrison Ainsworth's novel 'Witches of Pendle'.

South of Clitheroe on the B6246 is **Great Mitton,** a particularly attractive village. Until 1974 Great Mitton with its church was in Yorkshire, but the other part of the village, **Little Mitton,** divided by the River Ribble, lay in Lancashire.

A sweeping drive leads to **Mitton Hall,** which is a stone's throw from the medieval church at Mitton. This imposing manor house, with stately mullioned windows, was built for a cousin of Henry VII in about 1514. It stands in woodland surroundings extending to nearly 18 acres in all, with the River Ribble flowing nearby.

These days, the north wing houses a restaurant called **The Old Stone House Eating Establishment,** which allows a far greater audience to appreciate its spectacular dining room. Almost unbelievably, the minstrel's gallery and breath taking wood panelling are mostly original. The centre-piece is a vast stone fireplace with arched inglenook on the grandest scale. Hidden away at the back of the fireplace is a priest's hole - a relic of the early days of this manor house, when the observance of the 'Old Faith' of Catholicism was forbidden in England.

The high raftered ceiling has oak beams and vaults emanating from ornate carved bosses. From high vantage points, Coats of Arms, shields, lances and a stag's head look down on the families, friends and business people below who are enjoying relaxed and informal meals, from pizzas and steaks to full three course meals.

Over the years, the old hall has been added to, linking it with another old house. In the middle section, **Owd' Ned's Riverview Tavern** is named after a highwayman who is believed to haunt the old house. Stone-flagged floors and low, beamed ceilings provide a contrast to the hall's grandeur. Here, there is something to eat at almost any time of day - from sandwiches and finger snacks to pub meals of three courses, if required.

Off the main room, the seating area extends to a bright and airy conservatory with a patio and children's play area outside. Continuing through to the other old building, a comfortable lounge has leather chairs and Chesterfields, with a beautiful original fireplace carved in dark oak. This is shared with residents staying in the **Mitton Hall Lodgings** upstairs, which stretch overhead across the Tavern and have their honeymoon suite in the original manor house. Pine furniture and floral drapes make these very pretty rooms, and some have views over the river and countryside. With the facilities of the adjoining tavern and restaurant, this establishment succeeds in providing good, en-suite accommodation with a range of eating styles, against an authentic Old English background - and all for a sensible tariff.

*Mitton Hall*

Mr and Mrs Hargreaves who own **Mitton Green Barn** are a particularly friendly couple who always extend a warm welcome to their visitors. This large, detached and imposing house is a superb example of first class renovation and modernisation completed to a very high standard. It has taken seven years of dedicated hard work for Mitton Green Barn to finally offer its guests luxurious accommodation and wonderful views of the Ribble and Hodder Valleys. Located in Church Lane, there is an interesting medieval church at the top of the lane. The accommodation is luxurious and comfortable and offers guests a double and twin en-suite, plus a further double room. A comfortable resident's lounge is also available to relax in. A full English breakfast is served in the dining room and Sandra will happily accommodate special dietary needs. The position of Mitton Green Barn makes it ideally situated for visitors wishing to explore the superb Lancashire countryside and the nearby Yorkshire Dales.

*Mitton Green Barn*

**Gisburn,** a large former coaching village on the A59 to the north, has a wide, partly cobbled main street and a number of 17th and 18th century houses. Gisburn Park was once famous for its herd of white hornless cattle, belonging to Lord Ribblesdale. They are said to have been native to the area, but sadly became extinct in 1857. They are recalled in the name of Gisburn's White Bull public house and also in a famous painting of Gordale Scar by James Ward in the Tate Gallery in London.

**Waddington,** on the B6478 north of Clitheroe, has links with the ill-fated Henry VI, who lived for a year, in secret, in Waddington Hall before being betrayed to the Yorkists. He allegedly escaped via a secret panel from the dining room, only to be captured at Brungerly Bridge, down river near Clitheroe.

Situated on Waddington Fell, **The Moorcock Inn** is a famous old coaching inn with comfortable lounge bars, a superb ballroom, a cosy restaurant, and seven elegantly furnished bedrooms, each with private bathrooms. Under the ownership of Peter and Susan Fillary, this 17th century property has been carefully restored to its present condition.

The restaurant is open for a la carte dinner every evening, and the menu includes house specialities such as fresh fish and game dishes. Other dishes include steaks and poultry. Susan personally supervises the preparation of food and this is reflected by the way the menu changes with each passing season. Wherever possible, fresh local produce is used. Home cooked meals are served in the bar at lunchtimes and evenings, and the range of food available is extensive.

The ballroom at the Moorcock makes it an ideal venue for special occasions such as wedding receptions, dinner dances and private parties. During the summer months, the gardens are used for such events, and this proves to be ideal with the backdrop of the Ribble Valley and Pendle Hill.

*The Moorcock Inn*

West of Clitheroe, a network of quiet roads and lanes lead past Longridge Fell, a long wooded hillside from where there are magnificent views across the Ribble and Hodder Valleys and across the Forest of Bowland, and a choice of attractive walks along and around the summit.

Browsholme Hall, near Bashall Eaves, is the ancestral home of the Parkers, Forest Bow Bearers of Bowland. The house dates from Tudor times, and has wood carvings, arms and armour, period furniture, textiles, and a portrait of Thomas Parker, a former Lord Chancellor of England. The Hall is open to the public, but opening times are restricted.

Set deep in the heart of the beautiful Ribble Valley, on the Chipping Road in **Chaigley,** is the **Hodder Bridge Hotel.** On a main road position, the hotel is a large, imposing black and white building of considerable charm. It is owned and run by a very successful team, namely Mel and David Clay, who are father and son. Without wishing to be personal, we would describe them as two lovely Liverpudlians with ever-endearing Scouse charm. They have been at the Hodder Bridge Hotel for just four years and appear to be making a great success of their new found profession.

The hotel suffered an extensive fire just after Christmas in 1990, but with hard work and determination, it was back in service after just four weeks, and able to maintain its reputation for excellent service and value for money. A Freehouse, the hotel has five well furnished bedrooms, two en-suite, one family room and two twin bedded rooms. The restaurant is in the form of a carvery and offers excellent value for money when participating in the three course meals. The weekends are always extremely popular, as dinner dances are held as well as a disco. If you are looking for typical Liverpudlian humour, the personal touch, and never a dull moment, then we would definitely recommend a visit, as we thought it was superb.

*The Hodder Bridge Hotel*

Lower Hodder Bridge across the Hodder is also known as Cromwell Bridge, because Cromwell's army used it to travel westwards in 1652 before the Battle of Preston. It is now an ancient monument and there are some fine riverside walks from here.

**Hurst Green** is celebrated for Stonyhurst, the famous Roman Catholic public school, set in magnificent parkland with two huge ponds which were excavated in 1690.

**Ribchester,** an old weaving settlement to the south of Longridge Fell, on the banks of the Ribble, occupies part of the Roman fort of Bremetonacum. Many of the archaeological treasures from the site, including pottery, tools, masks, household implements, jewellery and altars, are displayed in the excellent Roman Museum in the village. There is also a small Roman bath house close by.

A very different kind of museum in Ribchester is the Museum of Childhood, with its remarkable collection of toys, models, dolls, dolls' houses and a twenty piece working model fairground.

To the north of Longridge Fell, another village not to be missed is **Chipping,** an attractive former weavers' settlement which once boasted no less than five water mills in medieval times. These utilised fast flowing streams from nearby fells. One of them survives as a restaurant, another, a former textile mill, as a centre of hand crafted furniture. The village has a handsome church, dating from the 13th century but with restoration over later centuries. An interesting feature is the 17th century school and almshouses for the poor of the village, built and endowed by one John Brabin, a wealthy Chipping cloth merchant and dyer.

A visit to the **Brickhouse Hotel and Restaurant** in Chipping is to be transported back in time into a world of old fashioned courtesy where the atmosphere is friendly, relaxed and informal. With its magnificent views of the Pendle and Longridge Fells, the hotel is an ideal retreat for weary travellers or diners alike. It provides an ideal hideaway for lovers of country pursuits, with plenty of nearby leisure facilities such as golf, trout fishing, tennis, riding, clay pigeon shooting and canoeing, to name but a few.

The hotel itself is an 18th century farmhouse, and can lay claim to being the first brick built house in the Forest of Bowland. Recently modernised and refurbished, the accommodation is of an excellent standard. Today, the Brickhouse enjoys an excellent reputation for its fine wine, food and atmosphere. Freshness and flavour is something that owner Heather Crabtree takes very seriously. 'The approach to preparation is simple, there is very little point buying the freshest produce to leave it standing - waiting to be used', explains Heather. Brickhouse cuisine can best be described as modern with traditional roots.

*The Brickhouse Hotel & Restaurant*

Presentation plays a vital part in the meals served in the restaurant, but this is not at the expense of quality and flavour. Choice is an important ingredient of the Brickhouse experience and usually includes at least six varieties of fresh vegetables with a la carte meals. Perhaps this is why it

72

is renowned as being one of the North West's finest countryside hotels and restaurants.

**Hough Clough Farm** is an attractive traditional stone built Victorian Farmhouse, tucked under the Bleasdale Moors just one and a half miles west of Chipping. It is within easy reach of Beacon Fell and is ideal for those who enjoy walking. Doreen and David Ingram are the proprietors, and they like to ensure that their guests have a thoroughly enjoyable stay.

Double or twin rooms are available and children are welcomed at reduced rates. The size of the breakfast served is not for the faint-hearted, and is synonymous with the traditional hearty British farmhouse breakfast. If required, guests may have the option of an evening meal at a very reasonable cost, and this is complemented, by the residential license thereby enabling guests to relax after a day of walking or touring without having to go out again.

All of the bedrooms are en-suite or have exclusive use of a separate bath. Other facilities include tea and coffee and colour television. For further details and information, we suggest you telephone Doreen or David on (0995) 61272.

*Hough Clough Farmhouse*

**Longridge** is a busy market, below the western edge of Longridge Fell and serves a wide hinterland of farm country. The town has three churches, all of interest, and boasts the first houses in Britain, in Club Row, to be purchased with the assistance of a Building Society. The town has a busy and popular shopping centre and is noted for its antique shops.

**The Corporation Arms** in Longridge has been in the Gornall family for 25 years. During the last decade since Tony's mother retired, Tony and his wife Stephanie have won a fine reputation for this attractive restaurant.

Its name somewhat belies it's appeal, but is nevertheless a part of its history. The title, 'Corporation', now extinct, refers to a period when the property was owned by what was then known as Preston Corporation. It bore a much more rural name in around 1865 when it was known as 'The Black Bull', and before that it was a farm dating back to the 17th century.

Tony and Stephanie have created an atmosphere of warmth and comfort in extremely pleasant surroundings. Passing through to the lounge, the oak panelling of the bar is echoed in the oak slats on the walls. Plants and pictures (some for sale) feature here, with a log-burning stove, a mirrored wall, and breathtaking views over the hills creating a relaxing ambience.

In the two cosy and inviting dining rooms, dark oak furniture adds to the charm of the building. The excellent traditional English cuisine is typified by dishes such as Venison in Ale and Steak and Kidney and Mushroom Pie. Equally traditional is the generosity of the portions.

*The Corporation Arms*

East of Longridge on the B6243 is **Knowle Green.** Here you will find **Meadow Side,** which offers superb bed and breakfast accommodation and is delightfully situated in the Forest of Bowland. It is ideal for golf, walking and fishing. The house has recently been extended to provide accommodation to a very high standard, and offers spacious guest rooms, a superb bathroom and a luxurious resident's lounge with colour television and panoramic views of the beautiful surrounding countryside.

South-east of here, on the A59 at **Copster Green, is The Brown Leaves Hotel.** This establishment has seen many changes since the site was established in 1926. It has progressed over the years from being a roadside cafe to a hotel, and in the intervening years, the present owners established a garden centre specialising in trees, shrubs and plants. It was in 1989 that Mr and Mrs Fisher, the proprietors of The Brown Leaves, decided to re-develop the site and turn the premises into a licensed 12 bedroomed hotel.

September of 1990 saw the opening of the hotel, and in this short time it has fast become popular for travellers between Lancashire, Yorkshire and the surrounding districts. It is ideally situated and provides extremely comfortable accommodation for the weary traveller. The bedrooms are attractively furnished and provide the conveniences one would expect from a larger hotel.

The hotel is managed by the resident proprietors, who like to extend a very warm and friendly welcome to their guests. Although new to the business of running a hotel, Mr and Mrs Fisher thoroughly enjoy their new-found profession and take great care to ensure that the hotel is run with the minimum of fuss but to the highest of standards. A drink at the bar in the company of the Fishers will confirm this and make for a very enjoyable evening.

*The Brown Leaves Hotel*

Just to the south of Longridge lie the Alston Reservoirs, and close by on the B6243, you will find a beautiful Georgian farmhouse. **Charnley House** is set on the edge of the lovely Ribble Valley, only 4 miles from the M6 and M55 at junctions 31 and 32. The accommodation available is a top floor family unit which is completely self-contained, and has a television area as well as toilet facilities. On the first floor of the house is another bedroom of character with a double bed. An English or Continental breakfast is served in the dining room on the ground floor, which overlooks an extensive garden and open country beyond. Attached to the house is an interesting Gallery, filled with beautiful Victorian paintings both in oil and watercolours. These are for visitors to both enjoy and purchase if so desired. One thing is for certain - if you are seeking peace and tranquility, superb accommodation, and the type of hospitality offered by the owner Mrs

Crosbie, then this is definitely the place for you to stay.

About six miles north of Longridge, close to the village of Whitechapel, is Beacon Fell Country Parks, one of the most popular countryside destinations in this part of Lancashire. This is a beautiful wooded hill-top, commanding magnificent views of the Bowland Fells. There are well-signed car parks, picnic places, and a choice of attractive well-marked walks across the summit and through the woodlands, and the area is rich in wildlife interest.

*Charnley House*

This western area of Bowland lies within a network of quiet lanes, with hidden villages such as Claughton, Calder Vale and Oakenclough. From the higher lanes along the moorland edges, you get sudden, unexpected views of the Fylde Coast and often magnificent sunsets looking across the Irish Sea. Best of all, this is an area to explore on foot. Leaving the car and the tarmac roads, you can take a choice of footpaths, for example, winding along the litte River Brock, or onto the higher fell country around Bleasdale.

*Slaidburn Bridge*

# North Lancashire

## CHAPTER FOUR

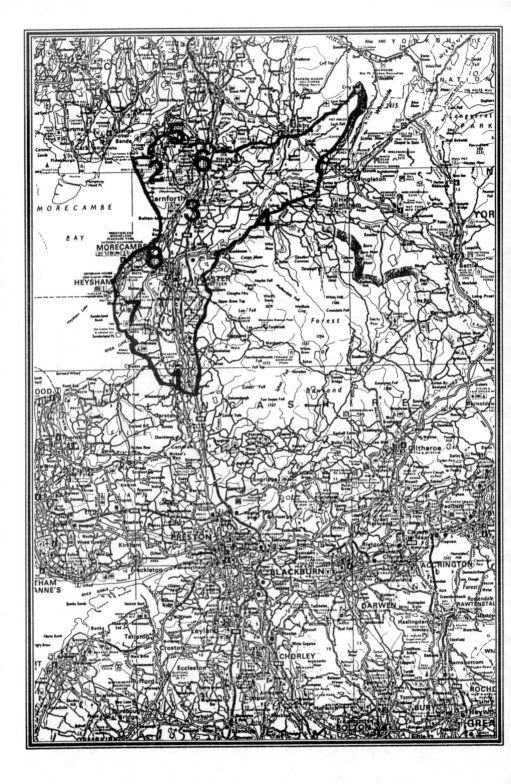

# Chapter Four
# Map Reference Guide

| Name | Map Ref No |
|------|:----------:|
| The Bower | 6 |
| Castle Hotel | 4 |
| Globe Hotel | 7 |
| Grosvenor Hotel | 8 |
| Middle Holly Cottage | 1 |
| Pine Lake Motel | 3 |
| Stonegate Guest House | 5 |
| Trailholme Farmhouse | 7 |
| Wood 'n' Wool Miniatures | 2 |

*Borwick Hall*

# North Lancashire

The northern edge of Lancashire sweeps from Morecambe Bay up along the valley of the River Lune to the edge of the Yorkshire Dales.

Indeed, high up on Leck Fell east of Kirkby Lonsdale, you are in true Dales country, with a typical craggy limestone gorge along the little valley of Leck Beck, as well as one of the most extensive cave systems in the British Isles for the experienced potholer to explore.

**Cowan Bridge** is another bit of Lancashire with strong Yorkshire associations, for here was the school for clergymens' daughters, where the young daughters of Parson Patrick Bronte of Haworth suffered harrowing experiences. These were to lead to the premature death of two of them - Marie and Elizabeth. The third, Charlotte, lived to record those experiences in one of the most powerful of all mid-19th century novels, 'Jane Eyre'. You can read a description in the novel not only of that nightmarish school, but of the beautiful countryside of Leck and Lunesdale that the young Jane glimpses all too infrequently.

The actual school at Cowan Bridge survives, now a private house (with no public access) on the main A65 road. A plaque on the gable end recalls the Bronte connection.

**Kirkby Lonsdale** is actually just over the Lancashire border in the county of Cumbria, but it serves as the focal point for the whole of this part of the dale. Architecturally, this little market town is a jewel, with a considerable number of fine Georgian, Regency and early Victorian houses and shops.

If you approach the town along the main A65 from the east, your first sight of the town is across Devil's Bridge, a slender triple-arched bridge across a wooded gorge of the River Lune. This bridge was recorded as being in existence in 1365 when a grant of pontage - the ability to collect a toll from travellers crossing over the bridge - was granted to the Vicar, who in return had to maintain it. It takes its name from a legend about the Devil and an old lady who wanted to get her cattle to the other side of the river.

She was promised a bridge by the Devil, providing she gave him the soul of the first creature who crossed it. Next morning, the Devil lay in wait for his victim, but was frustrated by the ingenious old lady, who threw a bun across the bridge. Her little dog chased it and the Devil had to be content with its soul.

The lovely church of St. Mary, also beautifully positioned above the river gorge, dates mainly from the 13th century, but almost certainly replaced a much earlier building. When it was being restored in 1866, burn marks and charred timbers suggested that the building had been attacked by the Scots in the 14th century. The view from the terrace beyond the churchyard up the Lune valley towards Underley Hall was described by John Ruskin in 1875 with his usual hyperbole as 'one of the loveliest scenes in England - and therefore the world'. You can walk down the steps from the churchyard and along the riverside to Devil's Bridge.

The town has a fine Market Square (market day is Thursday) with a tall Market Cross, no less than three car parks, a number of old inns, and a wide choice of shops, especially antique and bookshops. A Victorian Fair, when local people dress in period costume and Morris Dancers throng the streets, takes place each September.

From Kirkby Lonsdale, there is a lovely network of quiet lanes and roads to explore in this green and sheltered valley between the high fell country of the Dales and Lakes to the north, and the open spaces of the Forest of Bowland to the south. Villages such as Whittington, Wennington, Melling, Tunstall, Wray, Priest Hutton, Borwick and Gressingham repay exploration, whilst at **Hornby,** there is the romantically situated castle immortalised in a painting by Turner - though it was only built last century, incorporating the ruins of an older castle and transformed into a grand and picturesque country house.

**The Castle Hotel** on Main Street in Hornby has been run by Stanford and Rosalynd Robinson for the past nine years. It was formerly a coaching inn, providing rest and refreshment to travellers between Lancaster and Kendal. The old stables and smithy are still in existence at the rear of the premises.

A warm and friendly atmosphere greets the visitor to this comfortable establishment. There are twelve guest rooms, eight of which are en-suite. Two of the rooms are on the ground floor and are suitable for disabled persons. A large bar lounge has two open log fires and there are two very pleasant restaurants for which Mrs Robinson caters excellently, making the best use of local produce. The hotel also provides morning coffee and afternoon tea, and bar meals are available at lunchtime and in the evening.

A beer garden offers an attractive setting for drinks outside on a warm summer's day, and the distinctive 'real ale' to be enjoyed here is brewed locally at Lancaster.

The Robinsons are happy to organise river fishing and pony-trekking for their guests and there are squash courts and four golf courses within easy reach, as well as many places of interest to visit.

*The Castle Hotel*

For active visitors, there is a very good network of footpaths and cycleways to explore along the River Lune down to Lancaster, and beyond Lancaster as far as Glasson Dock, utilising old railway lines to provide quiet, level, traffic-free walking and cycle ways past the Crook of Lune and into the City. Car parks provide access to the route at Bull Beck (near Brookhouse), Crook o'Lune, Halton and Lancaster, by Skerton Bridge off the A6.

Another good opportunity for walking and also boating, canoeing and angling, lies along the Lancaster Canal, sadly severed by the M6 motorway north of Borwick, but otherwise open as a leisure waterway. The Lancaster Canal, which has a link to Glasson Dock, was opened in 1797, designed by the great canal engineer John Rennie. It contains the longest lock-free stretch of canal in Britain - 41 miles between Preston and Tewitfield, north of Lancaster. It is rich in items of architectural interest for the canal historian and boat enthusiast, including warehouses and bridges and a splendid colonnaded aqueduct over the River Lune at Lancaster. It is also a rich haven for wildlife - mallard, mute swan and coot are usually to be seen, as well as heron and kestrel. Water lilies and yellow flags also thrive along quieter fringes. Boats can be hired and there are leisure trips in the summer months.

**Carnforth** was once a busy railway junction town whose station has a claim to fame as the setting for the 1940s film classic 'Brief Encounters'. Though the station has declined in importance, being an unstaffed halt, the old engine sheds and sidings are now occupied by Steamtown, one of the largest steam railway centres in the north of England. Here you are likely to see such giants of the Age of Steam as Flying Scotsman or an A4 Pacific being stabled there, together with a permanent collection of over 30 British and Continental steam locomotives. There are steam rides in the summer months on both standard gauge and miniature lines.

The town of Carnforth itself lies around what used to be a busy crossroads on the A6. It has a choice of inns and shops, including one of the largest bookshops (new and secondhand) in Lancashire.

**The Pine Lake Hotel, Watersports and Leisure Resort** at Carnforth is modern and luxurious, and offers splendid views of the 70 acre lake. The resort has a feel of Sweden about it - clean living, fresh air, and saunas in the lodges to relax you after a strenuous day. There are 128 lodges with warm pine-clad walls, and 52 of these are available for hire. The resort is a successful combination of privacy, helpful service, the choice of self-catering (although you can have optional maid-service), the comfort of hotel rooms, and the freedom to wander round this beautiful complex and enjoy the many water activities.

This is an ideal opportunity to try out those sports you always wished to have a go at, but were too nervous to try! Waterskiing and Parascending (which we are reliably informed is a lot easier than it looks) are there for the more adventurous guests. Alternatively, you can splash about in row boats, skim across the lake in canoes, and with a stiff breeze behind you, sail over the water in a sailing dinghy. There are even giant inflatables for those who wish to float on the water but not necessarily go anywhere! Windsurfing can be arranged next to the watersports centre at Morecambe Bay, and if you want to stick to terra firma for a while, you can hire a bike and head off into the hills.

The gentle art of fishing can be indulged in here, and the lake is well-stocked with rainbow and brown trout, roach, perch and tench. There is also an indoor leisure centre, appropriately called Splashers, together with a Games Room, shops, bars, pool - in fact it is rather like living in an exclusive self-contained community.

The a la carte restaurant is there for those who wish to treat themselves to a really special dinner, while the family restaurant is also of a high standard. There are magic shows for the children during the day, and quality entertainment for adults in the evening. Creches are available free to guests during the day, which is an excellent way for parents to get out and make use of all the facilities. Knowing the children are safe is half-way to knowing that you can relax and enjoy yourself.

Situated just off the M6 at Junction 35, Pine Lake Resort couldn't be easier to reach, whatever part of the country you are travelling from.

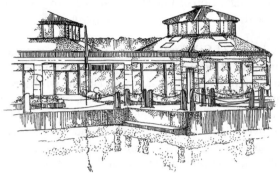

*Pine Lake Hotel, Watersports & Leisure Resort*

North of Carnforth is once again limestone country, with a remarkable area of wooded limestone headland and marshland jutting out into Morecambe Bay.

This area forms the Arnside and Silverdale Area of Outstanding Natural Beauty, and though on a small, even intimate scale, has much to interest the walker and the naturalist. The area is noted for its limestone pavements and crags, and its rich variety of natural history.

Warton Crag, just to the north of **Warton** village, is a noted viewpoint, and on the shoulders of the hill are the remains of a prehistoric hillfort. Warton village has links with George Washington, for the President's ancestors lived here for about 300 years and their coat of arms - the Stars and Stripes - is to be seen on the 15th century tower. Thomas Washington, the last of the Warton Washingtons and vicar of Warton, died here in 1823 and is buried in the church. The church font is Norman.

North of Warton is the delightfully named **Yealand Conyers.** Situated in this tiny, unspoilt village is **The Bower,** a listed 18th and 19th century house which offers bed and breakfast facilities. The views from the house are extensive and spectacular, taking in the surrounding hills and countryside. The Rothwell family purchased The Bower in order to escape from the rat race of London life, and they run their computer company here in relative peace and quiet.

The house is Regency in style and is set in a charming garden. The delightful dining room, which includes a seating area, has French windows leading out onto the garden, and a fine marble fireplace where log fires are lit on chilly evenings. The young owners are keen bridge players and love classical music. In the spacious hall is a recently commissioned harpsicord which Michael Rothwell plays with skill and pleasure whilst entertaining his guests. If our description of The Bower appeals to you, then we suggest you telephone for details and perhaps slip away from the rat race for an enjoyable break.

Whilst the villages of **Silverdale** and **Arnside** are small and mainly residential, a network of footpaths crosses the escarpments whose limestone woodlands are a joy for the botanist, being rich in wildflowers in spring - primroses, violets, orchids, bird's eye primroses, rockroses and eglantines abound. You can take a choice of footpaths from Arnside village to the summit of the lovely little limestone hill called Arnside Knott, to enjoy breathtaking views of the Kent Estuary, and across Morecambe Bay. Another footpath follows the shoreline around the little peninsula, following a miniature cliff above the muddy estuary which is particularly rich in birdlife - both seabirds and a variety of waders. A medieval defensive Pele Tower can be seen at Arnside Tower, a farm on the shoulders of the Knott.

Leighton Moss near Silverdale is a nationally known RSPB Bird Sanctuary, whilst bird lovers will also enjoy a visit to nearby Leighton Hall. As well as being a handsome neo-Gothic with exceptional collections of Lancaster-made Gillow furniture, the Hall has extensive grounds which are used for displays of falconry in the summer months.

If miniature fixtures, furniture and ornaments for serious dolls' house enthusiasts are your interest, then you simply must seek out renowned national experts Joan and Ken Manwaring at their cottage shop in Silverdale, **Wood 'N' Wool Miniatures.**

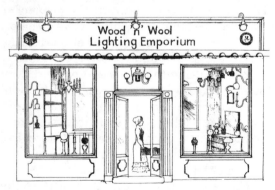

*Wood 'N' Wool Miniatures*

The family specialise in the manufacture of miniature lighting in 1/12th scale, and stock a range of over 40 different candle, oil and gas lights which are made to the highest standards. Most of the lamps are hand-turned in brass. Ken stresses that the miniatures are for serious collectors, and no lighting can be sold direct to children. The firm offers a complete mail order service.

Arnside enjoys a particularly lovely setting alongside the Kent estuary, with the Kent Viaduct carrying the railway to Barrow forming a dramatic feature. The river is tidal at low tide, being nothing but a narrow channel, but fills to a broad expanse of water at low tide. It is worth a trip to Grange over Sands by train, just to enjoy the experience of crossing the viaduct with its superb Lakeland mountain and estuarial views.

**Stonegate Guest House** on the promenade at Arnside is owned and run by Doreen Nesbit. Although she basically offers bed and breakfast, Mrs Nesbit can provide an evening meal if required and also specialises in afternoon teas with plenty of homemade fare. The house was built in 1882 and has been thoroughly modernised inside for the comfort of guests. It is an excellent example of the architecture of the period and many features, such as the original fireplaces, have thankfully been retained.

*Stonegate Guest House*

**Morecambe** has long been one of the most successful and popular seaside resorts in the North, and it can truly be said to enjoy one of the finest views from its promenade of any resort in England - a magnificent sweep of coastline and bay, looking across to the Lakeland mountains. Like other resorts, Morecambe has changed with the times, and major new attractions include the multi-million pound Bubbles Leisure Park and Superdome, as well as a Wild West Theme Park. There are also popular seafront Illuminations in late summer, together with all the usual facilities, lively shops and variety of entertainments of a busy seaside resort.

For both the tourist and businessman alike, **The Grosvenor Hotel** in Morecambe proves an ideal place to stay. Whether it be for a business trip, a special conference, or even a summer holiday and mini break, you will find that the Grosvenor will cater for your every need. The hotel is privately owned, and situated at the southern end of Morecambe Bay, it commands panoramic views of the Lakeland Hills. Occupying a prime position on Sandylands Promenade, it is in a peaceful area just far enough away from the hustle and bustle of the centre. Originally built in 1899, it is a superb example of Victorian architecture. The interior is a wonderful reflection of the elegance and splendour of a bygone era. Tastefully decorated and furnished, the 40 bedrooms are light, airy and spacious, with views which have to be seen to be fully appreciated. Most have en-suite facilities and the usual hostess trays, telephones, colour television and radio. A large three bedroomed apartment is also available which offers luxurious accommodation.

The Victorian dining room of the Grosvenor offers an extensive a la carte menu, and can cater for an intimate dinner for two or a gourmet creation for up to 200. Furnished with a subtle co-ordinating colour scheme, the seating is reproduction button backed chairs, and the tables are beautifully laid with fine china. Weekends are especially popular, as the hotel holds regular dinner dances in the ballroom. Other facilities include a games room and bar, a lounge bar, and a carvery restaurant. James Neilson has carried out a programme of extensive renovations and re-modernisation in his hotel, and he is determined to maintain the high standards which had previously been achieved.

*The Grosvenor Hotel*

It's worth strolling along Morecambe promenade as far as **Heysham,** Morecambe's twin, which has retained its quaint old main street which winds down to the shore. It is also a town with considerable historic associations, because it was here in the 8th century that Christian missionaries arrived from Ireland to convert the heathen Viking settlers in the north of England. They built the chapel of St Patrick on a rock on the sea edge. Its ruins, with coffin-shaped rocks - one of the most curious graveyards in England - can still be seen.

The little church of St Peter's on the headland is equally interesting. It dates back to Saxon and Norman times, with an Anglo-Saxon cross on which the Madonna and other figures have been crudely carved by 9th century masons, and there is a rare Viking hog-back gravestone.

Yet alongside these antiquities is the modern port of Heysham, with regular car-ferry sailings to the Isle of Man and to Northern Ireland.

For anyone with a sense of the past, it is worth making your way further down the pensinsula formed by Heysham and the River Lune, via Middleton and Overton, from where you can either walk or drive (though be careful - the road is closed at high tide, and parking is extremely limited in the village) to **Sunderland Point.** This is, unbelievably, an old port and seaside resort, which flourished until larger berthed ships, silting channels and the growth last century of rail-served Morecambe caused it to decline. A little wharf, quiet cottages, some with faded and evocative elegance, a sandy shore where sea thrift flourishes among the pebbles, are all that remains. The estuary is now a Site of Special Scientific Interest because of its wildlife value. You are likely to see such birds as redshank feeding on the rich food supplies of worms, shellfish and shrimps on the saltmarshes, whilst a variety of wildfowl such as shelduck, wigeon and mallard, are to be seen in the autumn.

A particularly sad story is associated at Sunderland with Sambo's grave. Sambo was a sea captain's servant at the time of the Slave Trade into Lancaster, who probably died of a fever in 1736 after a long and difficult voyage from the West Indies. Because he was not a bapitised Christian, he was not allowed to be buried in consecrated ground. In later years, his death and grave became a potent local symbol of the anti-slavery cause.

His grave can be still seen, in a field at the west side of the point. It is reached by walking along The Lane from the village foreshore, past Upsteps Cottage where Sambo died, and turning left at the shore then over a stile on the left which gives access to the simple gravestone. Fresh flowers are usually to be seen here, mysteriously placed on the grave.

During the last few years, a company by the name of Mitchells have made quite a name for themselves within the leisure industry. One of the premises run under the auspices of the Whittakers is **The Globe Hotel** in **Overton.** As long ago as the 17th century, The Globe was a thriving business offering refreshment and hospitality, and it has kept up this tradition. Nearby Sunderland Point was once one of the busiest ports in the country. It was here that ships returning from the West Indies with their cargoes of spices, rum, sugar, timber and cotton would unload their wares. The sailors then retired to The Globe for entertainment, food and drink.

The nature of The Globe's trade has changed considerably since then, but the quality of the hotel has gone from strength to strength. John and Janice Whittaker offer an exclusive range of food seven days a week, lunchtimes (12 noon until 2 pm) and evenings. The recently added conservatory makes a delightful setting in which to enjoy the excellent food. As Overton is a small fishing village, local seafood often features on the menu. Small weddings and parties are also catered for, and during the summer, the beer garden and children's play area are very popular. The Globe has excellent accommodation for the traveller, consisting of six en-suite rooms, decorated in the style of Laura Ashley. This is a truly hidden place, and a visit is a must.

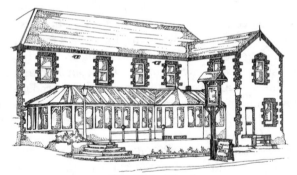

*The Globe Hotel*

We were pleased to discover that Overton also has farmhouse accommodation to offer its visitors. **Trailholme Farmhouse** is owned and run by Susan Graves, a very friendly lady who previously owned a hotel in Morecambe. Her experience ensures that guests are thoroughly satisfied when they choose to stay with her. Guests are accommodated in large, warm, comfortable rooms in the main house. The views from the farmhouse are spectacular, and take in the Lakeland Hills across to the Pennines and Fylde. If, like us, you enjoy the prospect of seeing local wildlife, then you will be amply rewarded with a visit to Trailholme. Rabbits, hawks, foxes and herons can all be spotted in the surrounding area.

On the opposite side of the Lune estuary from Sunderland Point (and only reached by a long road journey through Lancaster) is Glasson Dock. The silting of the Lune that ended Lancaster's importance as a port was the reason for the building of Glasson Dock in 1787 to hold 25 seagoing ships. In 1825, the Lancaster Canal was built to provide a better link between the city and the docks, and this was, in turn, supplemented by a railway line in 1883. This railway is now the footpath and cycle way to Lancaster's St George's Quay. At **Conder Green,** just to the east of Glasson, there is now a picnic site and car park at the site of a former station, with access onto the old railway line. Competition from other Lancashire ports, notably Preston and Heysham, caused Glasson to decline as a commercial port.

However, the village of **Glasson** is now a sailing centre, with the old canal basin now a popular marina, and the old wharves and warehouses transformed into an attractive leisure area, with pubs and shops serving a different kind of sea-going clientele.

You can walk, cycle, or drive from Glasson round past Plover Scar where a lighthouse guards the estuary, and where you'll find, near the point where the little River Cocker flows into the Lune, the ruins of Cockersand Abbey. The Abbey was founded in 1190 by the Premonstratensian Order on the site of a hospital. This had been the abode of a hermit, Hugh Garth, before becoming a colony for lepers and the infirm. The Chapter House of the Abbey remains, and was a burial chapel for the Daltons of Thurnham, descendants of Sir Thomas Moore. The village of **Cockerham** to the east serves outlying farms in land reclaimed from the marshes. It has a church with a fine 17th century tower, though the rest has been restored this century. Some of the graves in the churchyard are filled with plague victims.

About three miles east of Cockerham, just over the Lancaster Canal, is the village of **Forton,** where you'll find **Middle Holly Cottage.** This is a guest house which was once visited by one of Lancashire's most famous daughters - Gracie Fields. This is no idle boast - a photograph of Gracie, dressed in casual 'slacks' and wearing a jaunty beret, shows her standing in front of the Cottage. Her signature on the photograph offers conclusive proof. Apparently, she was in the area whilst filming 'Sing As We Go'.

Guests staying at Middle Holly will be able to enjoy the superb countryside of the Trough of Bowland, rural canalside walks, nearby Glasson Dock, the old market town of Garstang, and historic Lancaster with its famous castle.

Within five minute's walk are two local pubs and three popular restaurants. Situated just three miles south of Exit 33 on the M6, the guest house is conveniently placed for exploring further afield - it's only a half hour drive to the Lake District.

This mid-19th century house has been a coaching inn and also a farmhouse in its time, and now it is run as a family bed and breakfast venture by Jeanne and Mike McChrystal. Retaining the cottage style with exposed beams and antique furniture, their recent renovations included en-suite facilities in the five bedrooms. Jeanne and Mike receive all their visitors with a friendly, cheerful welcome, and we are sure that your stay will be very comfortable.

*Middle Holly Cottage*

*Hornby Castle*

# The Lancashire Coast and the Wirral

## CHAPTER FIVE

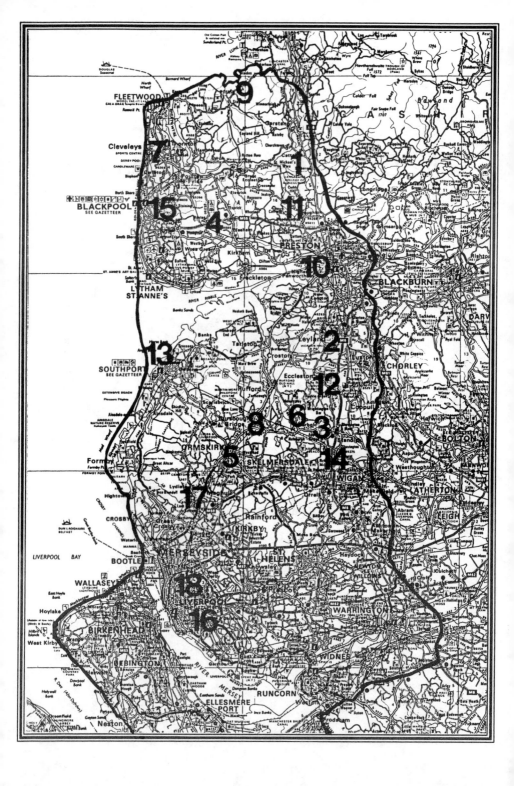

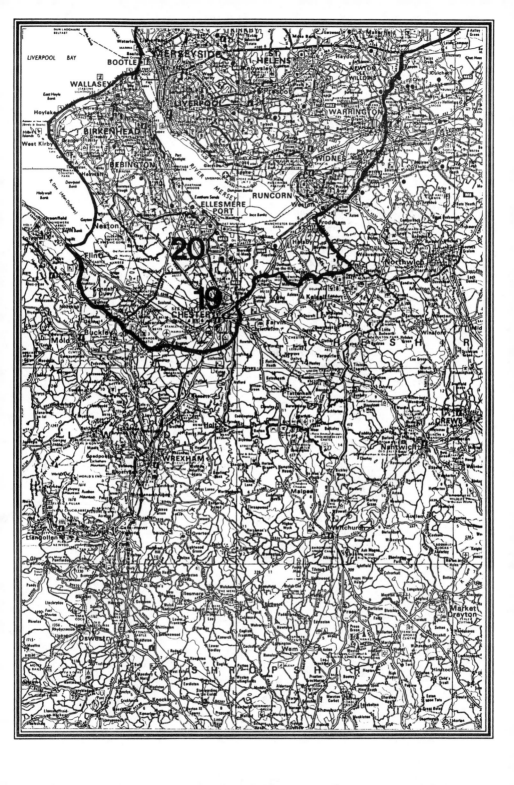

# Chapter Five
# Map Reference Guide

| Name | Map Ref No |
|---|---|
| Abbey Farm Caravan Park | 6 |
| Brandreth Barn | 8 |
| Bygone Times | 12 |
| Calverts Farms | 2 |
| Chester Court Hotel | 19 |
| Cottage Fish & Chip Restaurant | 16 |
| Dicconson Arms | 14 |
| Guys Eating Establishment | 1 |
| Italian Orchard | 11 |
| L'Alouette | 16 |
| Martin Inn | 8 |
| National Museum & Gallery | 18 |
| Olde Duncombe House | 1 |
| Olde Ship | 9 |
| Peggottys | 13 |
| Pheonix Hotel | 17 |
| Rake Hall | 20 |
| Rigbye Arms | 3 |
| Robin Hood Inn | 6 |
| Smithy Guest House | 2 |
| Smugglers Cove | 7 |
| Speke Hall | 18 |
| Springfield House Hotel | 9 |
| Swarbrick Hall Farm | 4 |
| Turbary House & Garden Centre | 10 |
| Wesley House | 10 |
| West Lancs District Council | 5 |
| Worden Arts & Craft Centre | 2 |

CHAPTER 5

# The Lancashire Coast and the Wirral

You would perhaps hardly describe **Blackpool,** with its world famous seven mile long Promenade, its three busy fun-loving piers, its elegant 518 feet high tower copied from Paris's scarcely more famous Eiffel, and its reputation for extravaganza, as a Hidden Place of Lancashire.

But a little over 150 years ago that might well have been true, when Blackpool was little more than a fishing village among sand dunes on the Irish Sea coast. But then came the great Victorian railway companies who laid their tracks to the coast, built their stations (Blackpool had three) and helped to develop 'Cottonopolis by the Sea' in all its splendour over a few hectic decades. Year after year, during the summer 'Wakes Weeks', inhabitants of the Lancashire cotton towns came in huge numbers by excursion and special train to escape from the smoke and grime, and to spend a week in a resort devoted to providing not only sunshine, seaside and fresh air, but every conceivable fairground and wet weather entertainment for the family.

Though Lancashire Wakes Weeks are long in the past, Blackpool has now become an international resort and conference centre, as fully absorbed as ever in the entertainment business, and one of the busiest and liveliest resorts of its kind in the world.

Yet even Blackpool has its quiet corners, where you can escape the hustle of crowds. You only have to walk or take a tram along a few of the seven miles of its long promenade past North Shore and Bispham, or down to Squire's Gate or Lytham St Anne's, to find life moving at a much gentler pace, with much quieter beaches and promenades, rolling dunes, and pleasant town centres, yet still enjoying the bracing sea air that makes Blackpool famous.

There's no nicer or more enjoyable way of exploring the quieter sides of Blackpool and Wyre than by tram. Blackpool Trams are special in many

101

ways. Until very recently, this tramway system was the only remaining street tramway in Britain, if only now about to be rivalled by the new Metrolink system in Manchester and by Sheffield's Super Trams. Many of Blackpool's unique 'streamline' trams date from the 1930s or 50s, and the Tramway Company have a fleet of vintage cars used on special occasions, including during the famous late summer Illuminations. But there are also comfortable modern vehicles which make a trip out to Cleveleys or Fleetwood a delightful experience. It's possible to combine a tram ride with a walk along the foreshore to enjoy surprisingly fine coastline views, with excellent birdlife including a variety of seabirds, waders, and at certain times of the year, wild duck and geese.

Whilst visiting Blackpool, we strongly recommend a visit to 'The Famous' **Cottage Fish and Chip Restaurant** which is in **Great Marton,** just on the outskirts of the town. Not only is the food served here excellent and the portions large, but you might just be seated next to one of the many stars appearing in Blackpool at the time. The Cottage is renowned for being a favourite eating house within theatrical circles.

Just a few miles to the east of Blackpool, and in complete contrast to the busy pace of the town, lies the peaceful village of **Weeton.** Here, travellers seeking comfortable accommodation will find the warmest of welcomes at the beautiful Georgian farmhouse at **Swarbrick Hall Farm,** nestling in the tranquility of rural Fylde. Built in 1802, it is said to have once been Lord Derby's shooting lodge. Today, it belongs to Heather and John Smith, who take great pleasure in inviting their guests to relax and enjoy the delights of their 200 acre working farm. The farm is surrounded by wooded gardens which are great fun for children, and there are opportunities to fish and take long rambles.

*Swarbrick Hall Farm*

There is a choice of accommodation here between the beautifully decorated and spacious en-suite double room at the farmhouse, which is complete with all necessary facilities, or a well-appointed and luxurious self-catering cottage which sleeps five. The room in the farmhouse will comfortably convert for a family of four, and the price includes a full traditional English breakfast. Members of the Farm Holiday Bureau, the accommodation has been awarded two crowns for bed and breakfast and four keys for the self-catering cottage by the English Tourist Board.

**Cleveleys** still has a village atmosphere, with a busy main street and excellent shops, as well as a pleasant seafront.

**The Smugglers Cove** in Cleveleys can easily be found by its gold-coloured sun-canopies. Guests are left in no doubt, as they enter, that this small and friendly restaurant specialises in fish and seafood dishes. Black fishing nets are festooned across the ceiling, and fishing barrel-ends are a prominent feature along one wall.

Laid out on two levels, this is a casual and relaxed place to eat, and it is particularly popular with local businessmen. In the evenings, soft music creates an intimate atmosphere and the ladies all receive a red rose. The Smugglers Cove is run by a husband-and-wife team, Steve and Joanne, and although Steve specialises in crayfish, lobster, and dover sole, the menu is very comprehensive, with an international flavour. Escargot and grenouilles are offered, and a wide range of meat dishes includes steaks with a choice of four sauces. The blackboard announces the day's specials, which take full advantage of the local fresh produce available.

Steve and Joanne are very proud of the restaurant's reputation for especially generous portions. Their boast is that no-one's appetite has ever been less than fully satisfied.

*The Smugglers Cove*

It's only a short walk from the centre of Cleveleys to Marsh Mill at Thornton. This is a superbly restored windmill - open to the public - which now forms the focal point of a delightful craft and garden centre, with organic farm produce.

**Fleetwood,** where the Blackpool trams terminate, is a fishing port that was largely created as a model port by a local landowner, Sir Peter Hesketh Fleetwood, in the 1830s. The port enjoyed perhaps its busiest period during the Second World War, when East Coast harbours were more vulnerable to enemy attack. It was also once the rail terminus for Scotland, as the name of its principal hotel, 'The North Euston', indicates. This was linked to the more famous London Euston by the London and North Western Railway, and was the embarkation point for packet steamers travelling northwards to Scotland before the railway was built across Shap. Queen Victoria herself embarked here for the Highlands.

Sadly, the rail links have now all gone with the closing of Fleetwood's Station in the 1960s, though the port remains important as a Road Freight ferry terminal to Ireland, and the old fish docks are being rebuilt as a marina. Isle of Man Steam Packet Company boats also go to the Isle of Man during the summer months.

Fleetwood also has attractive seafront gardens and promenades, with magnificent views across Morecambe Bay to the Lakeland hills, a busy main shopping street, and a famous and varied market - Market Days in the summer months are every day except Wednesdays and Sundays. There is also the excellent Museum of the Fishing Industry close to the market.

An enjoyable trip to make is to take the passenger Ferry across the Wyre estuary to **Knott End.** Whilst Knott End is little more than a hamlet, the estuary itself and the coastline are particularly interesting, with areas of mud flat, salt marsh and dunes, all rich in birdlife. Much of the area has been declared a Site of Special Scientific Interest for its unique environmental quality, and you can follow the public right of way along the coastline almost as far as Pilling, overlooking Presall Sands.

A small Country Park is being created slightly higher up the Wyre estuary at Stanah, where there is a small car park, and riverside footpaths leading up to Skippool, a narrow, picturesque creek crammed with sailing boats of every conceivable shape and size.

But to discover Over Wyre, that part of Wyre District east and north of the river that gives the District its name, you must take the A588 across Shard Bridge (toll) to **Hambleton,** from where a network of quiet and sometimes extremely narrow lanes winds through a countryside of great charm. In medieval times, Hambleton was a centre for shipbuilding. North of Hambleton and to the west of the A588, a unique feature is the numerous Brine Wells, where brine is extracted for the chemical industry from many undergound wells.

**Pilling** is a quiet, scattered village on the edge of richly fertile marshland. For many years, the village was linked to its market town of **Garstang** by a little, winding, single-track branch railway, known affectionately to locals as 'the Pilling Pig'. According to an old timetable, the last train of the day only continued to Presall and Knott End on Sea if there was anyone left on the train before it trundled home for the night.

The **Springfield House Hotel** in Wheel Lane, Pilling, is situated just off the A588, midway between Blackpool and Lancaster. It is ideally positioned for business people and holidaymakers alike, as access to the M6 motorway and A6 trunk road is close by. Springfield House was built by a Yorkshire family who settled in Pilling in the early 1800s, and is a fine example of Georgian architecture. This imposing residence has been carefully looked after and nurtured by Elizabeth and Gordon Cookson, who are the resident proprietors.

*Springfield House Hotel*

Set in the peaceful surroundings of the Fylde countryside, it is only a quarter of a mile from the sea, yet conveniently placed for visits to Blackpool, Morecambe, the Lake District, and the Trough of Bowland. The hotel is beautifully furnished in keeping with its original splendour, and lends itself to sales conferences, private house parties and small exhibitions. Throughout the hotel, guests will find an abundance of fresh flowers, and most of the guest bedrooms have lovely four poster beds and spotlessly clean en-suite bathrooms. The restaurant is superbly appointed and caters for weekday lunches, evening meals and traditional Sunday lunches. Wedding receptions are a speciality of the house, and the beautifully

105

manicured gardens are ideal for wedding photographs. Springfield House is more than just a hotel - it is an experience not to be missed.

Pilling is said to be the second largest village in Britain, and is steeped in history. **The Olde Ship Restaurant** can be found right in the centre of the village. It was built in 1782 by George Dickinson, a slave trader trading out of the busy port of Lancaster. Originally, this Grade II listed building was built as an inn, and is reputed to be haunted by a lady dressed in Georgian attire, wandering around with a pale and worried look on her face!

The Olde Ship was purchased in 1990 by Mr and Mrs Smedley, who have worked hard to renovate the premises and convert it into a charming restaurant. It is closed on Tuesdays, but open for the other six days of the week from lunch through to 11.30 pm. The menu is varied and comprehensive, with the choice of starters including homemade soups, prawn cocktail, pate, and garlic mushrooms. The main courses are equally appetising, with poached Guinea Fowl in red wine and apricot sauce, seafood crepes, Rainbow Trout with almonds, Duckling a' l'Orange, and a variety of steaks with delicious sauces. Whilst compiling the menu, provision has also been made for vegetarians. Whatever your choice, we are sure you will thoroughly enjoy the hospitality and excellent service extended by your hosts.

*The Olde Ship*

Garstang is an ancient town, whose market dates back to the time of King Edward II, who gave monks the right to hold a market here. It was also important as a stage coaching town on the great high road to Scotland, and Bonnie Prince Charlie is reputed to have stayed in the town in 1715. The main road, later the A6, now by-passes the town, as does the M6. Garstang also had a period of glory as an inland port on the Lancaster Canal, and to the immediate south of the town, there is a fine aqueduct over the River Wyre which was built by John Rennie in 1793. There are also a number of fine canalside features, and trip boats operate on the canal during the summertime.

About half a mile east of the town on a grassy knoll are the ruins of Greenhalgh Castle, built in 1490 by Thomas Stanley, the first Earl of Derby. The castle was involved and severely damaged in a siege against Cromwell in 1645-46, reputedly one of the last strongholds in Lancashire to hold out against him. The town now has a fine Discovery Centre in the High Street, which deals with a variety of aspects of the region, including the canal and countryside history, both in Over Wyre and in the nearby Forest of Bowland.

South of Garstang, there are some attractive villages to explore. **St. Michael's-on-Wyre** has a superb church, mainly 15th century, but with Jacobean pews and some unusual stained glass.

In **Bilsborrow,** on the main A6, there is a picturesque stopping-place for bed and breakfast called **Olde Duncombe House.** With white walls, contrasting black sills and hanging baskets, it lies within well-kept gardens spreading alongside the Lancaster Canal. Cruising boats and walkers can now enjoy the tranquility of this stretch of water, which was constructed last century for transporting coal and stone.

Jayne and Alec Bolton are a friendly couple who came here five years ago, and soon found that their house had an interesting history. Its name refers back to the time when Bilsborrow was actually the village of Duncombe. The house was originally three cottages and a barn, and probably dates back to the 1500s. Long ago, the barn sheltered some of Bonnie Prince Charlie's men overnight, but in modern times, it forms the lounge and bedrooms of the main building.

*Olde Duncombe House*

107

Beautifully furnished, the cottage style emphasises the character of the house, with spacious bedrooms that are most attractive and extremely well equipped. Pine furniture features throughout, and each room is quite individual. Exposed beams and pictures on the walls enhance a warm and peaceful atmosphere. Jayne and Alec give extraordinarily good value for money.

The beams in the dining room are old ship's timbers and the traditional English breakfasts served here are substantial! Although Jayne and Alec can provide evening meals, this service is rarely needed - four neighbouring restaurants and inns cater for most tastes, with another 20 or so just a few minutes walk or drive away.

Nestling along the canalside at Bilsborrow, a pleasantly higgledly-piggledy group of thatched roofs with 'eyebrow' windows welcomes visitors to **Owd Nell's Tavern** and its adjoining restaurant and newly constructed 'Lodging House'.

An 18th century farmhouse, still surrounded by countryside with tow-path walks, forms the core of these pretty white-washed buildings. Its sympathetic conversion, some five years ago, emphasised many old features. While the stone-flagged floors and collections of curios have been repeated at 'Owd Ned's' at Mitton Hall, this is no rigid formula: here at 'Nell's', the farmhouse origins are recalled in the high, raftered ceilings, so reminiscent of barns, and also in the thatched roofs. Again, a relaxed and informal atmosphere holds sway, and a range of tastes in food and refreshments is easily satisfied.

A penny-farthing bike and a collection of clay pipes are attractively featured, and there is even an old 'skiff' suspended from the ceiling. A large semi-circular brick fireplace also catches the eye.

**Guy's Eating Establishment** was built in 1973 to the left of the Tavern, great care being taken to match this extension with the appearance of the original building. An old well, which was discovered at the time, has been preserved and renovated. Guy's offers mainly Italian and International fare, as can be seen from the large, brick pizza-oven, which dominates one corner of the dining room. There are also some rather different fish specials, depending on the freshly caught fish available at the time. A gallery, with dark oak spindle rails, is suspended from the vaulted ceilings. Those dining here gain a good view of the numerous items of interest on display near the main entrance, amongst the leather-clad seating of the reception area.

**Guy's Lodgings** is a two storey building which also has a thatched roof in keeping with the rest of the establishment. All rooms are en-suite and furnished in pine with traditional floral fabrics. There is no room service here, but guests obviously have the use of all the other facilities on site.

*Owd Nell's Tavern*

Further south on the A6, at the crossroads with the B5269, is the village of **Broughton.** Here you will discover what is undoubtedly one of Lancashire's finest Italian restaurants. **The Italian Orchard** is a family run business that has been operating for the last six years. The Bragagnini family originate from the north-east, Friuli region of Italy, situated between Venice and Trieste. Since opening their restaurant, the family have earned themselves an excellent reputation. The atmosphere is relaxing and warm, with soft Italian music being played continuously in the background.

The interior of the restaurant is most impressive. Set on two levels, diners are afforded the luxury of beautifully laid tables with sparkling cutlery and glasses. The restaurant also has the facility to cater for up to 250 people at any one time. In fact, it is not unusual on a Saturday evening for as many as 300 - 400 people to dine there, so the Italian Orchard is an excellent choice for large party bookings.

The kitchen area is open plan, and guests are able to watch the preparation of their meal. As one would expect, the menu offers the finest Italian cuisine. Continental dishes are also available, and a large board informs customers of the daily specials. A typical choice might be Antipasto Misto - a selection of hors d'oeuvres, or Peperoni Farciti - peppers filled with meat and rice, or something perhaps from the selection of English starters. There is a choice from upwards of 15 different dishes.

As well as traditional pasta and pizza, fish is considered to be a speciality of the house, with Seafood Pancakes, Fillets of Sole, and King Prawns being just a few to choose from. The Continental dishes are just as mouthwatering, with Chicken, Veal, Steaks and Pork featuring prominently. The meat dishes are served with delicious sauces and beautifully presented fresh vegetables. The wine list is alleged to be the largest and most comprehensive available in Lancashire, with over 200 different labels plus their own house wine.

If you should decide to dine at The Italian Orchard, you are sure to enjoy a superb meal in the congenial company of the Bragagnini family, who will undoubtedly wish you 'Buon Appetito'.

*The Italian Orchard*

Most roads in this part of Lancashire lead to **Preston,** Lancashire's county town. Preston is a fine central point from which to explore the whole region. It is a town of ancient history, strategically situated on the highest navigable point of the River Ribble. It is still an active port, with cargo vessels and even an occasional special passenger boat, though most maritime activity nowadays comes from sailing and windsurfing in the Riversway Marina. There are an impressive range of public buildings. The Parish Church occupies a site which has been in use for Christian worship since the 7th century, and the present church has an elegant 205 foot high spire which soars over the town centre. Preston Town Hall was designed by Gilbert Scott in suitable Gothic style, whilst the fine Harris Art Gallery, Museum and Library, in equally impressive neoclassic style, provides a civic focal point close to the busy covered markets. The Harris Gallery has, incidentally, some of the most impressive collections of sculpture and paintings in the county. There are also a number of covered shopping centres and pedestrianised areas, including the Guild Hall and Charter Theatre Complex which host a wide variety of events from straight theatre to classical and pop music and sporting events.

Only a few minute's walk from the busy town centre lie the green walkways, ponds and shrubbery of Avenham Park, which is itself linked by a riverside walk to Miller Park.

The unique **Turbary House Garden Centre** has absolutely everything for the enthusiastic gardener in a landscaped setting, offering hours of interest and enjoyment for all the family. In addition to an extensive display of indoor and outdoor plants to suit every home or garden, there is also a wide selection of garden accessories, tools, books and gifts, including basketware, ceramics, and fresh, dried and silk flowers. All of the afore-mentioned are attractively displayed in Turbary's well-stocked shop.

We cannot think of anywhere else that visitors can take a lakeside or woodland stroll and wander around hundreds of trees, shrubs and conifers whilst selecting their purchases, happy in the knowledge that the children are playing safely in the adventure playground. New innovations include a birds of prey aviary with fascinating Falconry displays and lectures. Every Wednesday is Senior Citizens Day at Turbary House, with a special discount on most items.

The Centre offers a unique gardening advice service, and can arrange special displays, demonstrations and functions to suit club and party bookings. They are happy to tailor events to suit the individual party, and it would be wise to enquire about the morning coffee, afternoon tea, hot pot suppers, barbeques or buffets which can be made available, in order to ensure a really special social event for all attending. Turbary House Garden Centre is open all year, with the exception of Christmas Day, Boxing Day and New Years Day.

*Turbary House Garden Centre*

The **Wesley House Restaurant** can be located on the outskirts of Preston at Lostock Hall. Situated in a main road position, the restaurant is housed in a large, detached red brick and black and white timbered building.

Josephine Jump is the proprietor, and she told us that until five years ago it was an Italian restaurant, but sadly, due to a fire, this was destroyed. It wasn't until Josie came along and saw the potential for another business venture that it came alive again as a restaurant.

Josie is a charming lady who comes from Southern Ireland, and being a typical native from this part of Ireland, she exudes the warmth and friendliness normally associated with the people from that part of the world. The restaurant has been completely renovated and refurbished to a high standard, and offers an excellent choice of menu.

Starters range from Melon and Port Caribbean and Baked Mushrooms and Prawns in Garlic Sauce, to Chicken Celery and Apple Mayonnaise. The choice may be made from around nine different starters. Main courses are just as appetising, and include Steaks of up to twenty ounces, Game, Poultry and Fish. Various Pasta and Vegetarian dishes are also available. The cost of a meal for two is very reasonable, with the average price being only ten pounds a head for starter and main course. We thought this represented excellent value.

*Wesley House Restaurant*

It's only a short drive south of Preston to Worden Hall, close to **Leyland.** **The Worden Arts and Craft Centre** is surrounded by 157 acres of parkland and can be found just off the B5243. Opened in 1984, the Centre occupies the remaining buildings of Worden Hall, home of the Farrington family until 1947. The Centre houses a fully equipped theatre, eight craft workshops, a coffee shop, and an exhibition-cum-display room. It is fascinating to watch crafts such as Pyrography, Woodturning, Knitting, Ceramics, Landscape Painting, Stained Glass and Blacksmithying in the process of being worked on.

Adjacent to the Centre is the Lancashire branch of the Council for the Protection of Rural England, a registered charity which seeks to improve, protect and conserve the countryside. CPRE has a gift shop and an exhibition area, which features permanent displays of Worden Hall 'Then and Now'.

The main features of Worden Park include a 17th century ice house, a miniature railway, a maze, a garden for the blind, an arboretum, a children's play area, and several picnic areas. There is ample parking which is free in the main car park, and in the Centre car park. Coach parties are also welcome, but prior notice is requested.

*Worden Arts & Craft Centre*

Leyland is a small town, and it has seen a lot of changes in the last 20 years. In many ways, despite the demise of much of the commercial vehicle industry which previously dominated it, it has moved into a period of renewed prosperity and taken on a more leisurely and attractive character.

Characteristic of this revitalisation is the recent renovation of the old blacksmith's, now the **Smithy Guest House,** which was a working smithy until about 25 years ago. When Christine Marland and her family moved here in the early 1980s, she insisted on retaining all the available original features when it was rebuilt and converted. The smithy dated from the 17th century, and the old stone walls have been made into a feature in many of the bedrooms, all of which are on the ground floor. This and other special amenities make it ideal for disabled guests. A large, pleasant garden can be enjoyed in the summer months.

An additional attraction is the lively personality of Christine herself. She combines an efficiently run guest house (of excellent value) with a friendly informality. Nothing is too much trouble - Christine offers to babysit for children, and she happily caters for vegetarian or special dietary needs. She is also an excellent cook and she does not believe in stinting! The four-course evening meals are usually traditional, with homemade soup and a roast. Although there are no tea and coffee facilities in the bedrooms, these are always available in the residents' television lounge.

*Smithy Guest House*

It is hard to believe that **Calverts Farm** at **Ulnes Walton** lies less than half-a-dozen miles from the M6, because this is a 54-acre haven of idyllic isolation.

At their working stock-farm, John and Dorothy Mercer offer cosy and comfortable accommodation. Dorothy's traditional farmhouse fare is much appreciated and includes large breakfasts and homemade specialities such as Lancashire hotpot and steak-and-kidney pie for evening meals. Although the farm is busy, all their visitors will receive a personal and friendly welcome. Children are well catered for and dogs are permitted by prior arrangement, so that true family holidays may be enjoyed here.

*Calverts Farm*

Not only is it a very convenient base for visitors to the Cumbrian Lakeland and Blackpool, but there is also plenty to do close to and around the farm. In these tranquil surroundings there is a large pond which is well stocked with perch, carp and tench for coarse fishing. These will give a great deal of pleasure to anglers, while ornithologists will enjoy the interesting bird population attracted to the farm.

South of the Ribble lies a region of richly fertile countryside - an area of potato fields, greenhouses and market gardens. It's also an area of quiet villages reached along meandering lanes.

**Croston** by the little River Yarrow has some 17th century almshouses and a 15th century church, by the side of which is a stone bridge with a single arch, whilst Eccleston Church has the remains of a Norman font. **Eccleston** is neat and tidy and relatively modern. It also has its surprises.

One of the most remarkable businesses we have ever called into has to be the fascinating company in Eccleston known internationally as **Bygone Times**. As the name suggests, this company has the best collection of antiques and Americana in Europe. In total there are five warehouses covering over 100,000 square feet of floor space. All five of these are crammed full with the most incredible and amazing array of objects, all of which are either for sale or hire. Because Bygone Times is so fascinating, visitors return time after time just to enjoy the spectacle, or to buy something unique, unusual, or impossible to find anywhere else. Visitors travel from all over the country to purchase specialised items. Children, adults, professional buyers and amateur collectors are all equally enthralled with the vast array of objects they see before them.

The proprietors of Bygone Times have the most comprehensive collection of Americana in this country, all imported direct from the U.S.A. Next time you walk into a shop, bar, restaurant, or even perhaps pay a visit to the fairground, you will possibly be confronted with articles which have been obtained from these premises. It would be impossible to list everything contained within these warehouses, so we will simply give you food for thought by naming just a few. Bulbous fridges dispensing coke and nostalgia, wurlitzers, electric guitars, baseball bats, telephone kiosks, store and road signs and traffic lights. The more spectacular items range from large Statues of Liberty to Moose Heads and Street Furniture. There is also a garage sale where the more discerning can purchase all American 50's classic cars, laden with gleaming chrome.

Bygone Times particularly appeals to Interior and Set Designers. The stock can be purchased outright, and covers every style from Victorian to the 1960s and beyond. They supply film, theatre and television companies with everything from individual props to complete sets. For Interior Designers looking for an entire theme, Bygone Times has the widest range of desirably dated, designer objects in the country. They supply to clients such as The Great American Prop Company in Orlando, Florida, Windsor Safari Park, Rock Island Diner, Piccadilly and Liberty Street Restaurants, as well as speciality shops and major breweries and architects throughout Europe. Without any hesitation whatsoever, we suggest you call in and browse around. We can guarantee that you will be delighted with the many things to see.

*Bygone Times*

Although it is only three miles from the M6, **The Rigbye Arms** at **Wrightington** nestles in the heart of rural Lancashire. This is a family run country inn with a well-deserved reputation for excellent traditional country fare. The menu changes daily and is very much dependent on seasonal availability and what can be bought from local suppliers. A large blackboard advertises the wide choice available, all homemade, ranging from specialities such as wood-pigeon casserole and beef in Guiness to old-fashioned bread-and-butter pudding. Vegetarian and special diets are catered for, and children's portions may be ordered.

Enjoyment of the delicious food is sure to be enhanced by both the friendly hospitality of Barbara and Keith Guest and the old world charm of the inn. Real Ale is on tap in the aptly named 'Foxhole', where walkers and farmers can drink their pints whilst considering the wildlife trophies and nostalgic bygones which adorn the walls and beams. A log-burning stove is a feature of the carvery within the attractive lounge bar, which is otherwise warmed by open coal fires and also includes a small snug area where children are welcome. In the warmer weather, guests are welcome to enjoy the bowling green, barbecue, garden and children's play area.

*The Rigbye Arms*

At **Mossey Lea,** south of Wrightington on the B5250 and just west of the M6, is Tunley Presbyterian Church, built in 1691 and the oldest Presbyterian Chuch in England. Skull House at **Appley Bridge** contains an ancient skull which reputedly goes back to its resting place from wherever it is moved.

We were greeted in a warm and friendly manner by Ron Cripps the manager when we visited **The Dicconson Arms,** in Appley Bridge. This charming pub and restaurant is situated near to the summit of Parbold Hill, which is the highest point between The Pennines and the sea. An interesting feature of The Dicconson is the stained glass windows depicting local scenes. The pub derives its name from Lord Dicconson, who once owned most of the surrounding land in the area. The bar is renowned for its traditional ales and wide choice of bar snacks. The restaurant can seat up to 78 people and is very comfortable as well as providing good food which is well presented and excellent value for money. The staff have a lovely friendly manner and do their upmost to ensure that diners enjoy their meal.

To the rear of the premises is a beer garden which is ideal during the summer for children to play in. Parking does not pose a problem, as the car park is large and spacious. We are quite convinced that if you decide to visit the Dicconson Arms, you will not be disappointed. Close by to the Dicconson is the notorious 'Parbold Bottle'. For those of our readers who have never heard of it, it is a huge, roughly hewn stone, shaped like a bottle. It was erected here in 1832 to commemorate the passing of the Reform Act. The site of The Dicconson Arms is known locally as 'Dangerous Corner', and it apparently got its name when an undertaker's hearse travelling too fast unfortunately deposited a coffin in the middle of the road!

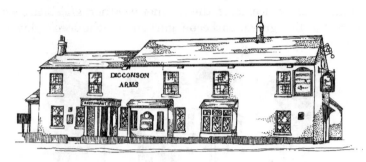

*The Dicconson Arms*

An alternative way to begin a journey into West Lancashire is to start at the top. There is nothing quite like standing at the summit of Parbold Hill on a warm summer's day, taking in the splendour of West Lancashire. Acres of lush, green countryside, laced with quaint villages and church steeples, stretch out as far as the eye can see, as the tranquil waters of the Leeds-Liverpool canal flow gently between them. Nestling at the foot of Parbold Hill lies the pretty village of **Newburgh.** The 'Best Kept Village of 1989', Newburgh is a delight to visit, and if you're feeling in need of fortification at this stage of your journey, be sure to stop off at the village's only inn, The Red Lion, which is also a well known restaurant and hotel.

Also very close to the motorway, but hidden away in the centre of a triangle formed by the villages of Croston, Eccleston and Mawdesley, **The Robin Hood Inn** has a charm which is no secret in this area. Standing at a 'T' junction about one and a half miles from each of the three villages, it has a pretty, white exterior, with black sills and lintels setting off the rather fine pub sign. This depicts Robin Hood and his band around a table in Sherwood Forest. Asked why the legendary outlaws are remembered here so far from Nottingham, licencees David and Margaret Cropper regret that somehow the story has been lost over the 300 years of the Inn's history. However, this is the only disappointment at this deservedly popular pub and restaurant.

Stone walls, beams, and brasses are much in evidence inside, and on chillier days an open fire burns in the 'snug'. The restaurant is upstairs, and extends throughout three adjoining and interconnecting rooms, seating 50 in all. This layout enables parties of 12 or more to enjoy relative privacy. The menu has a good selection of traditional grilled dishes, and the succulent steaks are particular favourites due to their excellent value. Booking early is the only way to ensure a table at weekends - the restaurant is very much in demand. At lunchtimes, only bar meals are available, either in the restaurant or in the pub, and, as with the a la carte menu, these are freshly prepared on the premises. A particularly wide choice of ales is offered, including real ale, and their wine list is good too.

A family room is set aside for those with children, and there is also a play area outside. A new acquisition, an 'enchanted tree', ensures that little ones are engrossed at play whilst their elders relax in the beer garden.

Margaret and David have been here for 25 years, and took over from Margaret's father. Oddly enough, the previous landlords were also father followed by son - near enough to a strong family tradition, surely!

*The Robin Hood Inn*

Rufford Old Hall, also close to the Leeds-Liverpool Canal at **Rufford,** is one of the finest 15th century buildings in the North. It is a superb, late medieval half-timbered country house, notable for an ornate hammer-beam roof and screen. There are collections of 17th century oak furniture in the Carolean Wing, which was altered in 1821, as well as 16th century armour and tapestries. It is now a National Trust property, and is open from 1 pm on most days except Fridays from Easter until the end of October.

A friendly welcome is assured when visiting **The Brandreth Barn Country Farm Hotel and Restaurant** in **Burscough.** Whether dining in the restaurant or staying at the hotel, guests will be delighted with the homely atmosphere which has been created by Margaret Wilson and her husband Bill. This charming couple make excellent hosts, and one cannot fail to admire the initiative they have taken by creating two successful businesses that complement each other so well. The name of Brandreth Barn is thought to have been derived from a former 18th century Chief Constable of Lancashire, who went by the name of Brandreth and lived locally.

When it comes to the catering side of the business, the farm provides excellent fresh produce for the kitchen in their use of first class home cooking. Much emphasis is put on using only the very best quality produce. Although relatively new as a hotel and restaurant, the business has fast gained an enviable reputation. The restaurant comfortably seats 45 people and the choices available from the menu are varied and mouthwatering. Many of the wines from the wine list are produced locally, and they are steadily increasing in popularity.

All of the bedrooms are en-suite and provide the usual facilities, with the added advantage of very comfortable accommodation. Margaret and Bill thoroughly enjoy their new-found profession. This is evident from the standards they have set and the policies they have adopted in order for their guests to have an enjoyable stay whilst at Brandreth Barn.

*Brandreth Barn Country Farm Hotel & Restaurant*

Also at Burscough, the **Martin Inn** is a traditional Lancashire Inn with super landlords. It is always a joy to come across a real family run hostelry with pleasant, friendly staff who aim to please their customers. The Inn can be located just four miles from Ormskirk and seven miles from Southport, and is easily reached from the M61, M58 and M6. This part of rural Lancashire is unspoilt and renowned for its hospitality and genuine friendliness to visitors.

John, Peter and Dianne who run The Martin Inn actually live on the premises, so guests are guaranteed that quality is maintained. The Mere bar is frequented by regulars who create an atmosphere of jovial hospitality. For lovers of real ales, the Inn provides a wide variety to choose from and has won numerous awards for their excellence. Accommodation is also available in the form of 12 comfortable en-suite bedrooms with extensive views of the surrounding countryside.

THE LANCASHIRE COAST AND THE WIRRAL

Anyone wishing to enjoy a quiet weekend in the country, with good food and good company at a price that won't break the bank, should not pass up the opportunity of visiting The Martin Inn. The surrounding area has a wealth of leisure activities ranging from golf to water sports, and a little further afield is Liverpool's famous Albert Dock Village which is well worth a visit.

*The Martin Inn*

While in Burscough, you will be able to view the Leeds-Liverpool Canal at close quarters. An abundance of wildlife can be seen around the canal banks and hedgerows, and if this is where your interests lie, your next port of call in West Lancashire will not disappoint you. Martin Mere Wildfowl and Wetlands Centre is home to about 1,600 resident swans, geese and ducks of 120 species from all over the world. This 350 acre site includes a host of attractions for all the family. The acres of fine landscaped gardens are a joy to stroll around. A peaceful nature trail also links nine bird watching hides, where you can see wild flowers and plants, woodland birds, and butterflies and other insects. Added to all this is a cafe, a shop, and plenty of parking space which makes Martin Mere an ideal place to spend a day out.

Travel north next, and situated just off the main Preston to Southport road at Mere Brow you will find Leisure Lakes. Ninety acres of countryside, woodland and lakes with sandy beaches, windsurfing, canoeing and fishing. There's also an adjacent pub. Time to head back towards the start of your journey, but there are still one or two places to see yet.

A much smaller Nature Reserve and Wildlife Refuge than Martin Mere is to be found at Haskayne Cutting, west of **Ormskirk.** Here, the Lancashire Trust for the Conservation for Nature have developed a one and a half mile Nature Trail in an old railway cutting. It can be reached off the lane to

Barton, from the A567 south of Halsall.

Between the 16th and 18th centuries, the Stanleys, Earls of Derby, were Lords of the Manor. The Parish church dedicated to St Peter and St Paul is particularly impressive. Founded in Anglo-Saxon times (hence 'Orm's Kirk'), the church is one of only three in England to have both a tower and a steeple, the steeple actually being older than the tower, dating from the 14th century. The tower was in fact added in 1548 to house the bells which were being moved there from Burscough Priory, which was being demolished. The carving of two figures in stone in the outside wall at the east end are probably Saxon. In the Derby Chapel are the tombs of the Stanley family, notable Royalists.

*Ormskirk Parish Church*

Ormskirk remains an attractive town, with some interesting 18th century and Victorian buildings - shops, inns, and public buildings, as well as some attractive terraced houses of the same period.

*The Clock Tower, Ormskirk*

No trip to West Lancashire would be complete without a visit to Ormskirk Market. As you stroll through the wide and varied range of stalls, you can see the history of this charter market that dates back 700 years to the Burscough Priory Monks. Held on Thursdays and Saturdays, each stall holds many bargains for you to choose from, and whether it's clothing, china, or just about anything else you can think of, you're sure to walk away with a smile on your face.

After a hectic day sightseeing, the time has come for gentle relaxation in a peaceful setting. Where better then, than Beacon Country Park? The Park boasts a superb Golf Course and Driving Range, walking trails second to none, a pizzeria where you can indulge in the finest Sicilian pizzas prepared by Salvatore, and a relaxing bar, all of which adds up to 360 acres of pure enjoyment. West Lancashire is a delight to discover, so prior to visiting, why not telephone (0695) 577177, extension 342, and ask for a free West Lancashire Fact Pack.

*Buck i' th' Vine, Ormskirk*

Only 10 miles from Southport's beaches, there is a particularly attractive caravan park, just north-east of Ormskirk. **Abbey Farm Caravan Park** is set in 22 acres of wooded farmland on the site of the 12th century Burscough Priory.

Mature trees and shrubs form a garden setting here. The owners, Joan and Alan Bridge, emphasise that the atmosphere is that of friendly, old-fashioned caravan holidays. None of the caravans are residential or sub-let, and they prefer not to provide commercialised features such as club and games rooms. However, there is nothing old-fashioned about the amenities, including those for disabled people and the nursing mothers' room - everything in this respect is very up to date.

With thoughtful organisation, Joan and Alan have ensured that everyone can thoroughly enjoy the park. Plenty of space and a special recreation field with an adventure playground enables children to play safely, while those with or without dogs appreciate a specified dog-exercise area. Touring caravans are welcome, and a separate field is set aside with facilities for camping.

Open all year round, the park is within easy reach of many places of interest, and within walking distance of a good variety of country inns. Anglers have no further to go than just outside the park!

*Abbey Farm Caravan Park*

A notable landmark between Ormskirk and Southport is Scarisbrick Hall. It was built in 1867 to the designs of Pugin, and with its tall and slender clock tower it is one of the grandest, if most extravagant, buildings of its period in the North. It is now a public school.

**Southport** is, and remains, one of Lancashire's most popular seaside resorts. If it doesn't have quite the bravura of Blackpool, it does have style, with Lord Street and its arcades still being one of the region's most elegant shopping streets. Even though it is a seaside resort, you sometimes have to travel some distance across broad expanses of sand to reach the sea, and the pier is so long that a railway takes you out to the pier end, where at low tide the sea and the Mersey estuary can still be some way off. There is all that you would expect to find at a seaside resort: lots of sand (especially dunes), refreshments, funfairs, rides, walks, boating pools, toy trains, and fine gardens, including superb herbacious borders and dahlia beds in late summer. But it's also worth travelling out to Hesketh Park or to the delightful Botanic Gardens at Meols.

If you are in the Churchtown area of Southport and are looking for a restaurant to stop at, we would suggest you pop into **Peggotty's** in Botanic Road. Charles and Ann White are the owners, and they pride themselves on their standards of excellence. We were greeted warmly by this friendly couple and immediately felt at ease. Peggotty's is fully licensed, and the a la carte menu is always available to choose from. An early evening set menu is also on offer.

This charming restaurant has a real olde worlde atmosphere, and is frequently patronised by local members of the community. The cuisine has a strong traditional English flavour to it. Sunday lunch is always popular and although there is sufficient seating for 40 people, it is advisable to give Charles or Ann a call to reserve a table. The Botanic Gardens are just a short distance away, and this makes an ideal place to visit either before or after a meal.

*Peggotty's Restaurant*

The Sefton Coast south of Southport and towards **Formby** is of national importance for its nature conservation interest - past Birkdale, also famous for its golf course, Ainsdale and into the Formby Hills, where pine woods flourish on the dunes. Lying between the Mersey and Ribble estuaries, Formby Point is an area of constant change where Man battles with the elements in an effort to prevent the merciless erosion of the coastline. The dunes protect the hinterland from flooding like a natural sea wall, but they also bring their own problems. Sand blown by storms has in the past threatened inland villages with engulfment and since around 1700, leaseholders in the area were required by law to plant marram grass to help stabilise the dunes. The woods were first planted at the beginning of this century for the same reason, and the intention was that an esplanade would be constructed along the coast if the sand could be held at bay.

The fact that Nature refuses to be so easily tamed has proved to be of great benefit to nature lovers who visit the area, as much of it is now a National Nature Reserve. Almost 500 acres of Formby's dunes and woodlands were bought by the National Trust in 1967, and it now provides a natural habitat for a wide range of animals and plants. Two animals in particular make Formby Point well known. The red squirrel colony descends from the variety introduced here from the Continent many years ago, and owes its success largely to being so well fed by visitors. The fact that so few trees grow on Formby's hinterland means that the colony is also well protected from its enemy, the grey squirrel, which is prevented access. The other animal which is eagerly looked for, but far more difficult to spot than the red squirrel due to its nocturnal habits, is the rare Natterjack Toad. Artificial freshwater pools have been dug to encourage this protected creature to breed. As you explore this fascinating area, please be careful to keep to the marked footpaths, as the erosion of the dunes is caused as much by the trampling feet of visitors as by wind and wave erosion.

**Liverpool,** like Manchester, is a city discovering itself as a major northern tourist centre. Much is linked to the city's maritime history, which began when the port was granted its first charter in the 13th century, and expanded with the coming of the railways and the great liners in the 19th century. It became Britain's Irish and great Atlantic Seaport, through whose wharves thousands of emigrants from Britain and from Continental Europe set sail, in often cramped conditions, to the New World - to America.

If you make your way to the great Albert Dock, now superbly restored as a Shopping, Heritage and Craft Centre, you'll find the Maritime Museum, which among many other exhibits has the interior of a 19th century emigrants' ship to give an impression of what it was like for so many people seeking a new life across the Atlantic.

Few cities in the world have a more impressive waterfront than Liverpool, with the great dockside buildings, including the famous Royal Liver Building, the Cunard Building and Port of Liverpool Building with its proud eagles, forming a thrilling skyline and attractive walkway. But many of the great merchant warehouses, banks and trading houses of this once mighty port survive along broad streets to give Liverpool a sense of grandeur which lives on. Behind the great warehouses and the new centrally pedestrianised areas, run narrow streets and alleyways, some with old inns and restaurants, which were once the haunt of mariners. But since the 1960s, these have been linked to the names of four young men who gave the city a new fame - the celebrated Beatles, whose music and Liverpool Sound in the Cavern Club became known worldwide. You can now take a daily Beatles Magical History Tour to visit such places that influenced their music as Penny Lane and Strawberry Fields - details from the Liverpool Information Centre on 051 709 3631.

This is a city of two great Cathedrals, the Anglican Cathedral, built in the 20th century in red sandstone in Gothic style and the largest Anglican cathdral in the world, contrasting with the modernistic Roman Catholic Cathedral, whose elegant crown-like structure is so very distinctive and impressive in a different kind of way.

Liverpool is also a great cultural centre. The Royal Liverpool Philharmonic Orchestra has an international reputation, and is based in the Philharmonic Hall in Hope Street. The Liverpool Playhouse in Williamson Square is Britain's oldest repertory theatre, whilst the Everyman Theatre nearby also has an outstanding reputation, in addition to the Empire, and the Royal Court Theatres. Walker Art Gallery has a splendid collection of Great Masters from early Flemish painters to the 20th century, including fine Rembrandts and Cezannes, whilst you'll find the Tate Gallery Liverpool devoted to modern art at Albert Dock. Transport enthusiasts will find much to admire in the Large Objects Collection in New Quay, whilst social historians will be fascinated by the Museum of Labour History, which lies close to the superb Liverpool Museum and Planetarium in William Brown Street.

Nor is the city devoid of green spaces. Croxteth Hall is set in 500 acres of Country Park. Keen walkers can follow the Mersey Way, following the coast from the Albert Dock via Otterspool Park almost as far as Widnes, whilst cyclists have use of the 20 miles of the former Liverpool Loop Line, now a country park.

**Sefton Park,** close to the city centre, is notable for its magnificent Palm House. If you wish to relax here in very pleasant surroundings and wake up refreshed, ready to begin another day's sight-seeing, we would suggest staying at **The Phoenix Hotel** in Aigburth Drive. With or without a car, it is ideally situated, with the city centre, train station, bus terminus and airport only a few minutes away. The hotel is a beautiful, distinctive house and serves as a genuine reminder of bygone days. Built originally for a shipowner engaged in South American trade, many of the period features of the premises were retained whilst restoration and modernisation were taking place.

After 10 years in the hotel trade, the proprietors of this professionally run hotel pride themselves in the knowledge that personal service is the key to the comfort of their guests. The accommodation is spacious, well furnished and comfortable, and is centrally heated throughout. All the rooms have colour television, and an additional advantage for disabled guests is the ramp, lift and wheelchair which give access to all of the facilities within the hotel.

The private lounge bar is fully equipped, and residents may relax here after lunch or dinner with a drink from the bar, or just take coffee. An additional lounge, with its quaint turret, sitting area and peaceful atmosphere, overlooks the gardens and is most enjoyable if you prefer a quiet afternoon or evening. The food served in the restaurant ranges from wholesome home cooking to a la carte, with a fine choice of meals available.

*The Phoenix Hotel*

Situated on the corner of Siddeley Street in **Aigburth,** the **L'Alouette Restaurant** is an imposing building of Victorian stature. Once inside, the theme of this large restaurant is typically French. Catering for large numbers of diners, it is popular with both local residents and visitors to the area.

*L'Alouette Restaurant*

It is not strictly necessary to book in advance as the staff will do their best to accommodate diners walking in off the street. The cuisine is as typically French as the decor, and represents excellent value for money. Close to all the local places of interest and popular attractions, L'Alouette is an ideal stopping off point after a long day's sightseeing. Established seven years ago, the restaurant has maintained an excellent reputation for business lunches and dinners, special occasions and party bookings.

At **Knowsley,** to the east of the city, there is a five mile Safari Park through six game reserves, whilst Stadt Moers Country Park close by is a fine example of a former derelict area being restored to natural beauty.

**Speke Hall** is a beautiful half-timbered Elizabethan manor house, and its grounds have a wealth of interesting features for the whole family to explore. When visiting the Hall you can discover the secrets behind the eavesdrop chamber, or find out what life was like below stairs in the servant's hall and kitchen. You may even bump into the tapestry ghost on your travels. The oldest parts of Speke Hall were built nearly 500 years ago by the Norris family. Over succeeding generations, the building developed around a cobbled courtyard which is dominated by two yew trees, known locally as Adam and Eve. The Great Hall dates back to Tudor times, but has considerably altered over the years. The house as we see it today owes much to the refurbishments carried out in Victorian times, with many of the smaller panelled rooms containing fine furnishings from the arts and crafts movement, designed by William Morris.

*Speke Hall*

Outside, there are superb grounds and gardens. The moat which surrounded the house in the 17th century has now been drained and forms a feature of the grounds, which include a Victorian Rose Garden, a Croquet

129

lawn, ancient woodland and the raised walk, which offers fine views across the Mersey. To make a visit even more enjoyable, the National Trust has an on-site tea room, serving light lunches with home baking, teas and ices, and a shop where you can purchase books, stationery, souvenirs and gifts. For the disabled, lavatories have been adapted to facilitate wheelchairs, and free use of a wheelchair is also available. Special events are arranged throughout the year and include music, drama and walks. Situated on the Northern bank of the Mersey, Speke Hall is just six miles east of Liverpool city centre and only thirty minutes from Chester.

For a real Merseyside experience, you have to cross the Mersey Estuary in a Famous Mersey Ferry, historic ships working Europe's oldest ferry. It was founded in 1207, the route being from Liverpool (Pierhead) to Birkenhead (Woodside) and Wallasey (Seacombe). These powerful little vessels, strong enough to withstand the Mersey tides, have recently been refurbished in traditional style to provide a miniature cruise across to the Wirral Peninsula. The views from the vessels down the estuary, which still carries big vessels - usually with containers, coming into the port - are back to the famous Liverpool waterfront, and are truly memorable.

You can also reach the Wirral in less grand style via the Mersey Tunnel and the M53 Motorway, which links to the M56 from Cheshire. Or you can go by Merseyrail, Liverpool's efficient underground railway, whose Wirral Line serves the northern part of the Wirral extremely efficiently, with electrified lines and frequent services to the traditional seaside resorts of New Brighton, Hoylake and West Kirby.

The Wirral describes itself, with good reason, as the Leisure Peninsula. Though the once great industry of shipbuilding at Birkenhead has declined, much of the area has undergone a change, not only with the restoration and smartening up of ferry terminii, but with the creation of attractive walkways along the seafront. If elegant Hamilton Square no longer contains the smart town houses of sea captains, Birkenhead Priory, the Chapter House of a Benedictine Monastery established in 1150 AD, now a church, has changed little and contains a Heritage Centre and Museum.

Birkenhead Park to the east of the town centre is a remarkable example of an early Victorian urban park, with lake, rockery, lawns, and formal gardens, which interestingly enough became the model for an even more famous park - Central Park in New York.

If you take the train from Liverpool Lime Street's Merseyrail Underground Station to West Kirby, then only a few minutes from the station, you're on the Wirral Way. This is a 12 mile long walkway along the old West Kirby-Hooton railway line, leading into Wirral Country Park. At **Thurstaton,** some three miles along the line and just off the A540, there is a car park and an excellent Countryside Centre close by. Here you'll find a choice of walks and trails along the coast, or continuing along the railway to Neston and Hooton via Hadlow Road, where you'll discover a perfectly restored railway station - without any trains.

Thurstaton village itself, with its impressive red sandstone church, lies close to Thurstaton Common, a long red sandstone ridge around which heather, bracken and gorse grow in profusion. From the summit, with its viewfinder, there is a superb view of the whole of the Wirral Peninsula, across the Dee estuary to the hills of Wales, and back across Liverpool to the Lancashire coast.

An equally fascinating walk from West Kirby, only to be undertaken when the tide is low, is to Red Rocks and Hilbre Island, a nationally important bird sanctuary in the Dee estuary, noted for the variety of wading birds to be seen. Access is on foot only (it's a five mile return trip) and is restricted to certain times of the day, as indicated by tide tables posted at the Dee Lane slipway.

Not far from Neston, into Cheshire, are Ness Gardens, Liverpool University's Botanic Gardens, where you'll find a splendid collection of herbaceous plants, primulas, rhododendrons, azaleas, heather, rose, and rock and water gardens, in a setting of sweeping lawns with magnificent views across the Dee estuary.

Wirral is full of the most fascinating villages to explore. **Bidston** has a hilltop observatory and windmill close by, and **Oxton,** a conservation area, is noted for fine views. **Willaston** also has a windmill, as well as a number of 17th century cottages and a village green.

Most fascinating of all perhaps, though relatively modern, is **Port Sunlight Village.** This is a model garden village, founded in 1888 by William Hesketh Lever to house his soap factory workers. It was named after his most famous product, Sunlight Soap. The village is officially rated as an Outstanding Conservation Area. In March of 1888, Mrs Lever cut the first sod of Port Sunlight, and thus helped to lay the foundations of a village which was to be appreciated by many generations to come. It was the aim of her husband, who later became the first Viscount Leverhulme, to provide for his workers 'a new Arcadia, ventilated and drained on the most scientific principles'. He took great pleasure in helping to plan this most picturesque garden village, and he employed nearly 30 different architects to create its unique style.

Port Sunlight is now a conservation area, still within its original boundaries. The history of this village and its community is explored in

Port Sunlight Heritage Centre, where there is a scale model of the village and of a Victorian Port Sunlight House, the original plans for the buildings, and displays of period advertising and soap packaging. The Village Trail shows you the Village's attractions, including the Lady Lever Art Gallery, which contains Lord Leverhulme's world famous collections of pre-Raphaelite paintings and Wedgwood. Guided tours of the Village are available for parties and schools, and a Village Trail leaflet enables visitors to find their way around.

If you are looking for somewhere different to eat, then why not try the restaurant which is situated in the grounds. It offers fine foods, a wonderful setting, and fascinating and beautiful treasures to appreciate.

*Port Sunlight Heritage Centre*

Further up the river is another Museum of national importance - The Boat Museum at **Ellesmere Port.** Situated in a historic dock complex where the Shropshire Union Canal and the Manchester Ship Canal meet, you'll find here a remarkable collection of canal craft, from a little weedcutter to 300 ton packet boats. Many are open to visitors, as are restored warehouses and canal workshops. These contain exhibitions, displays, workshops, a working steam engine, craft workshops and a picnic area. There are boat trips from the Museum in the summer months.

South of here at **Little Stanney** is **Rake Hall.** This is a magnificent old hall which over the years has been converted into a public house and hotel. Set in seven acres of attractive gardens, the views from the premises are superb, and incorporated within the grounds is a huge pond. It was built in the 19th century as a private residence, and the staircases, fireplaces and some of the windows are listed. As well as providing the usual facilities of first class ales and food, Rake Hall also has a private function room accommodating up to 140 guests, making it ideal for weddings and private gatherings. The exterior of the hotel has excellent facilities for children, with swings and slides for them to play on. There is also a large barbecue which is ideal for warm summer evenings. Rake Hall has been tastefully refurbished throughout during the last year, and it is an ideal stopping off point for a drink and a bite to eat, or indeed for a large family gathering.

*Rake Hall*

**Chester** has been described as one of England's finest walled cities. It has a history going back almost 2,000 years to when, in 79 AD, the Romans established a military settlement on the Dee estuary known as Deva, as a port and important frontier outpost against the wild Welsh tribes to the west.

Over ensuing centuries it became an important port and commercial centre, and the county town of Cheshire. Among places to visit are the magnificent 900-year-old Cathedral, two miles of red sandstone city walls with medieval towers around which you can walk, the ruined St John's Church, an Anglo-Saxon Cathedral with a coffin in the wall, the famous medieval Rows with galleries of speciality shops, and the ancient bridge over the River Dee.

You'll need more than one day to explore this remarkable city. It's worth starting a visit at the Chester Heritage Centre in Bridge Street Row, where an audio-visual show gives a stimulating introduction to the city's history and heritage. Other places to see include the Chester Visitor Centre with life-sized reconstructions of a Victorian street, the Castle Street Period House - a carefully restored 17th century town house, the King Charles Tower on the City Walls, the Toy Museum on Bridge Street Rows, the Chester Military Museum in The Castle, and the Grosvenor Museum in Grosvenor Street. This is Cheshire's major regional museum, packed with treasures from the city including Roman and medieval archaeological finds and local history material, as well as a collection of paintings and watercolours.

The main Tourist Information Centre is in the Town Hall in Northgate Street.

**The Chester Court Hotel** offers a friendly, warm and intimate atmosphere. It is situated within easy walking distance of the city centre and is an ideal spot for visitors holidaying in the area or business travellers looking for overnight accommodation. It is a detached building with a lot of character, set in its own grounds with ample parking facilities. Fully centrally heated throughout, all the bedrooms have colour television and most have bathrooms and showers en-suite. A rather nice touch is the bed linen which is crisp cotton, and tea and coffee making facilities, direct dial telephones, hairdryers and trouser press are standard within all of the rooms. The restaurant offers excellent home cooking, using only the freshest of produce, and a superb Full English Breakfast is served in the mornings. The menu in the restaurant caters for both table d'hote and a la carte and is very popular with guests. The proprietor, Mrs Southworth, told us that she tries to offer her guests every attention and comfort, in the hope that they will have an enjoyable stay and return again.

*The Chester Court Hotel*

Most people on a visit to Chester make their way to the riverside, perhaps to enjoy a trip on the Dee by motor launch, or even to take a horse-drawn canal boat along the Shropshire Union Canal from Tower Wharf.

Only a short drive or bus ride (frequent shuttle services in the summer) from Chester City Centre is Chester Zoo in Upton-by-Chester, just off the A41 to the north of the city. Set in 110 acres of superb gardens, this is currently Britain's largest zoo outside London, and bearing in mind the probable fate of Regent's Zoo, it looks likely to claim the crown. Among the many special attractions are a penguin pool with underwater viewing panels, the Chimpanzee Island inhabited by 22 chimps who also have a custom-built winter house, one of the finest Tropical Houses in Europe, a nocturnal house, a children's farm, elephants, a monkey house and collections of many rare and exotic animals and birds. The Zoo has gained an international reputation for the conservation and breeding of otherwise endangered species. Chester Zoo is open all the year round every day of the week.

*Lytham Hall*

# North Cheshire

## CHAPTER SIX

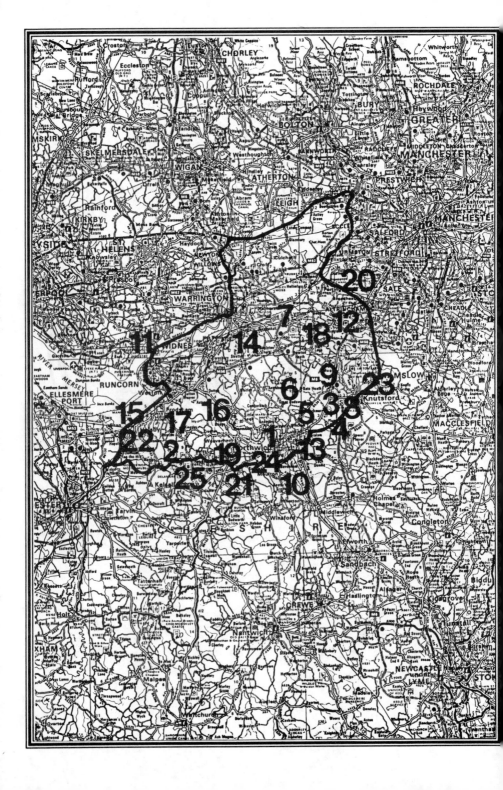

# Chapter Six
# Map Reference Guide

| Name | Map Ref No |
|---|---|
| Actons Of Lymm | 7 |
| Arley Hall | 1 |
| Ascol Drive Nursery | 8 |
| Ayreshire Guest House | 1 |
| Barratwich | 21 |
| Beechwood House | 19 |
| Brindley's Waterside Tavern & Restaurant | 4 |
| Casa Maria | 7 |
| Coppelia Antiques | 8 |
| Forest View Inn | 2 |
| Friendly Floatel | 1 |
| George & Dragon | 6 |
| Groundwork Discovery Centre | 13 |
| Hartford Hall Hotel & Restaurant | 10 |
| High Legh Garden Centre | 18 |
| Hilltop Equestrian Centre | 17 |
| Kingsley Mill | 15 |
| Lymm Bistro | 7 |
| Norton Priory Museum & Gardens | 11 |
| Nunsmere Hall Hotel | 24 |
| Old Broken Cross | 1 |
| Old Hall Hotel | 15 |
| Pickmere House Hotel | 3 |
| Railway Hotel | 20 |
| Red Bull | 16 |
| Rowlands | 15 |
| Salt Barge | 13 |
| Salt Museum | 1 |
| The Smoker | 8 |
| Springfield Guest House | 25 |
| Statham Lodge Hotel | 7 |
| Tattondale Carriages | 23 |
| Tattondale Farm | 23 |
| Tatton Park | 23 |
| Turners Arms | 12 |
| Victoria Hotel | 14 |
| White Lion | 22 |
| Wincham Hall Hotel | 6 |
| Yew Tree Farm | 9 |

*Sundial, Gt. Budworth Church*

# North Cheshire

The County of Cheshire blends qualities of both the North of England and the Midlands. To the east lie the high moorlands and crags of the Peak District, to the west the soft red sandstone country of the Mersey and the Dee, to the south a rich, pastoral landscape which blends into the Shropshire Hills. It is a county of contrast, fringing onto the great Metropolitan areas of Greater Manchester and Merseyside, with its share of industry, and yet with areas of deep rural countryside, as remote and unspoiled as anywhere in England. Here too you'll find black and white half-timbered cottages and thatched roofs more typical of Herefordshire and Shropshire.

North Cheshire is one of the less well known parts of the North West, and if it has less of the more dramatic scenery of other parts of Cheshire, it is rich in interest. Its miles of quiet lanes, shady waterways and forest footpaths linking pretty villages and interesting historical sites so close to the busy urban areas, creates its own charm. It is a landscape that was first shaped by the retreating glaciers of the last Ice Age, which carved out the many attractive small lakes or meres. Many of these make attractive features in the landscape, and are often important wildlife refuges for a variety of birds and wildfowl. A later influence on North Cheshire's landscape was the Salt industry, with salt in the form of rock salt or brine taken out in large quantities along the region's navigable rivers and canals. It also caused less welcome subsidence in parts of the county, creating many small ponds or flashes, which you'll find peppering the countryside throughout the area.

**Warrington** is North Cheshire's largest town and the main focus for industrial development in the region. It lies both on an important bridging point of the River Mersey, mid way between the huge conurbations and ports of Manchester and Liverpool, and on a nodal point of communications close to where the M6, M62 and M56 motorways intersect and where the electrified West Coast Main Line railway links London and Scotland. Not for nothing does Warrington, with its excellent communications, claim to

141

enjoy Britain's most central location.

In past years Warrington was most famous its heavy industry, including the manufacture of chemicals and the production of steel rope and wire for industry. Today the town is also an important centre for brewing, soap manufacture and scientific research, but it still has several fine Georgian and Victorian buildings around the town centre and a pleasant central shopping centre around Horsemarket Street. The Town Hall is a former country house, built in 1750 for Lord Winmarleigh, before being acquired with its park by the Council in 1872. Some of the windows are framed in copper and the magnificent cast iron gates, which are 25 feet high and 54 feet broad, were given to the town in 1893.

Warrington's oldest building is in fact the Church of St Elphin which dates from the Middle Ages, though its spire is 19th century and is one of the tallest in England. On the nearest Friday to June 1st every year, members of the local congregation celebrate a 'Walking Day' with a procession around the town, a custom that is believed to have originated in the 19th century.

Another good reason for visiting Warrington is its excellent Museum and Art Gallery in Bold Street, one of the earliest Municipal Museums in the country, dating from 1857, and a real Aladdin's Cave in the very best Victorian tradition. The museum collection dates from 1848 and contains everything from shrunken heads, a unique china teapot collection, a scold's bridle, Egyptian mummys, a rare Roman actor's mask and other Roman artifacts discovered in nearby Wilderspool. There are some fine paintings as well, most of which are Victorian watercolours and oils, but also a rare Vanous still life.

To the north east of Warrington lies Risley Moss Nature Park, over 200 acres of scattered woodland, mossland, ponds and pools. Make time to visit the visitor centre and climb the Observation Tower with its magnificent views of the Peak District fells nearly 30 miles away. Close by is Birchwood Forest Park, which lies about half a mile from the Birchwood/Warrington intersection of the M62.

Warrington lies on three important North West waterways - the River Mersey, the Bridgewater Canal and the Manchester Ship Canal.

The Bridgewater Canal, which lies to the south of the town, was one of the first canals to be constructed in England. It was built in 1767 by James Brindley for the Duke of Bridgewater, to transport coal from Worsley to Manchester and then on to Runcorn for outward shipment to sea via Liverpool. The canal cuts across Walton Hall Park on the outskirts of Warrington, where you'll also find 50 acres of formal and informal gardens and attractive glass houses, as well as a fine Victorian house open to the public every Sunday afternoon throughout the year and on Thursdays, Fridays and Saturdays in the summer months.

Widnes and Runcorn are busy industrial towns, but both have features of interest.

In **Widnes,** you'll find Catalyst, the Museum of the Chemical Industry. This fascinating museum is located close to the River Mersey and the Runcorn-Widnes Bridge, and is open daily except Mondays. The Museum, which claims to be a world first, explores various aspects of one of Cheshire's greatest industries, with an emphasis on 'hands-on' scientific exploration for the whole family. There is also a programme of special events throughout the seasons.

**Runcorn** is largely a new town with modern shopping precincts and radial roads. But it is also the home of Norton Priory, Britain's only monastic museum.

Rain, shine or snow, **Norton Priory Museum and Gardens** is always a fulfilling and fascinating place for a family visit or afternoon stroll. Situated in a peaceful oasis on the edge of Runcorn, the Augustinian Priory was built as the prosperous abode for 12 canons in 1134. Since then, it was transformed into a Tudor and then a Georgian mansion before it was abandoned in 1921. Daily life for the canons was strictly disciplined and a typical day would consist of prayer, worship and work duties, with some time set aside for relaxation according to the rule of St Augustine.

The main activity would be worship, so the day was mainly taken up with attending the church services. The canons were known as 'Black Canons' because their outer garment was a cape of black woollen cloth, worn over a white linen surplice. Their hair was tonsured and they wore leather boots or shoes. Life for the canons was not as spartan as one would imagine because they ate two meals a day in the refectory or dining room. We know they were allowed to eat meat because when excavations were carried out, many bones of animals were found. As well as a staple diet, beer was the drink that accompanied their meals.

Day-to-day life in 12th century Cheshire is reflected through the exhibitions which have been created in the prize winning Museum. Age old crafts and art forms such as tile making and sculpture are revived and celebrated in workshops and demonstrations which are held periodically throughout the year. Just a short walk away is the estate's 18th century walled garden. Visitors can enjoy a tranquil walk through the gardens and follow this with a visit to the gift shop. Refreshments are available on site and there is a specially designated picnic area. More information may be obtained by telephoning (0928) 569895.

As well as the excavated ruins of the Priory with the 12th century undercroft, there are beautiful woodland gardens which go back to the 18th and 19th century country home built at Norton Priory. These gardens include such features as a stream glade with azaleas and rhododendrons and a fine Laburnum arch.

*Norton Priory*

At Spike Island, just off the River Mersey between Runcorn and Widnes, there is an area of reclaimed landscape and industrial archaeology, with walks along the riverside and along the St Helens Canal, as well as a Mersey Way Ranger information point. Spike Island is to be found just to the north of the Runcorn-Widnes bridge.

There's also a five mile 'linear park' along the Sankey Valley from Runcorn, through which the historic St Helens Canal runs. Here you'll find a butterfly garden, a bog garden, and an adventure playground for children. Bird watchers will also find much to interest them at Pickerings Pasture on the Mersey Way footpath alongside the Mersey at Widnes, with wildflower meadows and a picnic site as well as estuary views.

But North Cheshire also has some remarkable unspoiled villages awaiting exploration, some with interesting literary connections.

**Grappenhall,** just off the A50 south-east of Warrington, is a village of traditional Cheshire thatched cottages, with its church standing by the banks of the Bridgewater Canal. If you look carefully above the west window of the church tower, you'll find the carved figure of a cat with a grin. This is thought to have been the original Cheshire Cat which featured in Lewis Carroll's 'Alice in Wonderland', and which has become a symbol of the County of Cheshire.

Lewis Carroll - his real name Charles Lutwidge Dodgson - was born in 1832, son of the local vicar, not far away in the village of **Daresbury.** The village can be found on the A56 south-west of Warrington. There is a special memorial window to him in Daresbury Church, with illustrations from his book including the Mad Hatter, the March Hare, the Dormouse, the White Rabbit, the Queen of Hearts, and of course Alice and the Cheshire Cat.

North of Daresbury is **Stockton Heath,** where we came across **The Victoria Hotel.** It is conveniently situated in the centre of Stockton Heath with a wide variety of restaurants, welcoming public houses and pleasant shops all within easy walking distance. Ideal for business travellers, the M6 and M56 motorways are just three miles away and Manchester Airport can be reached within 15 minutes. Arthur and Beryl Cunningham run this lovely three storey Victorian hotel, and one of the things they pride themselves on is the hearty English breakfast which they serve. The Hotel is a large, imposing, detached timber fronted building, beautifully decorated, spotlessly clean, airy and spacious.

The accommodation comprises one family room, five doubles, three twins and five singles. The majority have en-suite facilities and are fully equipped with colour television and tea and coffee trays. Arthur is a particularly interesting person to speak to, and he related to us the story of his boxing career. A former member of the famous Lowe House Boxing Club in St Helens, by the time he retired at the age of 21 he had won the Army Cadet Championship, the Junior ABA British Championship, and had also won the Lancashire and Cheshire Boys Club Championship four times. He fought all over the country and remains to this day an avid boxing fan. The accommodation at The Victoria Hotel is very reasonably priced, and reservations may be made by calling 0925 63060.

*The Victoria Hotel*

145

Another delightful village close to Warrington is **Lymm,** also on the Bridgewater Canal, with half-timbered houses, a market cross and village stocks. Lymm developed as an important centre for the fustian cloth trade in the 19th century. Lymm Dam is a large man-made lake in a lovely woodland centre, which is linked to surrounding countryside and to the canal towpath by a network of footpaths and bridleways. The Dam is popular for angling and birdwatching.

We were delighted to find the exclusive **Casa Maria** at the entrance to the village, situated close to the famous fustian cutting cottages in Church Road. Casa Maria is a beautiful beamed cottage which stocks some of the best of Italian and other European designer gowns. The dress agency is run by Maria Cunningham, a Portugese lady with plenty of flair. She stocks clothes that are nearly new, in absolutely immaculate condition. This 'recycling' of garments is becoming a growing trend amongst those who enjoy the thrill of changing their style frequently, and it is being adopted by many of the chic fashion shops. Maria's main concern is that you should feel totally relaxed as you browse. It is pretty certain that you are bound to find something special that you simply must have - so why not give yourself a treat!

*Casa Maria*

**The Lymm Bistro** in Bridgewater Street can be found in an attractive 200-year-old building which has been run for the past three years by Jo Shenton and Michael Venning. Since opening the Bistro, Jo and Michael have earned themselves an excellent reputation for providing first class food and wines. Michael Venning is the chef, and he has obviously gone to great lengths to ensure that his diners receive only the very best and freshest of produce. Meals are cooked to order and served in the cosy, friendly atmosphere which the Bistro exudes. Michael's speciality is fish, and this can be anything from a simple but exquisite whole Dover Sole, to really exotic and exciting dishes. For example, it is not unknown for Michael to offer amongst his daily specials such unusual dishes as giant Australian Snow Crab, Barracuda Shark, or Parrot Fish. As one can imagine, offering dishes such as these makes the Lymm Bistro very popular, and it is not surprising that diners travel from far and wide to sample such excellent cuisine. Jo and Michael are on hand every evening to look after the personal requirements of their diners. In order to do justice to the menu which Michael has so thoughtfully put together, we feel we must enlarge upon the dishes which are offered.

Blackboard specials are always popular, and a selection of starters may consist of Avocado filled with Smoked Salmon and topped with a tomato vinaigrette, fresh Squid cooked with tomato and red wine, or perhaps plump Frogs Legs sauteed with onions and garlic and flamed in Brandy. The main courses are just as mouthwatering. We particularly liked the sound of the Norwegian Red Fish - a fillet of this unusual fish poached with various Shellfish and Smoked Salmon, served in a cream sauce, sounds marvellous. We were just as impressed with the Wild Boar - a roast saddle of Wild Boar served in a sauce made from its own juices, Juniper Berries and Port. By now we are quite sure that we will have whetted your appetite, and can only conclude by suggesting that prior to visiting you telephone and reserve your table. As you can imagine, the Lymm Bistro does become extremely busy and represents superb value for money.

*The Lymm Bistro*

Canal holidays are increasingly popular these days, so it will not suprise you to learn that we popped in to visit **The Wharfage Boat Company** whilst in the village. This is a proprietary operated business run by Norma and Ben Faulkner, situated on an old wharfage site at Lymm. The excellent location of the business offers holidaymakers a host of cruising routes which include the Cheshire Ring and the Llangollen, or a journey to the fair city of Chester. Alternatively, the northward route will take you to Leeds, Liverpool and Skipton. For those who enjoy an even more leisurely pace it is also possible to stay on The Wharfage Boat Company's own lock-free section of the canal.

The business is engaged in narrowboat construction, refurbishment and a trip-restaurant boat operation. With considerable experience in the hire of water craft for holidays, the company has ensured that the narrowboats have superb facilities, with many personal touches. For example, wall decor is standard, and garden chairs, barbecues and board games are all to be found on board. Differing from the large operators of narrowboats, the Wharfage Boat Company is open seven days a week for visitors to admire the standard of work when construction is under way. Old hands at steel narrowboat holidays will know that there can be no finer holiday than to cruise along the tranquil Waterways of England and Wales at a truly leisurely pace.

*The Wharfage Boat Company*

We also made a point of stopping to browse around a particularly well-known showroom in the area. As lovers of fine leather furniture, we had been advised to call in and meet Bob and Lynn Mynett, who have established a unique family business known locally as **Actons of Lymm.** Bob and Lynn acquired the business in 1985 from Mr and Mrs Acton, and since then the transformation that has taken place is remarkable. Whilst the building was undergoing major structural alterations, the Mynett family discovered a sandstone lined fresh water well, believed to be about 400 years old. Eager to preserve their find, they had the well dug out to its original depth of 25 feet and carefully restored it, thereby adding yet another feature to the historic nature of the property.

The building that the showroom is housed in is attractive in itself, but once inside, we were thrilled to discover a veritable treasure trove of magnificent leather and reproduction furniture. Besides furniture, there is an intriguing display of brass and copper, an extensive range of pictures including Victorian prints by Stephen Selby in handsome frames, an exquisite selection of figurine lamps, Limoges Castel Porcelaine and Arden sculpture by Christopher Holt.

The name of Actons has long been famous for supplying superior quality leather suites, custom made by skilled craftsmen, using only the finest hides from a selection of over 50 shades. The beauty of leather furniture lies not only in its attractive look, but also represents an excellent investment. As well as the furniture and furnishings, Lynn has added a variety of items suitable for presents, ranging upwards from a couple of pounds in price. There are also dried flower arrangements and a delightful range of gifts for both men and women. Whether you decide to buy or browse, you are assured a very friendly welcome and the opportunity to purchase one of tomorrow's heirlooms.

*Actons of Lymm*

If you are looking for accommodation in the area and you appreciate comfort, delicious food and personal service, we suggest you pay a visit to the **Statham Lodge Hotel.** Originally a Georgian country house, this elegant, privately owned hotel combines traditional charm with an atmosphere of relaxed and friendly hospitality. The M6 and M56 motorway intersection is only two miles away, giving easy access to the business and commercial centres of the North West. This beautiful manor house is set in extensive and impeccably maintained gardens, and has an air of peaceful tranquility. The management team at Statham Lodge specialise in arranging all kinds of social and business functions, from private dinners and lunches in the Roulette Room Suite, to large conferences, wedding receptions and dinner dances.

The restaurant receives many compliments for its consistently high standards. The menu offers a variety of freshly prepared tempting dishes to choose from, and consists of the very best of English and Foreign cuisine. Much thought was given to the accompanying wine list, which complements the menu exceptionally well. The accommodation consists of 38 en-suite bedrooms with first class facilities, including a link to the BSB movie channel. The bedrooms are very comfortably furnished and the tariff includes daily newspaper and early morning tea or coffee, followed by a Full English Breakfast served in the restaurant. Alternatively, Statham Lodge staff will provide a light continental breakfast which can be brought to your bedroom on request. Whatever your requirements, we know that you will be well looked after and will thoroughly enjoy your visit to Statham Lodge.

*Statham Lodge Hotel*

We also discovered a very friendly establishment just north-east of Lymm at **Heatley.** The village lies on the A6144 from Lymm and is right on the border with Manchester.

**The Railway Hotel** was built in the 1860s and stands beside the now redundant railway line between Warrington and Manchester. Mr Paul Burgess is the proprietor and he has run the Railway Hotel for the past six years. During this time he has actively encouraged visitors and locals to use the hotel as a family meeting place. The inn is open from twelve o'clock lunchtime until eleven o'clock in the evening from Monday to Saturday, with normal opening hours on Sunday.

Traditionally decorated, it has a pool and darts room which is very popular. There is a substantial play area for children to use and bar snacks are served all day. A large function room is also available for private parties.

*The Railway Hotel*

**The Turner Arms Hotel** can be found further south along the border in the small village of **Bollington.** It is a family run premises providing a good standard of accommodation and restaurant facilities. The hotel appears in several other publications and is a particular favourite with hikers and rambling enthusiasts, especially those who wish to walk the Pennine Way. Bernard and Brenda Dingle are the proprietors, and they make guests very welcome with their own special brand of hospitality. The hotel is situated on the edge of the village, and it is only 30 minutes from Manchester Airport. Children are always welcome and there is ample parking close by.

*The Turner Arms Hotel*

The hotel accommodation consists of eight bedrooms, and three of these are doubles with en-suite bathrooms. As well as having two bars, there is also a separate restaurant offering an a la carte menu. Excellent bar snacks

151

and lunches are available in the bars and Sunday lunch is so popular that it is always advisable to book in advance. The Turner Arms is renowned locally for its first class real ale and this obviously makes it a popular place to stop for a drink.

South of here on the A50 is **High Legh,** and this is definitely the place to visit if you are a keen gardener. **High Legh Garden Centre** was opened in 1987 and is truly a garden centre of excellence. With its huge range of plants, shrubs, tools and accessories, it is a mecca for any gardening enthusiast. A large car park gives immediate access to the many trees and shrubs on display. Huge polytunnels have been erected to ensure that all plant material goes on sale, and remains, in tip top condition. The primary aim of High Legh Garden Centre is that quality and service remain at all times a top priority. A wide selection of top quality outdoor plants are on view, and undercover areas protect the more vulnerable of species. There is a large range of speciality house plants which include Bonsai, Cacti and Airplants, as well as an Aquatics Centre with numerous aquaria, fish, plants and other accessories.

*High Legh Garden Centre*

One of the highlights of the Centre is the well-established gift shop which prides itself on the constantly changing selection of gifts. Many new and original items are to be found here and ideas range from china, glassware, ornaments and prints, to toiletries and men's gifts. The Centre also supplies a top range of greenhouses, conservatories and garden furniture. Their range of French furniture was recently awarded the 'Best Display' in the North West. One of the professional services the Garden Centre offers is a landscaping design service. There are also many demonstrations and events held during the year, but particularly around Christmas time, when the children's Grotto is always original and popular.

Also on site is a superb fern-filled Cafe which provides a welcoming opportunity to enjoy a full meal or a snack. Children are well-catered for and there is a very safe and well-equipped play area set aside for them. Only a short drive eastwards from Lymm will bring you to **Tatton Park.** A visit to the renowned Tatton Park has always been regarded as one of the best days out in the North West. Close to the delightful village of **Knutsford,** which boasts an amazing variety of architectural styles, Tatton Park is not surprisingly the National Trust's most visited property. It is the complete historic country estate. A magnificent Georgian Mansion by Wyatt rises from the glorious gardens, widely regarded amongst England's 'Top Ten'. The opulent staterooms contrast with the stark servants' rooms and cellars, working as they did for the Victorian household of the noble Egerton family.

The enormous Tenants Hall, sometimes closed to cater for private events, has been described as 'the most extraordinary room in England'. It contains the last Lord Egerton's collection of curios from his travels abroad during the 1920s and 30s. You will also find there a 1900 Benz, registered M1, the first car in Cheshire.

The original breeds of animals still live down on the Home Farm, a short walk from the Mansion. Working as it was in the 1930s, the farm is the heart of the estate with its workshops and old estate office. A 'new' steam engine has recently been restored in the engine house.

Old Hall nestles in a wood in the deer park. Visitors are given a guided tour through time from the late middle ages up to the 1950s. Flickering light from candles reveals the ancient timber roof of the Great Hall, supported by ornate quatrefoils. Underfoot the floor is strewn with rushes, providing a warm place for the medieval lord of the manor and his servants to sleep. Built around 1520, Old Hall conjures up a hauntingly real image of an authentic journey through history. Outside, deer roam around 1,000 acres of parkland. Many people visit Tatton just to enjoy the tranquility and walk round the meres watching the wildlife.

To complete the day's enjoyment, visitors can take lunch in the restaurant or have a drink in the Tatton Arms. Many public events are held indoors and outside in the Park, ranging from a giant classic car show to major equestrian events. Also of interest is the Japanese Koi Carp Show and many craft fairs. Opened in 1991, the children's playground is specially tailored for pre-school up to twelve year olds. Children can happily amuse themselves while parents relax in the picnic area. If you would like to telephone Tatton Park for further information prior to your visit, the number is (0565) 654822.

*Tatton Park*

**Tattondale Carriages** are situated within the grounds of Tatton Park. Stephen and Sonia Gray run this unique business where horse drawn carriages are restored. Also provided on the site are horse drawn carriage rides around the park itself. A regular feature is to see the carriages being prepared for a local wedding, just one of the few special occasions for which they are called upon to provide transport. The carriages are always turned out superbly and inevitably lend an atmosphere of elegance to any special occasion. It is not unusual to see as many as 20 horses on view in the stables, and these range from Shire horses to Shetland ponies. The stables also specialise in beautiful Black Fresian horses, which are very rare. These are indeed a sight to behold when harnessed to the carriages. Viewing is between the hours of 12 am and 4 pm, and once a week a blacksmith calls to demonstrate the art of forge work.

*Tattondale Carriages*

154

**Tattondale Farm** is also set in the grounds of Tatton Park. It is a 500 acre arable farm, and the house was built in the 1880s as the estate manager's home. Beautifully decorated throughout, bed and breakfast is offered by owners Susan and Richard Reeves, who have lived here for 10 years. There is a family room consisting of a double room with private bathroom and adjoining twin room for children, which assures you of privacy when you feel the need to escape the pressures of parenthood for a while! Another double room and a single room with wash hand basins are available upstairs, together with a further double room on the ground floor, which is particularly suitable for disabled visitors. Susan has provided bed and breakfast here for the past four years, and tells us that what she likes best about it is meeting so many different kinds of people. We have no doubt that what the guests appreciate most is the friendly welcome their hosts extend to them, which couldn't fail to make them feel immediately at home.

*Tattondale Farm*

The beautiful village of **Rostherne,** though outside Tatton Park, is actually an estate village. All the cottages lining the road to the Church are named after shrubs and trees, such as lilac, willow and apple. A group of 12 houses at one end of the village form a square. They were built by Margaret Egerton in 1909, complete with a bath house and a laundry with irons and free soap - a remarkable innovation for their day. Rostherne has the largest and deepest mere in Cheshire - over 100 acres and 100 feet deep, it is now a bird sanctuary. The Mere is best seen from the Churchyard, which provides one of the loveliest views in Cheshire. According to local legend, when the bells were hung in St Mary's Church, the largest rolled away into the mere and every Easter morning it is tolled by a mermaid. Inside the Church, there is a poignant monument to Lady Charlotte

155

Egerton who was drowned in the Mere on the eve of her wedding.

Cheshire is also a county rich in customs.

Every year, the village of **Appleton Thorn,** south of Warrington, celebrates 'Bauming' the thorn. This unique custom owes its origin to a Norman knight, Adam de Dutton, who according to tradition returned in the 12th century from the Crusades with a cutting from the Glastonbury Thorn to plant at Appleton as a thanksgiving for his safe return. The present tree outside the church was planted in 1967 and is meant to be a direct descendant of the original. The ceremony takes place on the third Saturday in June, when young children decorate the tree and sing the 'Bauming song', written by the 19th century Cheshire Poet, R.E Egerton-Warburton.

**Arley Hall** lies about three miles south-east of Appleton Thorn. The Arley Hall Estate is one of the few remaining houses and estates to have survived in Cheshire as a family home with resident owners still in attendance. The house and gardens have been owned by the family of the Hon. Michael and Mrs Flower for over 500 years. Arley is an agricultural estate set deep in the North Cheshire countryside, yet it is only five miles from the M6 and M56. The Hall, Chapel and Gardens provide visitors with hours of enjoyment and interest. The Hall contains fine examples of panelling, plasterwork, family portraits and furniture. It is set in 12 acres of one of the finest gardens in England, which won the Garden of the Year Award in 1987. On the site is a chapel, a gift shop with plants for sale, a tea room and a picture gallery with paintings by local artists.

The old estate yard is set aside for the workshops of local craftsmen. John Chalmers Brown makes custom built furniture and other wooden objects. Bob Dawson is a potter who specialises in fine bone china figurines, and Peter Holt produces garden furniture to grace any garden. It is also possible to watch the expertise of Stuart Mallett, who will make anything in stone from a bird bath to a terrace balustrade.

**Stockley Farm,** which is on the estate, is run by Reg and Joan Walton. They thoroughly enjoy welcoming guests to their award-winning modern working dairy farm, which is of particular interest to families. Visitors to the farm are taken by tractor and trailer from the Arley Hall car park. They are then able to see cows being milked, play with and feed the animals, and enjoy the milk bar, straw bounce and shop.

The Gardens of Arley Hall offer great variety and interest all through the season. Visitors can explore the gardens with use of a guide book written by Lady Ashbrook. The task of writing the booklet was one for which she was uniquely qualified, having known the garden intimately all her life.

156

The guide describes something of the historical development of the garden and is designed to lead the visitor round it in a logical sequence. Also of interest is the fact that in the past, each succeeding generation of Lady Ashbrook's family has contributed to the development of the gardens. We are certain that readers will thoroughly enjoy visiting this delightful Hall and Gardens and therefore recommend telephoning for more information. The number is (0565) 777353.

*Arley Hall*

Another old Cheshire custom still continues in the village of **Antrobus,** south of Lymm. It occurs every November and is called 'Souling'. On All Souls Day, prayers used to be said for those in purgatory and the poor of the village would beg for Spice Cake in return for saying prayers. The practice was banned at the time of the Reformation, but still continued in parts of Cheshire. In the public houses around Antrobus, souling is still performed with a Mumming Play, accompanied by a Hobby Horse, the 'Wild Horse of Antrobus'. This is built on to a horse's skull with moving jaws and brightly painted in various colours.

Nearby is **Great Budworth,** with its charming red brick and timber framed cottages with twisted chimneys, all clustered round a green hill and the handsome parish church of St Mary and All Saints. Great Budworth was once the largest ecclesiastical parish in Cheshire, encompassing 35 individual townships, most of which are now independent. The Church itself was built between the 14th and 15th centuries and is famous for its crowd of quaint carvings and odd faces that peer out at unexpected corners: some with staring eyes, others with their tongues poking out at the unwary visitor. Look for a man tired of too many sermons near the pulpit; under the roof of the nave you'll find a man with a serpent, another trying to turn a somersault, and a minstrel plays his bagpipes. In the Lady Chapel is buried the famous 17th century historian, Sir Peter Leycester, and in the Warburton Chapel is a fine carved Tudor ceiling and 13th century oak stalls - the oldest in Cheshire.

The village is one of the most picturesque and attractive we have ever come across. Mr and Mrs Curtin are the proprietors of the village pub, called **The George and Dragon.** Above the entrance to the pub is the following motto:

> As St George in armed array,
> Doth the fiery Dragon slay,
> So mayst thou with might no less,
> Slay that Dragon drunkenness.

Thankfully, few people have actually paid any heed to these words of wisdom, and the pub has survived and still proves to be extremely popular. It is a beautiful old building, dating back to 1722, and epitomises the phrase 'Olde Worlde'. The bars are typical of what we have come to know as 'old fashioned charm'. Attractively decorated and in keeping with its era, the seating is comfortable and the atmosphere most amenable. As well as keeping an excellent cellar and selling hand-pumped beer, the food available is wholesome, good value and well presented.

*The George and Dragon*

For daily specials, consult the blackboard. The regular dishes include Steaks, Poultry and Fish. It is one of the few public houses in the area to have a traditional roast lunch available on a daily basis. As well as being good value for money, there is also plenty on the plate. If you happen to be in the area on a Sunday we would advise you to call in early, as the price of £3.95 makes roast Sunday lunch very popular with locals and day trippers alike. On the first floor of the pub is the Horse Shoe Room, which is available for private functions and can seat up to 40 diners. During busier periods this room is used as a family room, and it is also designated a no-smoking area.

If horse riding is one of your hobbies and you are in the **Aston by Budworth** area, then you would be well advised to telephone (0565) 894100 and speak to Mr Frost, who owns and runs the **Yew Tree Equestrian Centre.** The stables are situated midway between Pickmere and Tabley. At present there is stabling for 18 horses, but in the near future plans are afoot to extend this facility. As well as a number of acres for cross country riding there is also an indoor schooling centre. Mr Frost's dedicated staff will obligingly teach clients how to ride and will also instruct them in the art of grooming and livery. Whilst at the Centre, we noted how well the horses were treated. If you should decide to ride, there is no need to worry about your standard as Mr Frost and his staff are happy to tailor rides and schooling to the requirements of individual clients, from the novice to the expert.

*Yew Tree Equestrian Centre*

Pickmere lies to the east of Great Budworth and is the busiest and most popular of Cheshire's many small lakes, with boat trips and boat hire available, and a small fairground at one end. To the west is Budworth Mere, one of the largest in Cheshire. It was created by the retreating glaciers. Sandwiched between the Mere and the Trent and Mersey Canal is Marbury Country Park. This 190 acre Park was created out of the former Marbury estate, once owned by the Smith Barry family. The house is reputedly haunted by the Marbury Lady. There is an Information Centre and a one and a half mile Discovery Trail through the woodland, which recalls the story of the vanished Hall and Park.

The village of **Pickmere** lies on the B5391. Commanding superb views of the Cheshire Plain from the Dee Estuary to the Pennine foothills, **Pickmere House** makes an excellent choice when looking for somewhere to stay in the Knutsford area. The proprietor, Mrs Brown, extends a warm welcome and assures her guests of personal attention. Nothing is too much trouble for this charming lady, who speaks both German and French. Perhaps this is why both business travellers and holidaymakers alike return time and again to sample her hospitality.

Pickmere House, a listed Georgian farmhouse, was built in 1772 and is exceptionally spacious. In addition to a large beamed dining room, there are two comfortable well furnished lounges. The choice of bedrooms gives excellent flexibility and ranges from family rooms, large doubles and twins to small singles, most of them en-suite and all with the usual television and drinks facilities.

Pickmere is not only ideally situated for exploring Cheshire's peaks, plains, parks and waterways, but is also close to Manchester Airport and just two miles west of junction 19 of the M6. This makes it an ideal stopover for both North and Southbound travellers. Chester, Manchester and Liverpool are all accessible within 40 minutes. Leisure activities in the area include golf, riding and watersports. Mrs Brown is happy to arrange special interest weekends, and these have been as diverse as Investment Management, Birdwatching and Italian Art.

*Pickmere House Hotel*

South of Pickmere is **Plumley,** just off the A556 near Tabley Mere. Here we discovered a very suitable place for sporting diners.

Once a village hall, the unique restaurant section of **The Smoker** in Plumley now serves as a restaurant, capable of satisfying the most discerning of diners. It can be found just one and a half miles from Northwich and three and a half miles from Knutsford. The Smoker has an intriguing history and has long been associated with that well known sport of Kings, horse racing. A brief history of The Smoker is explained on the inside cover of the bar and restaurant menu. It states that the picture on the front of the menu shows Lord De Tabley on his grey mare, 'Smoker', who was bred as a race horse by the Prince Regent, later George 1V.

Lord De Tabley raised the Cheshire Yeomanry as a means of defence against the threatened invasion of Napoleon. In nearby Tabley House, where the descendants of Lord De Tabley still live, there is a picture of him mounted on Smoker reviewing his troops on the beach at Liverpool. The inn was built during the reign of Queen Elizabeth I, and Lord De Tabley who owned it then renamed it as a memorial to his horse. Smoker was a well loved race horse whose record on the turf was impressive. An extract from Wetherby's Racing Calendar states that during his career from 1790 until 1793, Smoker started 19 times, won 12 races including two matches, was second three times, third twice, and unplaced twice.

John and Diana Bailey are now the proprietors of The Smoker. Built approximately 400 years ago, it is a charming inn and restaurant full of character. The open log fires and lovely old oak beams lend an air of superb ambience to the premises. The menus for both the restaurant and the bar are not only impressive but also varied, interesting and innovative. On the day we were there the specials, which change daily, were Whole Baked San Peters, Game Cottage Pie, and Grilled Shark Steak in Tomato Sauce. The restaurant menu contains no less than 21 starters and 27 main course dishes. These vary from fish and meat to poultry and seafood. The wine list accompanying this impressive selection is well chosen and offers French, German, Spanish and Portuguese wines.

*The Smoker*

If time is a problem, then we would advise our readers to pop in for one of the many bar snacks available. These include hot dishes such as Halibut Steak Mornay, Roast Sirloin of Beef, Kofta Curry with Poppadom, Chilli, and Homemade Steak and Kidney Pie. The menu also caters well for vegetarians. Cold dishes include Salads such as Smoked Salmon, Seafood, Beef, Poultry, and Cheese. The sandwich menu is just as mouthwatering and prices for the bar snack menu vary from £1.40 up to £4.75. When you visit The Smoker, we are sure you will agree with us that the standard of service, the presentation, and the value for money is hard to beat, and the welcome you are given ensures a return visit.

**Coppelia Antiques** is situated at Holford Lodge, Plumley. The building was once two Elizabethan farmhouses, and these were rebuilt in 1870 using the original timbers at the front of the building. The premises nestles right in the heart of the Cheshire countryside but is only four minutes from junction 19 of the M6 motorway. It has magnificent views of the surrounding area. Lovers of fine antiques will be in their element here, as Coppelia Antiques caters only for people with discerning taste. The showroom has a wealth of beautiful long case clocks. The restoration and repair of clocks and furniture are completed on the premises, and many of these items date back to the 18th century. At the time of our visit we saw approximately 120 differing types of clock on display. In order for clients to truly appreciate their beauty, they are displayed as closely as possible to a natural home environment. As well as clocks, Mr and Mrs Clements also deal in Georgian furniture and Victorian suites. Viewing is a must when you are in the area, and Mr and Mrs Clements are always happy to give constructive and expert advice.

*Coppelia Antiques*

If you enjoy strolling around garden centres and nurseries, then we recommend a visit to **Ascol Drive Nursery**. Situated just off of the A556 Altrincham to Chester road, take the turning opposite the sign for Northwich. Jacqueline and Dinkie Bristow who own the nursery have been here for just two years and in that time they have put in an incredible amount of work. Considering the way in which the nursery is laid out and organised, it is almost impossible to believe that they have been here for such a short time.

Besides the visual items grown and sold in nurseries, they also specialise in hanging baskets and Christmas wreaths. Conifers are grown from rooted cuttings and carefully tended. Prices are extremely reasonable, whether you purchase flowers, shrubs, bedding plants or seeds. Nothing is too much trouble for the Bristow family and they will happily impart their expertise to customers. The site covers four acres and allows visitors to leisurely browse around at their convenience. You may like to purchase one of their magnificent hanging baskets while you are here.

Wincham Wharf at **Lostock Gralam** has served the Trent and Mersey Canal since it opened in 1777, linking the industrial Midlands with the Mersey Basin and the Duke of Bridgwater's canal. From the first, this busy waterway carried coal to the factories, salt from Northwich, china clay to the Potteries, farm goods to the fast growing towns and finished wares for export.

At the Wharf, goods were received for transit and the draught horses hauling the trains of boats were changed, fed and farriered. The site served much the same function as motorway service stations do today. Now, Wincham Wharf continues as a working boatyard where you can see narrowboats and other craft being built, renovated and decorated. The original Warehouse building still stands, carefully preserved and restored to serve today's travellers as **Brindley's Waterside Tavern and Restaurant**.

Taking its name from James Brindley, the famous canal surveyor and engineer, the Tavern and Restaurant has been created in the historic warehouse. Many of the original architectural features have been preserved to provide an atmosphere conducive to the enjoyment of good company and excellent food, whether you take a pub lunch in the Tavern or a more elaborate meal in the 'Above the Salt' restaurant. Morning coffee and afternoon tea accompanied by delicious home-baked cakes and scones are also served.

Visitors can also cruise in comfort on the electric Packetboat which is available for daytime or evening charter cruises, of which a variety of options are available. In summer, it is difficult to beat one of the Barbecue evenings - silent electric cruising, charcoal grilled steaks, and the lively music of the Ceilidh Band. This is a superb way of entertaining friends, staff or company guests. The cruise menu ranges from cream teas and finger buffets, to chilli con carni and Hungarian goulash. Or you can enjoy more elaborate buffets of cold meats and salads and mouthwatering barbecues.

In autumn, and up to the end of December, visitors can take daytime and evening cruises in centrally heated comfort, with the above wide-ranging menu options to choose from. The Canal banks are illuminated as the cruise boat silently sweeps along, and for clients wishing for more lively parties, the Band is available. Those with a more adventurous spirit will be delighted to know that day hire boats are available on a self-steer basis. With a maximum capacity of 12, these small but well-equipped boats are an ideal way of spending a little time in the 'slow lane'. Passing landmarks such as the Lion Salt Works dating from 1870 and the Anderton Lift built in 1875 will enhance your cruise, and make the experience one to remember.

*Anderton Lift*

Increasingly, we find these days that the discerning holiday maker or business traveller is looking for the kind of service and value for money that the larger hotels are unable to provide. We can only assume that this is due to the personal service which you only find when the proprietors are resident on the premises and able to keep their finger on the pulse. **Wincham Hall Hotel** in **Wincham** is such a place. We are sure that this is due to the enterprising foresight of Mr and Mrs Clemetson, who are now the proud owners of a beautiful hotel which caters admirably for the afore-mentioned guests. Your first glance of Wincham Hall Hotel will surely confirm that our assessment is correct.

Wincham Hall is an historic establishment which dates back to the year 1100 AD. Set in five acres of attractive grounds, the approach road is flanked by a mass of rhododendrons and holly bushes, leading to the locally known babbling brook called Peover Eye. At the turn of the 20th century, the Hall was used as a girls school, and it subsequently became home to American servicemen during World War II. Under the auspices of Jane and Richard Clemetson, the hotel has undergone extensive refurbishment and now has 10 newly appointed bedrooms, all beautifully furnished and well equipped, with excellent views of the surrounding countryside. The Hotel provides a superb setting for weddings, parties and private meetings. The ground floor reception rooms sport a wealth of beams, creating a relaxed and informal atmosphere. The cocktail and lounge bar have wonderful open fires that immediately extend a warm welcome to guests.

The restaurant has gained an enviable reputation. This is not surprising, as the menu is varied, and ranges from light lunches such as open sandwiches to The Lobster Plate - half a prime Lobster with a salad and lime and dill dressing. The dining room has panoramic views overlooking the grounds, and the tables are impeccably laid with crisp tablecloths and sparkling cutlery, crockery and glassware. Again the fare offered is wide with both a four course Table D"Hote menu and an A'la Carte menu. If your preference is for fish there is a wide variety including fresh lobsters and oysters from the seafood tank. Whatever your preference, we are sure that a visit to Wincham Hall will leave you in no doubt as to the standards of excellence that Richard and Jane have achieved in the short time they have been there.

*Wincham Hall Hotel*

The town of **Northwich** lies on the confluence of the Rivers Weaver and

Dane. Its name derives from 'wych', meaning salt town. Salt has been extracted from Cheshire since before Roman times. In 1670 rock salt was discovered in nearby Marston, and Northwich developed as a major salt producer. In the 19th century, Brunner and Mond set up their salt works at Winnington to manufacture alkalai products based on brine. This company is now part of the Multinational corporation, ICI. Extensive pumping of brine has, however, caused subsidence and large holes often used to appear, even swallowing up buildings. Salt extraction is now carefully controlled, but you can still see flooded areas, or flashes, around the town and on Witton Street, the White Lion Inn has sunk an entire storey! The subsidence led to the design of a new type of timber framed building in the area which can be jacked up as required.

Situated in the Northwich Workhouse building on London Road is Britain's only **Salt Museum.** With its unique collection of traditional working tools, and lively displays which include working models and videos, the Salt Museum tells the fascinating story of Cheshire's oldest industry. Not only can ancient remains such as Roman evaporating pans and medieval salt rakes be seen, but there is much to remind visitors of the vital part that salt plays in the modern chemical industry.

The Salt Museum is open all year round, Tuesdays to Fridays from 10 am till 5 pm, and Saturdays and Sundays from 2 pm till 5 pm.

*The Salt Museum*

A relatively new name to the catering and leisure industry is a company trading under the name of 'Friendly Hotels'. Obviously this company has done well because of its forward thinking and ability to identify gaps in the market. With nine hotels in England, five in Scotland and one in France, we think this justifies the reputation they have gained for their standard of excellence.

166

One of Friendly Hotels' most innovative concepts is **The Friendly Floatel,** which can be found in London Road. It is the very first Floatel to be constructed in the UK and is situated close to the meeting point of the Weaver and Dane rivers. The Floatel has all the facilities of a modern hotel, including restaurant, bar, mini gym, syndicate rooms, and function room facilities for up to 150 people. To starboard on the Upper Deck is a restaurant fit for an ocean liner. Guests can 'Yo ho ho' with a bottle of almost anything in this splendid bar. The a la carte menu has been well thought out and ranges from poultry, steaks and lamb, to pork, fish and seafood. To port are sumptuous cabins, and on the lower deck there is an ultra cool trim gym, which includes the facilities of a sauna and solarium.

The staterooms are specially selected and have been finished to a very high standard. Regular guests particularly appreciate the extra facilities provided there. As well as a welcome aboard drink, there is teletext television, mini bar, hairdryer, trouser press and personal toiletries. Definitely worth a visit, the Floatel is brand new and designed for travellers with a little romance in their souls. The location is lovely, and guests can breathe clean air and listen to the birds amidst outstanding scenic beauty. Above all, this is a hotel that always provides guests with lots of fun.

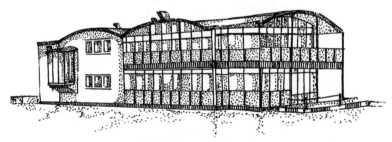

*The Friendly Floatel*

Northwich is an attractive old town with an interesting Town Trail (leaflet available from the Council offices), and it also owes its prominence as an inland port to the River Weaver. This was widened and improved in 1732 to create the Weaver Navigation, linking Northwich with the Mersey Estuary for larger vessels. It was also used to bring in the vast quantities of Lancashire coal needed to heat the salt pans for salt production.

The town was later linked to the Trent and Mersey Canal via the Anderton Boat Lift. This magnificent monument to Victorian Engineering has recently been restored. The Lift raises or lowers boats 50 feet between the River Weaver and the Trent and Mersey Canal in two huge water filled tanks. These can both carry two narrowboats and 252 tons of water, and the Lift is powered by a 30hp electric motor. It was designed by Edwin Clark and opened to traffic in 1875.

There are public cruises on the Weaver Navigation at weekends and certain mid-week days during the summer months, starting from the Tow Quay between the swing bridges.

Work is underway to develop a Recreational Footpath known as the Weaver Valley Way along this scenic and historic waterway from Winsford, south of Northwich, to Frodsham by the Mersey Estuary. At present, sections are open from Winsford and Northwich.

On the outskirts of Northwich on the A533, we found the **Ayrshire Guest House,** a Victorian family house with seven rooms, two of which have en-suite facilities. There are tea and coffee making facilities in all rooms and you are able to park your car off the main road. Centrally situated between the main motorways, the Ayrshire offers reasonably priced accommodation in a convenient location.

*Ayrshire Guest House*

**The Old Broken Cross Inn** is a delightful little public house, situated on the banks of the Mersey Canal at **Rudheath.** It was built over 200 years ago and was converted into an inn in 1777. Co-incidentally, this was the same year in which the Trent and Mersey Canal was completed. The belief is that the building was in fact an ale house prior to that, and was established to quench the thirst of the watermen of Middlewich. Originally called The Broken Cross, it wasn't until 1851 that the 'Old' was added. Jeff and Jackie Prior have been resident at The Old Broken Cross for almost 16 years, and during this time they have firmly stamped their own personalities on the place. The walls of the pub are lined with wonderful pictures of the canals, and this theme is followed through in each of the bars. It is a popular venue for the locals to meet in, and team sports include darts, dominoes, football and golf. It is also not unusual for deep sea fishing trips to be organised from here. The bar menu for lunches and bar snacks are available from 12 am until 2 pm and children's meals are exceptionally well priced.

*The Old Broken Cross*

On the site of The Lion Salt Works at Marston - the last remaining open pan salt works in Cheshire, which is currently undergoing renovation to become a working museum - is **The Groundwork Discovery Centre.** The building in which it is housed has a chequered history from being two houses to a pub with stables, through to an office and tea room for the Salt Works. Today it is the office and Discovery Centre for the Macclesfield and Vale Royal Groundwork Trust - a local environmental charity which promotes environmental improvement and helps to raise local awareness via informal leisure facilities.

The Discovery Centre plays host to a range of exhibitions from Easter until Christmas, featuring the work of local groups, for example the Cheshire and Wirral Badger Group, through to matters of local historic interest. There is information about the Salt Works as the restoration programme continues, and leaflets about other local attractions and a shop selling a range of gifts and local books and maps. The Centre is open every afternoon from Easter to Christmas.

Groundwork also operates a Cycle hire base in the Delamere Forest which is open from Easter until October every weekend and every day during July and August. For details about either forthcoming exhibitions and events or about cycle hire, please telephone (0606) 40555.

*The Groundwork Discovery Centre*

Whilst investigating the whereabouts of these famous salt works, we discovered **The Salt Barge.** Peter and Val Fay are the landlords of this super pub, and they offers drinkers and diners a friendly and comfortable environment in which to enjoy good food and first class ale. The pub is situated on the banks of the Trent and Mersey Canal, just opposite the Salt Works. Originally an 18th century ale house, the premises has recently been renovated and modernised. The decor has been sympathetically updated to enhance the character, charm and history attached to the pub. The walls are adorned with brass and objects relevant to life on the canal in years gone by. There are ample parking facilities and very well equipped play areas for children. The menu is varied and reasonably priced and a good selection of wines are available to accompany your choice of food. The positioning of The Salt Barge makes it an ideal place to stop for a drink and bite to eat, especially during the summer months when narrowboats are much in evidence on the canal.

*The Salt Barge*

South-west of Northwich is **Hartford,** and whether you are in the area for business or pleasure, we cannot recommend highly enough a weekend break at **The Hartford Hall Hotel**. If you should decide to stay here, you will easily slip into the relaxed life-style of days gone by. It is a most delightful 16th century building, set amidst beautifully manicured lawned gardens with mature trees and shrubs. This charming 21 bedroomed hotel has been tastefully and sympathetically restored to its original period splendour. Every detail of the furnishings and fittings, wallpaper and sumptuous fabrics has been chosen to enhance the traditional feeling.

The bedrooms at Hartford Hall are lavishly furnished, warm and homely, providing every modern amenity. Each has a private bathroom and shower, colour television, radio, trouser press, direct dial telephone, baby listening service, and of course the equipment for liquid refreshments. The lounge bar serves light lunches and excellent wines and spirits as well as afternoon tea or morning coffee. For those who wish to dine, an a la carte restaurant is situated on the ground floor of the hotel, overlooking the magnificent grounds of Hartford Hall. The standard of cuisine is comparable with some of the finest in England. Open to resident and non-resident guests, it is popular for both social entertaining and business dinner meetings.

*Hartford Hall Hotel & Restaurant*

The Nun's room is an ideal venue for a small conference or private function. It is steeped in history and the interior of the room is actually listed. The setting of the Hall is perfect for wedding receptions, and the management and staff ensure that careful attention to detail guarantees that an unforgettable day is enjoyed by the bride and groom and their guests. We are sure that visitors seeking peace and tranquility, personal service, sumptuous surroundings, and excellent restaurant facilities will

171

not be disappointed, should they decide to spoil themselves and steal away to Hartford Hall for a well earned break.

**Beechwood House** in **Weaverham** is within easy reach of both the M6 and M56 motorways. You will find this 1830s farmhouse only two miles west of Northwich, yet tucked away in a surprisingly rural valley. Janet Kuypers runs an excellent bed and breakfast establishment here, and the house has interesting architectural features and a very pleasant garden. This is an ideal place to relax after a long journey. Evening meals can be taken by arrangement, and vegetarians are well catered for.

*Beechwood House*

A couple of miles from the local beauty spot of Delamere Forest (which we will come to shortly) you will find a charming place to stay called **Barratwich.**

This comfortable Victorian cottage is to be found a short way off the main A556 on Cuddington Lane. The owner, Mrs Riley, told us that the property was once three separate cottages, but it now provides the visitor with tastefully decorated accommodation set in large gardens of over one acre.

*Barratwich*

The large drawing room leads into a conservatory with pleasant views over the surrounding countryside, and there is ample car parking space.

One of the most beautiful Country Hotels we have had the pleasure of visiting must surely be **Nunsmere Hall** near **Sandiway**. Set in the peace and quiet of the Cheshire countryside, it is ideally situated for Manchester Airport and the M6 motorway. Sitting well back from the busy A49, the house is approached via a long, winding private wooded drive, which has spectacular views of the lake. Originally built as a private residence for Lord Brocklebank, the Hall is now privately owned and run by a charming young couple called Malcolm and Julie McHardy. They opened the Hall as an hotel in 1987. Nunsmere offers its guests the wonderful atmosphere and hospitality of a fine country house. The 10 acres of wooded gardens are surrounded on three sides by a 60 acre lake, and provide a tranquil, relaxed setting. Close by are a host of leisure activities and sporting facilities, with two notable golf courses just a few minutes away from the hotel. Clay pigeon shooting, archery and a helipad are all available by arrangement in the grounds.

The interior of Nunsmere Hall is splendid, and the ornate ceilings, decor and antique furnishings lend an air of exclusive elegance to the building. Great care was taken when the furnishings were selected, and these are in keeping with the splendour formerly attributed to the Hall. The reception rooms are spacious and capable of affording privacy, and they all have outstanding views across to the grounds and lake. The 15 bedrooms and suites are light and airy, and beautifully furnished. All have private bathroom facilities, which are fully equipped with luxury toiletries and trouser press. Many of them have the advantage of overlooking the sunken gardens and croquet lawn. The old library is an ideal venue for senior executive meetings and special celebrations, and can comfortably cater for up to 16 guests.

To dine at Nunsmere Hall is truly an experience not to be missed. A selection of menus are available, and the chef takes great pride in using only fresh, local seasonal produce which is delivered on a daily basis. In order to do the menu justice and whet the appetite's of our readers, we cannot resist relating one or two of the dishes available. Comfit of Pork and Duck, with a raspberry vinegar and olive oil dressing. A salad of Scottish Smoked Salmon and Avocado with an orange yoghurt dressing. Main courses include a Ravioli of Calves Sweetbreads with wild mushrooms and a globe artichoke bottom accompanied by a chantrelle and Madeira cream sauce, Terrine of Scallops, Cauliflower, Ginger and Fine Herbs served with an olive oil and lemon water dressing, topped with sevruga caviar. As one would expect, the wine list has been equally well chosen and incorporates wines from as far away as Australia, New Zealand and California.

The brochure for Nunsmere Hall states that 'Nunsmere Hall offers all the time and space you need to simply relax over a delightful meal or meet for business'. This certainly sums up the feelings which we have for Nunsmere Hall, and we cannot improve upon it further.

*Nunsmere Hall Hotel*

**The Forest View Inn and Caravan Park** is ideally situated for holidaymakers who enjoy touring the countryside with their caravans in tow. To find the Inn from the A556 from Northwich, turn right at the signpost for **Norley** village (just before Oakmere) and look for Gallows Clough Lane, which is a turning just over the railway bridge.

The caravan park is open from 1st March until 30th September and there are 30 spaces available for touring caravans. Lyndon and Jane Carthew are the proprietors of The Forest View Inn, and we found them to be a very friendly couple. The Inn has stood for over 100 years and is a charming 'olde worlde' country pub. Although children are allowed to eat at lunchtime, they must be 14 or over to eat inside the pub during the evening. The beer garden can be used for meals at any time.

As well as daily specials, the Inn's menu consists of many varied dishes. Prawn cocktail or Pate Maison may be your choice for starter, and the main course may be selected from Salads and Basket meals, or old favourites like Steak and Kidney Pie, Roast Chicken, Chilli Con Carne, Moussaka or Lasagne. As well as sandwiches and special sized portions for children, vegetarians are also catered for. The Inn is ideal if you are staying at the caravan park and do not wish to cook in the van. The children will love it as there is plenty of room for them to play, and of course pets who are kept

174

under control are also welcome.

*The Forest View Inn & Caravan Park*

North of Norley is **Kingsley,** and if you are close to this charming village, be sure to enquire as to the whereabouts of **The Red Bull.** Not to be confused with the animal variety, this particular Red Bull is a super pub serving excellent ales and a fine selection of food. Chris and Gil Mason are the licencees, and Gil - not Jill! - goes to great lengths to ensure that his name is spelt correctly so as not to cause his new customers embarassment. He related a story to us about a new customer walking into the pub and saying, 'Hi Chris, where's Jill?' Rather embarassing really to have to reply, 'I'm Gil, Chris will be in in a moment.' Although this friendly couple have only been running the pub for about six months, they certainly seem to have the ability to make their customers feel at home. Chris has obviously had lots of experience in catering, and this is evident from the comprehensive menu on offer. Meals are served at lunchtimes from 12 am until 2 pm, Wednesdays to Sundays, and evening meals from 7 pm until 9 pm, Thursdays to Saturdays.

The choices are extensive and range from basket meals to steaks, including daily specials such as pork escalope. Chris and Gil have built up an excellent trade for Sunday roast lunches, and if in the area at that time, be sure to call in early. Gil is responsible for running the bar. Spacious and comfortable, with exposed brickwork and lovely open stone fireplaces, it extends into three different areas. Outside the pub is a large car park and childrens' play area. The gardens are beautiful and in the past have been awarded the Pub Garden of the Year Award. As well as tables and chairs to sit and eat at, there is a stream bordering the garden and a lovely childrens play area with swings. This is an ideal place to stop for a bite to eat or a refreshing drink, especially if you have the family with you.

*The Red Bull*

**The Hill Top Equestrian Centre** is set in the beautiful Cheshire countryside at **Newton-by-Frodsham,** and has outstanding views of the surrounding area. Pam and Eddie Ashby have been running the riding centre for three years. As well as providing livery for horse owners, the Centre has 31 stables, an outdoor menarge, and cross country fences. Riding lessons are available for horse owners, and people are encouraged to visit the centre to watch lessons in progress and obtain expert advice on all aspects of horsemanship. Every care has been taken to provide excellent livery for the horses, and their well being is the main priority at all times.

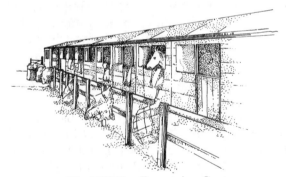

*The Hill Top Equestrian Centre*

**Frodsham,** to the north, has a broad High Street lined with thatched cottages and spacious Georgian and Victorian houses. It was once an important coaching town in the stage coaching days of the 18th and 19th centuries and there are several fine Coaching Inns. Built in 1632, The Bear's Paw with its three stone gables recalls the bear-baiting that used to take place nearby. But Frodsham dates back to at least Norman times when the Earls of Chester built a castle here. The castle was later destroyed in the 17th century, and only fragments remain on Overton Hill. Below the north face of the Hill is the Church of St Laurence, with views spread out over the town, the Mersey Estuary and the Manchester Ship Canal. The Church still has some fragments of Norman carving, but it is the exquisite north chapel with its 17th century panelling which is of particular note.

The Old Hall Hotel is a lovely 16th century building situated right in the heart of Frodsham, opposite the Mersey Estuary. The interior of the building is beautifully decorated and rather unusual, but of particular interest are the two areas of wattle and daub which have been left exposed. There are also lovely open fireplaces for added warmth in the winter. The bedrooms are extremely spacious and decorated to a high standard. All are en-suite and have colour television, telephone, and tea and coffee facilities. As well as eight single rooms, 11 doubles, and one family room, there is also a suite available. The restaurant serves breakfast, luncheon and dinner, with a la carte and table d'hote always proving to be popular with residents. The bar is well stocked and has a friendly, welcoming atmosphere. Mrs Winfield has run the hotel for the past 15 years and likes to provide her guests with first class standards and efficient staff. We thoroughly enjoyed our visit to The Old Hall Hotel and were delighted to have met with such friendly service.

*The Old Hall Hotel*

If all roads led to Frodsham, it would be a good thing, for here we discovered **Rowlands Restaurant & Bar,** run by brothers Nick and Matthew Rowland. They have only owned the 160-year-old former alehouse for a short time, but have already achieved an excellent reputation for their particular style of cuisine. Nick previously worked in Scot's of Mayfair, and

177

is quite determined to provide a menu which is exclusive and which would be at home in a top-class London restaurant, but at prices much nearer to what us mortals can afford!

The restaurant is already bright and cheerful, but the brothers intend to refurbish it to a greater standard and provide the very best setting for their extensive menu. We have only a small space to capture the imagination, but here goes! 'Poached Supreme of Pheasant' filled with wild mushrooms and served with a brandy and cream sauce. 'Strips of Venison' cooked in butter, with a Red Wine, bacon and mushroom sauce, served in a pastry tartlet. And one to set the tiredest of tastebuds quivering - 'Cornfed Chicken', which is stuffed most unusually with black pudding and served with pureed leeks. With an enormous range of buffet style dishes, an exciting wine list and facilities for intimate or large parties, it is well worth turning off the beaten track for a meal here.

**Kingsley Mill** near Frodsham has occupied this site for approximately 300 years. Originally, there was a water wheel attached to the mill, and this was dismantled only 25 years ago. The mill still produces and manufactures animal feeds, as well as being home to the Country Clothing Riding Equipment retailers. This has been developed over the last five years and sells everything that a horse rider may require. Whether you are a riding enthusiast or not, Kingsley Mill is well worth visiting and may be located on the B5153 Northwich to Frodsham road.

*Kingsley Mill*

**The White Lion** has been run under the auspices of Keith and Brenda Morris for the past seven years. It is set in the picturesque village of **Alvanley,** south of Frodsham on the B5393. Built around 1700, the pub and restaurant facility exudes charm, atmosphere and character. Decorated in the traditional black and white associated with the older type of premises, there are lots of old oak beams and interesting curios. Keith and Brenda pride themselves on the food which is served in the pub. Open seven days a week, meals may be obtained between 12 am and 2 pm, and 6 pm to 9.30 pm. Prices are exceptionally reasonable, and the choices available range from simple salads and sandwiches to steaks, poultry, lasagne and hot pot.

A blackboard advises diners of the specials of the day, and on the day we visited, there were no less than eight special starters and 18 special main courses. Quite a selection, and spoilt for choice, we opted for the Roast Duck and Salmon Steak. One of Keith's pastimes is to keep animals. He has sheep, chickens, ducks and geese, all of which roam freely around the rear grounds of the inn. Families are always welcome and there is a designated play area in which children can amuse themselves.

The stability of Alvanley was responsible for a way of life which changed little over the generations. Traditions were maintained, and even less than 200 years ago, a fire dance was still held at Teuthill. This was a practice stemming from heathen fire worship. By contrast, a more homely custom called 'Roping' was also practiced in the village. This consisted of a rope being held across the church gate, ensuring that newly wed couples had to pay a forfeit, thus enabling all the locals to drink their health at The White Lion. Alvanley has its roots in farming, and the surrounding area of fields and woods have a network of footpaths which are ideal for the walker.

*The White Lion*

It's a steep climb from **Helsby** village, about three miles south-west of Frodsham, along pretty woodland paths to the red sandstone summit of Helsby Hill, where you'll find the site of an iron age fort. The Hill is now owned and protected by the National Trust. The views across the Ship Canal and Mersey Estuary towards Liverpool are superb, and you can still see the artifical defences on the south and east sides of the fort, together with the remains of the man-made defensive earthworks behind the triangulation point at the summit.

The 32 mile long Sandstone Trail begins in Frodsham, a route taking its name from the underlying red sandstone which is such a feature of north and east Cheshire. The Trail ends at Grindley Brook on the Shropshire border. Details, leaflets and a guidebook about the Trail are available from Information Centres throughout Cheshire.

It's a pleasant walk along the Sandstone Trail to Delamere Forest - 2,400 acres of attractive plantations of conifers fringed with deciduous oaks and chestnut trees, and one of the loveliest areas of woodlands in the North of England.

Delamere Forest was once part of the vast medieval Forest of Mara and Mondrum that stretched from the Mersey, south to Nantwich and the borders of Cheshire. In Norman times, the word 'Forest' meant a protected hunting ground for royalty or nobility. Delamere was originally used by the Earls of Chester and it became a Royal Forest in the 14th century, with James I being the last King to hunt deer here. Large areas of oak were cleared from the Forest in Tudor times for ship building and boat construction, as well as for the familiar black and white half-timbered cottages of Cheshire. In the 19th century, much of the area was replanted with oak and pine. Since the early 20th century, Delamere Forest has been under the control of the Forestry Commission, who undertook an intensive programme of tree planting and woodland management. The Forest is now very much a working forest, in which 90 per cent of the trees are eventually destined for the saw mills.

However, Delamere Forest and the Forestry Commission welcome visitors. Close to Delamere Railway Station (frequent services between Chester and Manchester), about two miles north of Delamere village off the A566, there is the Delamere Forest Visitor Centre. This has exhibitions and audio-visual presentations on the history and ecology of the Forest, including a replica of the Horn of Delamere, the badge of office of the hereditary Forester and bow bearer, and now symbol of the Forest. There is also a small bookshop and cycle hire centre. Throughout the Forest are a network of waymarked walk trails, linked to car parks and picnic areas. For example, a popular walk from Delamere Station is to the pretty reed fringed lake at Hatchmere, or south to Eddisbury Hill and The Yeld (outside the woodland), once occupied by an Iron age community and used as a fortress by Aethelflaeda, daughter of King Alfred, in Saxon times. There is an Easitrail, specially designed for the disabled and wheelchair users. There are also waymarked nature trails around Linmere close to Delamere Station.

**Springfield Guest House** is run by a very friendly woman by the name of Mrs Mulholland. Built in 1863, the house is a large, imposing building with whitewashed walls, and beneath each of the windows are flower boxes full of glorious flowers. To the front of the property is a large car park and beautifully kept grounds, which guests are encouraged to use. The house is conveniently situated for visitors wishing to explore the surrounding local attractions.

It is situated on the edge of the Delamere Forest in the Vale Royal district of Cheshire. It is on the main A556, which is a direct route through to the M6 motorway and Manchester Airport. The interior of Springfield Guest House is charming, beautifully furnished and spotlessly clean. Since establishing the premises as a guest house, Mr and Mrs Mulholland have gained an enviable reputation for looking after their guests and providing home comforts. The seven bedrooms consist of four singles, one double, one twin and one family room, and all have good facilities and are tastefully decorated. Most of the visitors tend to return time and again to sample the hospitality extended to them by this charming couple.

*Springfield Guest House*

At **Mouldsworth,** west of the Forest, is an excellent Motor Museum housed in a former waterworks. This has a collection of cars and motor cycles particularly from the 1920s and 30s, but also boasts a 1906 De Dion Bouton, a 1970 Triumph TR6 and a replica 1920s garage, as well as examples of toy pedal cars and old Dinkey toys to make some not-so-young visitors nostalgic.

Further south is the village of **Tarvin** and the 14th century Church of St Andrews, which still bears its scars from the Civil War. Look for the smattering of bullet marks on the wall outside the main entrance. The Church also has some amusing gargoyles and grotesques, including one man with toothache and another holding a bell.

Other attractive villages in this part of Cheshire include **Kelsall,** with the remains of Kelsbarow Castle on the hill close by, **Great Barrow, Little Barrow,** and **Dunham-on-the Hill** - quiet communities all so very close to the busy tourist centre of Chester.

# Cheshire Peak and Plains

## CHAPTER SEVEN

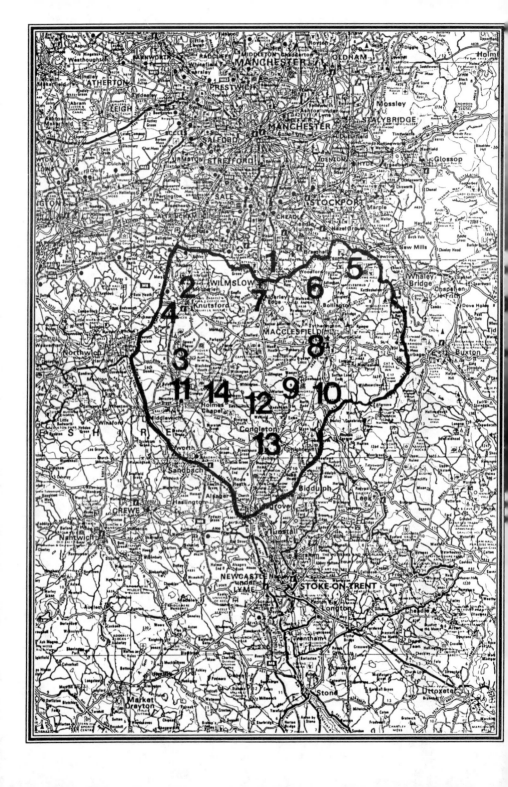

# Chapter Seven
# Map Reference Guide

| Name | Map Ref No |
|---|---|
| Barnshaw Smithy | 2 |
| Church Farm Produce | 9 |
| Crown Inn | 14 |
| Davenport Arms | 9 |
| Fernbank Guest House | 1 |
| Fiddly Bits | 4 |
| Heatherfield Hotel | 4 |
| Hillside Ornamental Fowl | 2 |
| Knutsford Heritage Centre | 4 |
| Laburnum Cottage | 2 |
| The Laurels | 3 |
| Longden Workshop | 8 |
| Longview Hotel | 4 |
| Lyme View Marina | 6 |
| Marton Heath Trout Pool | 9 |
| Oak Cottage Motel | 3 |
| Prince Studio | 5 |
| Prospect House Hotel | 7 |
| Railway Inn | 2 |
| Rough Hey Farm | 10 |
| Sandhole Farm | 13 |
| Sandpit Farm | 9 |
| Tiree | 11 |
| Yellow Broom Restaurant | 12 |

*Gawsworth Hall*

# Cheshire Peak and Plains

East Cheshire is often referred to as 'Cheshire Peak and Plains' to indicate the contrast between the high hills to the east and the gently undulating pastures and woods on the edge of the Cheshire Plain to the west.

And the contrast is sudden. Within half a mile you can find yourself travelling out of lowland Cheshire into some of the highest and wildest countryside of the Peak District - acres of lonely moorland and gritstone crags through which steep valleys and moorland streams wind their way. And on the summits of the bare and empty uplands you can enjoy a sense of grandeur and wide open space almost without equal in England.

This is part of Cheshire which has a magic of its own, especially for the rambler. You can cross an expanse of open moorland to suddenly drop down quiet hillsides into intimate valleys, or climb steep ridges and summits from where you can enjoy breathtaking views back across lowland Cheshire and across to the Shropshire hills. It was here, in the deeply cut valleys on the edge of the Peak, in towns like Bollington and Macclesfield, that the early textile mills, powered by fast flowing moorland streams and serviced by the new Macclesfield Canal, heralded a new industrial world. You'll find villages of weavers' cottages and industrial terraces close to the mills they served.

Yet travel only a few miles to the west and you are back in the Cheshire Plain, a gentler landscape of rich pastures, deep hedgerows, meandering lanes and quiet villages.

**Knutsford** lies on the edge of this gentle lowland countryside. It is an attractive market town of narrow streets, old shops and fine Georgian houses. The town dates from medieval times, but grew quickly in the 18th century into an important coaching town on the main London-Liverpool road, and it still has many former coaching inns. It is however as the setting of Elizabeth Gaskell's novel, 'Cranford', that Knutsford is perhaps best known. 'Cranford' is a chronicle of the daily events and lives of the people of a small Victorian country town, written with a blend of sympathy, sharp observation and gentle humour which still delights modern readers.

There is a memorial to Elizabeth Gaskell incorporated into the striking King's Coffee House on King Street which was designed by Richard Harding Watt in 1907. Further down the same street is Knutsford's Unitarian Chapel where Elizabeth Gaskell is buried in the churchyard. The Chapel is one of the oldest Dissenter buildings in the country, completed in 1688 and opened in 1689 after the passing of the Toleration Act. It's a simple red brick building with mullioned windows, and a flight of steps at each end leading up to an upper gallery.

Opened in 1989, **The Heritage Centre** in Tatton Street is a reconstruction of a 17th century timber framed building which had been a Smithy in the 19th century. During the restoration, the old forge and bellows were found in a remarkable state of preservation. The Macclesfield and Vale Royal Groundwork Trust - whose aims and work we have already described in Chaper 6 - undertook the rebuilding, using where possible the original materials. The wrought-iron gate which leads up into the courtyard in front of the Centre was designed as part of an environmental art project and depicts dancing girls taking part in the local May Day celebrations.

*Knutsford Heritage Centre*

With the help of local people, the story of the town will be featured in the Centre along with a changing range of exhibitions featuring local history topics, crafts and environmental topics. On the second Thursday of every month there is a lunchtime talk starting at 12.30pm, and there are a series of events linked to the exhibitions. The Heritage Centre is open Sunday to Friday 2pm - 4.30pm and on Saturdays from 11am - until 4pm. Additionally, there is a small shop selling gifts and local books and maps, and also local

188

information about other attractions and places to visit. Groundwork also operates a Cycle Hire in nearby Tatton Park every weekend from Easter until October and every day except Monday during July and August. We suggest you telephone for more information prior to visiting, during open hours on 0565 650506.

Whilst in King Street, we were intrigued to come across a little shop called **Fiddly Bits.** Always inquisitive, we decided to pop in and see just what kind of fiddly bits were for sale. Once inside the shop, you can imagine our delight to find before us a wonderful selection of enchanting doll's houses and shops, scaled down to one twelfth normal size. They have a vast range of accessories, all intricately put together. Being a former terraced cottage, the shop has lots of character and this is largely due to the fact that it was built around 1782. Hilary Swallow is the proprietor of the shop and she has been operating for almost eight years. Hilary's displays are magnificent and they will delight both young children and adults alike. The work that goes into the production of the doll's houses and miniatures is particularly intricate and the craftsmen that make them obviously exercise great patience. Even if you are not an avid collector of these items, we would still recommend calling in just to browse.

*Fiddly Bits*

Every year, Knutsford celebrates Royal May Day. The festivities, which are considered the most impressive of their kind in England, began in 1864 and earned their Royal prefix when the town was visited by the Prince of Wales in 1887. The celebrations consist of May Pole dancing and a large procession headed by Jack in Green and the May Queen in a horse-drawn landeau. The streets are carpeted with coloured sand in which patterns are traced. Sand is also scattered for local weddings, a custom said to have originated when the Anglo-Saxon King Canute crossed a ford over a nearby stream and scattered the sand from his shoes as a wedding party passed. It has also been suggested that the name Knutsford might even derive from 'Canute's Ford'.

Overlooking Knutsford's large Common, you will find a lovely, friendly little hotel of quality called **The Longview Hotel and Restaurant.** Here Pauline and Stephen West, who have enjoyed offering hospitality for the past 15 years, look forward to extending a warm welcome to their guests. They enjoy it and hope that their guests do too.

The hotel is both larger and more salubrious than it looks from the outside. Furnished with many antiques that reflect another age, the Wests have been careful to retain the character and elegance of this Victorian building. All 23 en-suite bedrooms offer the standard amenities required by today's traveller, and are carefully decorated with the use of cotton printed fabrics. Little touches like the dried flowers and pin-cushions give it that cared for feeling, which is echoed throughout the hotel. As soon as you step into the reception/lounge you will be greeted by the warmth of an open log fire crackling away in the cottage black leaded range. The cosy cellar bar offers a wide range of beverages, and there are old deep seated couches in which many an hour could be wiled away. The restaurant, which has a very good reputation, offers excellently prepared dishes which are served in this small comfortable period setting overlooking the Common, a racecourse in Victorian times.

Our views on this hotel are echoed by a number of other 'Good Sirs', such as The A.A., The Which! Hotel Guide, Michelin, Routiers and The Royal Automobile Club, as well as The English Tourist Board. It is definitely worth a second look.

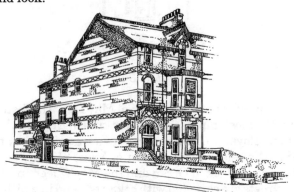

*Longview Hotel*

190

**The Heatherfield Hotel** also stands in spacious surroundings overlooking Knutsford Heath. Built around 1870, it was originally two houses, but these were later knocked through to form what is now an imposing detached residence. The hotel has belonged to the Pryor family for the last 48 years, and was originally run by Mr Pryor's grandmother. Many changes have taken place during those years and the hotel is now of considerable size, very spacious and tastefully decorated. There are 10 comfortably furnished bedrooms, including four doubles, four twin bedded rooms, one single and one family room. All are light, airy and well equipped. The gardens to the front and rear of the property are well cared for and provide plenty of car parking space. The hotel is ideally situated for visitors wishing to explore the surrounding Cheshire countryside.

*The Heatherfield Hotel*

Just to the north-east of Knutsford is the village of **Mobberley** and the Church of St Wilfred, famous for its richly carved rood screen of 1500, which is said to be one of the finest in England. There is also a memorial in the Church to George Leigh-Mallory, the famous climber who died whilst climbing the final summit ridge of Everest in 1924.

Whilst on our travels we always consider it a pleasure to watch true British craftsmen at work, so we were delighted to chance upon **Barnshaw Smithy** in Pepper Street. Dave Broadbent is the working blacksmith proprietor of Barnshaw Smithy and he has specialised in ornamental ironwork for the last 15 years. His expertise is evident from the articles which he produces and displays in the shop attached to the forge. Dave's reputation for the standard of his work is so well known that he often undertakes private commissions from the National Trust.

Visitors to Barnshaw Smithy are able to watch items such as weather

191

vanes, fire grates, signs and decorative brackets being made. Onlookers then have the advantage of actually purchasing the goods 'hot off the forge'. As well as smaller items, Dave can also produce more decorative work such as balustrades, dividing screens, light fittings, hand rails and brackets, and modern sculptural work to individual specification. One area which he particularly specialises in is the full restoration of antique gates, as well as all forms of restoration to ornamental metalwork.

*Barnshaw Smithy*

The superb private collection of Wildfowl to be seen at **Hillside Ornamental Fowl** was first begun over 30 years ago. Since the move to Damson Lane in Mobberley in 1974, the collection has gradually grown to include some rarely seen species amongst which are Pink-eared ducks, Magellanic Flightless Steamer ducks, Hartlaub's duck and Pacific Eiders. Situated around the grounds are various aviaries housing an interesting group of pheasants, some of which are quite rare. It is possible to glimpse the Satyr Tragopan or Bronze-tail Peacock Pheasant here.

A truly eye-catching sight are the three groups of Flamingos, Lessers, Greaters and Chilean, and other exotic species include African Spoonbills, Sacred, Puna and Scarlet Ibis, Pink-backed Pelicans, White Storks, and several species of Toucans, Toracos and Hornbills. A fascinating feature for adults and children alike is the Penguin Pool. Here several species can be seen, including a magnificent pair of King Penguins. The pleasant combination of pools, waterfalls, paths and plants make Hillside a haven for both birds and visitors, and it makes a pleasant outing for all the family. Hillside is open from Easter until the end of September on Sundays,

Wednesdays and Bank Holiday Mondays.

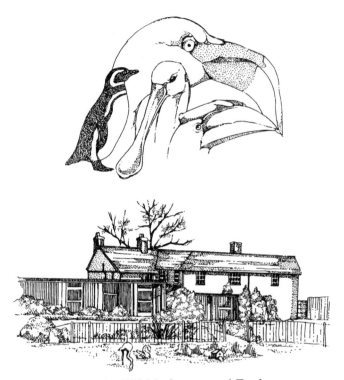

*The Hillside Ornamental Fowl*

We always like to pop into the local pub when we arrive at a village we haven't visited before, not just to sample its obvious pleasures, but because we find it the best way to gather local information. At Mobberley, we thoroughly spoiled ourselves and visited two separate establishments!

We found the **Chapel House Inn,** run by David and Tina Isaac, in Broad Oak Lane. Built over 200 years ago, the pub has retained its original charm and is delightfully decorated. One of the reasons the pub is so popular with locals is the flavoursome Boddingtons Ale, which is reputedly the best pint for miles around! There is a garden for families to sit and enjoy our English summers when they finally arrive, and with children in mind, David plans to build a play area at some time in the future. If you arrive in a peckish mood, then get your teeth around a 'buttie' - that's all they serve in the way of pub meals, but they are filling and very tasty!

*Chapel House Inn*

Tony and Lynda Davies are the publicans who run a lovely old pub in Mobberley called **The Railway Inn.** They are a very friendly couple who made us feel welcome from the moment we arrived. The building is over 200 years old and has lots of atmosphere and charm. It is situated next to Mobberley Station and is signposted from the village. Recently renovated, the Inn has managed to keep its character by retaining its old oak beams, which we are sure could tell a story or two. Whilst Tony is in charge of the bar and cellar, Lynda uses her skills in the kitchen and provides customers with excellent bar snacks, evening meals and also children's portions. All of the food available is very reasonably priced and from what we saw, it is very attractively presented. There is a bowling green outside, and at the time of writing we are reliably informed that The Railway Inn is about to join the local league. There is also a fully equipped children's area where the youngsters can play safely.

*The Railway Inn*

**Laburnum Cottage** in Knutsford Road is a superb, large detached guest house situated just a few miles from the M6 and conveniently placed for Manchester Airport. Shirley and Malcolm are the owners of this charming guest house, and they like to ensure that their guests are made welcome and encourage them to feel at home. The standard of accommodation is excellent and the tasteful decor and furnishings create a relaxing atmosphere.

The bedrooms are spotlessly clean and beautifully decorated and the smell of lavender is prevalant throughout the house. Laburnum Cottage has wonderful open views across to Tatton Park, and guests may take afternoon tea on the lawn surrounded by well-tended flower beds which are ablaze with colour during the summer months. Non-smokers will be pleased to know that this is also a non-smoking house. It really is a peaceful house that exudes charm and friendliness and is ideal for a relaxing break away from it all. If travelling by rail or air to this part of the country, Shirley or Malcolm will happily arrange to provide visitors with transport.

*Laburnum Cottage*

If you travel eastwards along the B5085 from Mobberley, you reach **Alderley Edge,** a town taking its name from a long wooded sandstone escarpment, nearly two miles in length and rising 600 feet above sea level, culminating in sandy crags overlooking the Cheshire Plain.

Alderley Edge itself is a popular area of countryside rich in history and legend. There is a network of footpaths through the woods with superb views over the surrounding countryside. A short walk takes you to the Wizard's Well, in which you'll find the following verse: 'Drink of this and take thy fill/For the water falls at the Wizard's will'.

Local legend tells the story of a farmer who was on his way to Macclesfield market to sell his white horse, when he was stopped by a Wizard who

195

wished to buy the horse. The farmer refused, but he failed to sell the horse at market, and on his return was forced to sell it to the Wizard. The Wizard showed the farmer a cave, barred by iron gates, in which a sleeping army of knights and their steeds lay ready to ride out to save the country in its hour of need. The Wizard, who in some versions of the story is portrayed as Merlin, explained to the farmer that he was a horse short and he rewarded the farmer handsomely. Readers of Alan Garner will recognise that this story and the setting of Alderley Edge forms the core of his classic children's adventure story, 'The Weirdstone of Brisingham'.

More factually, Alderley Edge once contained a large neolithic settlement, and many Bronze Age tools and implements have been found there. The area is also riddled with old copper mines, some of which are dangerous and should not be explored. It is now a National Trust property, and a car park on the main Macclesfield road gives access to the woodlands.

**Prospect House Hotel** is set in the heart of the Cheshire countryside, and it was built originally as a bakers to serve the community of Mobberley, Alderley Edge and the surrounding areas. It operated as such until approximately 38 years ago. The present owners have carefully restored the house into a small family run hotel which recaptures the atmosphere and grace of the Victorian era. While offering excellent service and modern amenities, they have managed to create the warmth and comfort expected of an English country house.

A 40 foot conservatory overlooking the patio and lawn is the most recent addition to the house. The accommodation comprises 12 en-suite bedrooms with bathroom or shower, and all are attractively furnished and very comfortable. The menu in the dining room changes daily and is varied. Prospect House is ideally situated, and can be located on the B5085.

*Prospect House Hotel*

From Alderley Edge there is a footpath that will take you to Hare Hills Gardens, a little known National Trust property. The Victorian gardens include fine woodland, rhododendrons, azaleas, a pergola and a walled garden themed in blue, white and yellow flowers.

In **Nether Alderley,** further along the A34, you'll find a delightful 15th century watermill that has been restored by the National Trust. The red sandstone walls are almost hidden under the huge sweep of its stone tiled roof. Inside is the original Elizabethan woodwork and Victorian mill machinery, which is still in working order. If you've time, visit the 14th century church of St Mary with its unusual richly carved pew set up on a wall like an opera box and reached by a flight of steps outside.

*Nether Alderley Mill*

To the north of Alderley Edge is **Wilmslow,** a busy but attractive commuter town, with a pleasant town centre, areas of green and an attractive Parish Church on the banks of the little River Bollin.

Not far outside the town is an area of peat bog, Lindow Moss, in which the perfectly preserved body of an Iron Age man - Lindow Man - was recovered. He had died suddenly, possibly as a result of a ritual execution.

From the centre of Wilmslow you can walk through the Carrs, a pleasant riverside park, to Styal Country Park.

Owned by the National Trust, this comprises 250 acres of woodland and riverside walks, as well as the model village of Styal with its delightful redbrick terraces and thatched cottages. Quarry Bank Mill, built in 1784, was one of the first generation of cotton mills powered by a huge iron waterwheel driven by the River Bollin. The Mill is now an award winning working museum where visitors can see demonstrations of spinning and weaving on historic looms. There are also exhibitions on printing and dyeing and on the lives of the mill workers. Samuel Greg, the owner of

197

Quarry Bank Mill, was both a pioneer of the factory system and a philanthropist. He took children from the slums of Manchester to work in his mill, providing them with food, clothing, housing, education and worship in return for their labour. Visitors can experience for themselves what life was like for the hundred girls and boys who once lived in the Apprentice House, with guides dressed in period costume.

There is an old Victorian vicarage in the village of **Handforth,** which has been transformed to provide most comfortable and interesting accommodation. Known as the **Fernbank Guest House,** it is set in the attractive North Cheshire countryside, only a stone's throw from the delightful rural setting of Quarry Mill. The excellent motorway system provides easy access to the Peaks, Lake District and North Wales, and Fernbank is also highly convenient for travellers using Manchester Airport. It is run by Barry and Christine Wright.

The character of the house has been carefully preserved and the public rooms are beautifully furnished in keeping with the period.

Christine contributes a unique interest to Fernbank. She is an expert professional restorer of china and porcelain and is happy to explain and demonstrate her art to guests. She teaches ceramic restoration and conducts courses in the subject at Fernbank at certain times of the year. Visitors to the studio are welcome, but are requested to make an appointment. Barry is a congenial and amusing host, pleased to provide information and every assistance to guests to ensure their enjoyment. He also arranges a courtesy car service to Manchester Airport and the nearby railway station.

*Fernbank Guest House*

Nearby Adlington Hall has been the home of the Legh family since 1315. It is an interesting building, incorporating two contrasting architectural styles spanning four centuries: Tudor and Jacobean timbered work and handsome Georgian stone additions. The Great Hall was completed in 1505 for Thomas Legh, and has a hammerbeam roof enriched with carvings and mouldings, and two large oak supports said to date from the original hunting lodge of 1040. Also in this room is an organ built by Father Smith, which is said to be one of the finest 17th century examples in Britain. It was played by no less a figure than George Frederick Handel when he visited the Hall in the mid-18th century. There is also a fine Timbered canopy displaying arms of important Cheshire families, and an elegant Georgian panelled dining room. The gardens were designed in the style of Capability Brown in the 18th century and there is a yew walk and a lime avenue, which was planted in 1688 to commemorate the Ascension to the Throne of William III.

The new cafe at **Lyme View Marina** in **Adlington** offers visitors a pleasant place to sit and have a cup of tea and relax after a stroll along the Macclesfield Canal. The owner, Mr Hodgkinson, has been here for 30 years, and what was originally a working farm now provides mooring facilities for up to 130 small river craft. In addition to these, two barges are available for hire, but visitors are recommended to book early in the season as they always prove popular. As a wise rat once said, messing about on the river must be one of the best ways to enjoy a lovely summer afternoon! Walkers can explore the Middlewood Way, a disused railway cutting which is close by, and with the annual Cheshire Canoe Races held here every July, there is something for everyone to enjoy. Disabled visitors are welcome with easy access to all parts of the Marina, and large groups can easily be catered for.

*Lyme View Marina*

Visitors to this part of the county may or may not have heard of the artist Ian Price. For this reason we recommend our readers to divert a little in their journey and visit Ian's studio at Higher Poynton. It is known as **Prince Studio** and can be found in Prince Road. Ian is a well known and respected artist with great talent who has lived in the area for the majority of his life. Educated at King's School, Macclesfield, The School of Art and also the former Regional College of Art, Manchester, he gained his NDD, ATD, and ATC qualifications and was also awarded the Heywood Special Prize for Book Illustration. He has spent over 25 years teaching in the area, as well as tutoring in Canada. Ian has published numerous articles on art education in newspapers, magazines and books on subjects such as Card and Paper Crafts, Printmaking, Christmas Decorations, Lettering and Display and Rockclimbing.

Most of Ian's efforts have concentrated on the development of his career as a painter, and his original paintings and drawings have been executed in a variety of media, as well as limited edition prints. His work can be found in collections all over the world, particularly in the USA, Canada, Japan, South Africa and Switzerland. Ian's main subject matter tends to be landscape, and his paintings of Cheshire, Derbyshire, Snowdonia and the Lake District are greatly admired. In recent years, he has devoted a considerable amount of time enlarging his range of greetings cards, and these have subsequently become extremely popular. A visit to Ian's studio will confirm what we have said, and we are sure it will prove to be most enjoyable.

East of here on the busy A6 road lies the village of **Disley,** a scattered village clustered around a classical fountain. The church is noted for some extremely old European stained glass, and a tower built in 1527 for Sir Piers Legh of Lyme Hall.

Disley lies close to Lyme Park, which is now owned by the National Trust and managed by Stockport Metropolitan Borough Council, but for over 600 years it was the home of the Legh family. Nothing remains of the original house built in 1465, but the later 16th century house was incorporated into the present building, which was designed by the Italian Giacomo Leoni in the 18th century. It is the largest house in Cheshire, a mansion built on a grand scale with 15 great bays fronted by four huge ionic columns. There are several Elizabethan rooms. The finest is the Drawing Room, once described as the most beautiful room in England, with superb oak wainscotting and an elaborate plaster frieze. The Salon and Dining Room are enriched with beautiful Grinling Gibbons carvings in limewood, depicting clusters of fruit, foliage, and scenes of fishing, painting and music. Greatly prized are items that once belonged to Charles I, a group of Chippendale chairs said to be covered with the material cut from his clocks, a pair of gloves, his dagger and a portrait showing him with his death warrant in his hand.

Lyme Hall is set in extensive parkland and woodland filled with red and fallow deer, a delightful area in which to stroll and picnic. On a hill stands a small square lookout tower, believed to be Elizabethan and known as The Cage. Within the 13 acres of beautifully laid out Victorian gardens are an Orangery (now a cafeteria) and a charming sunken Dutch Garden.

For keen walkers, Lyme Park is the start of one of Cheshire's finest walks, The Gritstone Trail, which, like the Sandstone Trail, takes its name from the underlying bedrock which so shaped the scenery. The Trail is over 18 miles long and ends in Rushton Spencer in Staffordshire, passing through beautiful remote moorland including the summit of Fat Betty and Kerridge Hill.

**Prestbury,** between Wilmslow and Macclesfield, boasts an attractive tree-lined High Street, flanked by old coaching inns and black and white buildings which mingle with the mellow red brick work of later Georgian houses. The Church of St Peter, which dates from the 13th century, still maintains a tradition which began in 1577. A curfew bell is rung every day at 8 pm during the autumn and winter, with the number of strokes corresponding to the date of the month. In the Churchyard is a glass case containing pieces of carved sandstone thought to have been part of a cross erected here in the 8th century by early Saxon converts to Christianity. The fragments were discovered embedded in a wall during restoration work, where they had been hidden for 400 years. Close by is a building known as the Norman Chapel, though only the impressive doorway actually dates from Norman times. Opposite the church is a striking magpie timber-framed building which was once the vicarage. It is said that during the Commonwealth, the rightful incumbent was debarred from preaching in the church by the Puritans, and so the Rector retaliated by addressing his parishoners from the tiny balcony.

**Macclesfield,** nestling below the adjacent Peak District hills, was once an important silk manufacturing town, and a market town with its origins in medieval times. The town's link with silk developed in the 17th century from a cottage industry, expanding in 1743 when Charles Roe built the first silk mill. There then followed a rapid expansion, the industry reaching its peak of activity in the 19th century. Man-made fabrics are still manufactured in the town, but textiles no longer dominate its economy.

Appropriately enough, Macclesfield has the country's only museum devoted to the Silk Industry, which covers all the aspects of the industry from Cocoon to Loom. The Museum has an award winning audio-visual presentation of the history of the Macclesfield Silk Industry, and there are also fascinating exhibitions on the silk route, silk cultivation, fashion, and other uses of silk. Nearby Paradise Mill, which was built in the 1820s, is now a working museum demonstrating silk weaving on 26 jacquard hand looms. Exhibitions and restored workshops and living rooms capture the working conditions and lives of mill workers in the 1930s. It is also possible to buy locally made silk products at the Museum.

Modern Macclesfield is an interesting town with small narrow cobbled streets and snickets to explore, and many streets lined with black and white timbered houses and old weavers' cottages. There is a fine market square with a market cross, and set on a hill, a handsome church that was originally founded by King Edward and Queen Eleanor. It is probably best viewed from the railway station first, before climbing the 108 steps to view its interior.

St Michael and All Angels Church was extended at the end of the 19th century, but it retains its 14th century core. Inside is the Legh chapel, built in 1422 to receive the body of Piers Legh who fought at Agincourt and died at the Siege of Meaux. There is also a tablet to John Brownswood, who was a schoolmaster at Stratford-Upon-Avon, and who is said to have taught Shakespeare before becoming Headmaster at the local Grammar School. In the Savage Chapel you'll find the famous Legh Pardon Brass, recording the medieval practice of selling forgiveness for sins.

Macclesfield Sunday School was built in 1813 for the education of local working children. It was finally closed in 1970 and as well as housing the Silk Museum, it forms the Heritage Centre with exhibitions on Macclesfield's rich and exciting past and on the story of the Sunday School itself. On the outskirts of the town is West Park Museum, a purpose built Museum, founded in 1898 by the Brocklehurst family. The collection includes Egyptian artifacts, fine and decorative arts, and paintings by Charles Turnicliffe, the well known bird artist. The Museum itself is set in one of the oldest public parks in England and has reputedly the largest bowling green in the country.

An interesting shop to visit when in the vicinity of Macclesfield is the **Longden Workshop.** This odd looking little corner shop in a back street close to Christ Church is the showcase for a group of artists and craftspeople who work in the studios above and behind it. Being built on a steep slope, the building is on five levels. A few steps up from the shop will take you to the printing studio, and a few steps down to the pottery. At an even deeper level you will find the potters glazing and firing their ware in the kiln, and on the upper floor there are painting studios and a dark room for photography. During the winter months classes are held here in Etching and Pottery.

The shop is situated on the corner of Shaw Street and Bridge Street, in a conservation area, but not far from a large car park on Churchill Way. Everything you see here is produced on the premises and includes etchings, screen prints and paintings, many of them inspired by the beautiful countryside around Macclesfield. The pottery is stoneware - unusual decorative pots and domestic ware in summery colours.

The workshops and gallery are open to visitors Monday to Saturday, from 10 am to 5.30 pm. You are welcome to call in and see the potters and print makers at work, without obligation to buy.

*Longden Workshop*

To the east of the town centre lies the Macclesfield Canal, one of the highest inland waterways in England, running for much its length at over 500 feet above sea level. It was surveyed by Thomas Telford and opened in 1831, linking the Peak Forest Canal at Marple with the Trent and Mersey Canal near Kidsgrove, a distance of 26 miles. Between Macclesfield and Congleton, the canal descends over a hundred feet in a spectacular series of 12 locks at Bosley, before crossing the river Dane via Telford's handsome iron aqueduct. Another unusual feature of the canal are its roving bridges which carried the towpath across the canal, thus allowing horses to pass beneath the bridge before crossing it, and therefore making it unnecessary to unhitch the tow line.

At **Bollington,** the canal crosses the River Deane on a stone aqueduct, passing several of the large textile mills which it once served. Bollington grew rapidly in the 18th and 19th centuries, and in its heyday had 13 cotton mills. The Victorian shops and cottages around Water Street and the High Street give the town a marked 19th century flavour. Above the town on

Kerridge Hill is White Nancy, a distinctive bell-shaped structure, erected as a monument and landmark to commemorate the battle of Waterloo in 1815. It's worth climbing up to the top (footpaths lead from the centre of Bollington to the summit) for a magnificent view of the town with its grey mills and the great railway viaduct that cuts across the town, and across the Cheshire Plain. You can continue along the ridge that forms Kerridge Hill, another magnificent viewpoint.

In the former Gate House of the Adelphi Mill in Grimshaw Lane, Bollington - an impressive stone building which used to be a thriving cotton mill - is the **Groundwork Discovery Centre,** with a changing range of exhibitions from local history through to nature topics and information on local groups. Each exhibition has a series of activities linked to it from making bat boxes with the younger members of the family through to crafts, demonstrations and illustrated talks and walks.

Macclesfield and Vale Royal Groundwork Trust runs the Centre, having rehabilitated the building in 1986. It is open every afternoon from Easter until Christmas and has a small shop selling gifts as well as books and maps and information about other attractions in the local area.

Also on the same site, there is the opportunity to hire a bike and ride along the traffic-free Middlewood Way - a disused railway line which now forms a linear parkway. Bikes are available each weekend from Easter until October and every day during July and August. For information about the Discovery Centre and Cycle Hire, telephone (0625) 572681.

*Adelphi Lodge*

To experience the rooftop of Cheshire, take the A537 road from Macclesfield (there is a regular bus service) up the winding Cat and Fiddle Pass to the Cat and Fiddle Inn. You'll find yourself in a wild, desolate landscape with open views over Axe Edge Moor. The Cat and Fiddle is the second highest pub in England at 1,690 feet above sea level. It was built in 1831 to serve travellers on the old turnpike road between Macclesfield and Buxton. You can still see two mileposts, one of iron and the other of stone, 164 miles from London.

The name Cat and Fiddle is probably a corruption of the name of a medieval Forester known as Catton Fidelis - Caton the faithful. The story goes that when deer poachers were apprehended, Caton would grin broadly - hence the expression 'to grin like a Cheshire Cat'.

East of Macclesfield, the Gritstone Trail passes through Teggs Nose Country Park, once a large quarry from where the pink 'Chatsworth' building stone was cut. The quarry closed in the 1950s and is now part of a country park with a welcoming Visitor Centre, a network of well-marked trails, and a display of quarry machinery. Views stretch across to Macclesfield Forest, a former Royal Hunting Forest once under the jurisdiction of the Davenports of Capesthorne Hall. The Forest is now controlled by the Forestry Commission and there are some pleasant woodland trails through it. Footpaths also lead to the summit of Shutslingsloe and on to the remote moorland hamlet of **Wildboarclough,** whose mill once produced carpets for the Great Exhibition in 1851. The last wolf in England is reputed to have been killed here in the 17th century.

In the nearby hamlet of **Macclesfield Forest,** there is a little 17th century chapel where rush bearing services are still performed, the rushes being brought to the chapel in brightly decorated carts.

High on the moors where Cheshire, Staffordshire and Derbyshire meet is Three Shires Head, close to where a packhorse bridge crosses Panniers Pool. Now it is a favourite place for walkers, but it is as the haunt of outlaws that this beautiful spot is best known, since it required sheriffs from each of these shires to make a successful arrest.

The hamlet of **Wincle** is in one of the remotest corners of Cheshire, reached by narrow roads that wind down the wooded valley of the River Dane. Its very isolation gives this moorland settlement a particular charm of its own amidst the rugged grandeur of the surrounding fells. The Ship Inn's sign depicts the Nimrod, the ship in which the local squire, Sir Philip Brocklehurst, sailed to the Antarctic with Shackelton in 1907. Wincle Grange, just half a mile away, once belonged to the medieval Abbey of Combermere. An earlier religious relic is the 11th century Cleulow preaching cross, hidden in a clump of trees a mile north-west of Wincle.

The River Dane meanders through a wooded valley down to **Danesbridge,** where a single-arch stone bridge spans the river. It is a short drive or lovely walk down the Dane Valley and up to The Cloud, an outcrop of distinctive gritstone rocks on the Staffordshire border that rises to over 1,125 feet above sea level. From here there are superb views south to Potteries around Crewe and Nantwich, north to Lancashire and east up the Dane valley into Derbyshire.

Close by are the Bridestones (reached by a minor road off the A523 at Ryecroft Gate), a neolithic chambered tomb, consisting of a chamber over 18 feet long and made up of two large stones and divided into two sections by a cross slab. There would have once been a large barrow over 300 feet long covering a tomb which has long since disappeared.

**Congleton** is still known as the Bear Town. There is a story that when the Town bear died, the Elizabethan townsfolk lent 16 shillings (80p) to the Bear Warden for the purchase of a new one. The money had originally been collected to buy a Town bible and hence the ditty, 'Congleton rare, Congleton rare, Sold the Bible To buy a bear.' Congleton was one of the last towns in England to end the cruel practice of bear baiting.

Bear baiting apart, Congleton has an historic centre. It was once an important medieval market town. It is also one of the few towns in Cheshire to keep its original medieval street pattern. The two oldest buildings are the White Lion Inn on the High Street, and the Lion and the Swan Inn on West Street, both dating from the 17th century. The former was believed to have been used as an office by John Bradshaw, the High Steward of Congleton and later President of the Court that tried Charles I. There is also an impressive Venetian Gothic Style Town Hall built in 1866, which contains some interesting exhibits including a bridle for nagging wives that could be fastened to a wall in the market place. Congleton developed as an important textile town in the 18th century with many of the mills involved with silk manufacture, cotton spinning and ribbon weaving. You can still see part of Congleton's oldest silk mill at Mill Green near the River Dane.

The traditional farmhouse and newly converted stable block of Sandhole Farm is situated just two miles north of Congleton on the A34, on the edge of Hulme Walfield village opposite The Waggon and Horses public house. Owned by Veronica and David Worth, this 180 acre working farm has been in the family for 21 years. During this time, considerable modernisation and renovations have been undertaken. It is an ideal base for exploring the Peak District National Park, as well as Jodrell Bank Telescope and the numerous stately homes and china world of potteries in the area.

Sandhole Farm has central heating throughout, tea and coffee making facilities, and televisions with teletext. An intercom service is in all of the bedrooms as well as the use of a hairdryer. The two bedrooms in the house have vanity suites and bathroom or shower, and the accommodation in the recently converted stable block overlooks rolling countryside and has en-suite facilities. There is a trouser press and use of a payphone for convenience. The superb lounge is warm and comfortable with a small bar area, complete with fridge, microwave and sink. Patio doors lead onto a barbeque area, which is popular during the summer and autumn. A full English breakfast is served in the house at all times to suit the guests. Reductions are offered for children under the age of 14 sharing a room, and for parties of 10 or more it proves an ideal place to stay during the Christmas and New Year period. David is a keen bee keeper and has a number of hives. The honey is extracted and bottled on the farm and is on sale to the general public. It tastes delicious and makes an ideal accompaniment on the breakfast table.

*Sandhole Farm*

Just south of Congleton is the village of **Astbury**. Its redbrick and black and white cottages, grouped round the village green, are quite a contrast from the grey-brown villages of the Peak. The splendid recessed spire of St Mary's church, that dominates the village, is considered one of the most striking in Cheshire. As you approach the church, you see that the spire is in actual fact detached from the nave. Though the church dates from pre-Norman times, the present building was erected between the 13th and 15th centuries, whilst the spire was only added towards the end of construction. Beautiful timber work inside the building has made the Church justifiably famous. A richly carved ceiling complements the intricate tracery on the rood screen and the lovely Jacobean font cover.

Little Moreton Hall, just off the A34 about five miles south of Congleton, is undoubtedly the finest black and white timbered and moated Manor House in England. It was begun by Ralph Moreton in about 1480 and the fabric of the magnificent house has changed little since the 16th century. Huge carved overhanging gables and distorted panels create a kaleidoscope of black and white patterns. A richly panelled Great Hall, parlour and chapel show off superb Elizabethan plaster and wood work. There is also a beautifully reconstructed Elizabethan knot garden with clipped box hedges and a period herb garden.

On a limestone ridge a thousand feet above the Cheshire Plain stands a striking landmark and folly, Mow Cop, built in 1754. This romantic ruin was erected by Randle Wilbraham of nearby Rode Hall and offers magnificent views over Staffordshire and Cheshire. In 1807 it was the scene of an extraordinary 12 hour prayer meeting, that led to the establishment of Primitive Methodism. Just to the north of Mow Cop is a single 70 foot high column of rock known as the Old Man of Mow.

Mow Cop is perhaps best viewed as it was intended from the gardens of Rode Hall at Scholar Green. Randle Wilbraham was a prosperous and eminent Cheshire lawyer, who built himself this elegantly proportioned house in 1752, extending an earlier house into the servants' wing. Inside the house itself are some fine rococo plaster work and family portraits, whilst the Hall is set in the formal and informal gardens from where the famous view of Mow Cop can be enjoyed.

Between Macclesfield and Congleton lies the village of **Gawsworth,** which is grouped around three small lakes. The Church is reflected in one of the lakes and has a noble 15th century tower and some fascinating gargoyles. Inside are various monuments to the Fittons of Gawsworth, including the sad kneeling figure of little Margaret who died when she was only seven in 1631 with her mother and father, Sir Edward and Jane Fitton. The most notable monument is to Dame Alice Fitton, who rests her head on her husband's tomb with her two sons and two daughters, one of whom, Mary, is said to be the dark lady of Shakespeare's sonnets. Mary Fitton became a Maid of Honour at Elizabeth's court and was renowned for her dark beauty. However, in 1602 she became pregnant, and her lover, the Earl of Pembroke, was imprisoned. Tragically, their child died at birth.

Gawsworth Hall, a half-timbered Tudor Manor house, was built for the Fitton family, and you can still see their shield on the chimney stacks. The 15th century drawing room remains unaltered, as does the main bedroom with its stone fireplace, oak framing, plasterwork and glass. There is also a handsome library and a Chapel built in 1365 which contains some beautiful stained glass, some of which is by William Morris who also designed the Rood. The Hall has a fine collection of sculptures and paintings which include works by Wilkie, Turner and Constable.

To the rear of the house is a rare example of a medieval tilting ground, that was used by knights until the end of the 16th century. In the summer it is sometimes the setting for outdoor productions of Shakespeare's plays. The Hall and Estate had its own drama in 1712, when Lord Mohun and the Duke of Hamilton were both killed in a duel over ownership of the property. The last professional jester and fiddler, Samuel 'Maggot' Johnson, is buried in nearby Maggoty Johnson Woods, owned by the National Trust. He died in 1773 and is said to have earned his nickname from the popular folk dance 'The Maggot', which he frequently played.

**Rough Hey Farm** in Gawsworth is a very busy Bed and Breakfast establishment and working farm. Whilst we were there, the owners, Mr and Mrs Worth, were busy with the lambing season. The history of Rough Hey dates way back to 1530 and the original site is mentioned in the Domesday Book. The word 'Hey' comes from the French word 'Haie', and we are reliably informed that it means 'fenced or hedged clearing'. The cottage was originally used as a hunting lodge. Rough Hey is delightfully situated some 800 feet above sea level, overlooking the Cheshire Plain. It is only three miles from Macclesfield and 12 miles from Buxton. The accommodation comprises a large family room with double bed and single bed, a twin bedded room and a single room, and a bathroom and shower. Guests have full use of a lounge with dining area and television, and they are assured of a warm and friendly welcome complemented by good farmhouse cooking.

*Rough Hey Farm*

A minor road leads west to **Marton** and the Church of St James & John, reputedly the oldest timber-framed church in Europe. It was founded in 1343 by Sir John de Davenport, and is a beautiful example of black and white style architecture, with an unusual tower roofed with wooden

209

shingles. Inside on the west wall are traces of medieval painting, and two stone effigies are thought to be those of Sir John and his son, Vivian.

Lovers of fishing will be delighted to know that Pikelow Farm at Marton has superb facilities for the avid fisherman or woman. David and Anne Taylor are the owners of **Marton Heath Trout Pool,** and they have been running their 60 acre working farm for the last 23 years. In 1987, this enterprising couple decided to build a man made trout pool, which they subsequently called 'Don's Pool'. A couple of years later they decided to build another, and this one was named 'St Mary's Pool'. The pools were named after the contractors, Don Scott and St Mary's Plant, and soon became jointly known throughout the region as Marton Heath Trout pools.

The pools are sited in such a way that the beauty of the surrounding Cheshire countryside can be appreciated by everyone. Fishing from either Don's or St Mary's pool can be a very pleasurable and tranquil experience, and is ideally suited for those wishing to get away from it all for a day. Both the pools are well stocked and the price of a day's fishing is very reasonable. Coarse fishing is also available on separate farm ponds, and during the summer months the farm opens for 'pick your own' fruit on six acres of mixed strawberries, raspberries, gooseberries and currants. David and Anne have created an ideal place for visitors who appreciate something a little different from the usual tourist attractions.

*Marton Heath Trout Pool*

If you appreciate comfortable farmhouse accommodation, we suggest you spend a day or two at **Sandpit Farm,** just outside Marton. The farm has been on this site since the late 16th century and it has survived through several generations of the family who own it. The Kennerley family have lived here since 1830, and the present Mrs Kennerley has been providing bed and breakfast for the past five years. Both the farmhouse and its interior are magnificent. The accommodation comprises one twin, one family and one single room, all of which are beautifully decorated and furnished to a very high standard. Guests may relax in the extremely comfortable lounge and enjoy a traditional English breakfast in the residents' dining room. The countryside surrounding this 200 acre working arable farm is both tranquil and peaceful, and the grounds surrounding the farmhouse are well kept and most attractive. Children are welcome and reductions are made for more than one child sharing a room. The farmhouse can be located following a winding lane from near the centre of the village of Marton. For further details or a brochure, we suggest you telephone Mrs Kennerley who will be happy to advise you. The number is (0260) 224254.

*Sandpit Farm*

Capesthorne Hall is the home of the Bromley-Davenports, whose ancestors were recorded as living here at the time of the Domesday Survey. The family crest, a felon's head with a rope around his neck, recalls the family's postion as Chief Foresters of Leek and Macclesfield Forest, where they had the power to grant life or death. The Hall was built in 1719, but after a disastrous fire in 1861 the centre portion was rebuilt to the designs of the Victorian architect, Salvin. The House is beautifully furnished, including some excellent pieces built by American cabinet makers in the 18th century. The tiny theatre in the stable wing was built for family theatricals, and the exquisite Georgian Chapel dates from 1720. The gardens are entered through a pair of 18th century Milanese gates from where there is a view of the Park and its chain of man-made lakes.

The **Davenport Arms** building was originally part of the Capesthorne Estate. Standing in the same spot for over 200 years, its original purpose was to serve as a court house. During a later period, the building was used as a collecting house where tenants living on the estate paid their rent. Rumour has it that when the rent was paid, the estate would provide them with a free meal or as much ale as they could drink in return, obviously an incentive for prompt payment! It was during the 1950s that the premises finally became a public house serving the local community.

In recent years, an 80-seater restaurant has been added. Situated inside the inn is an exposed well, which has been in existence since the inn was built and is now a feature of the premises. As well as a good selection of ales, there is an a la carte menu and a cold table and bar snacks menu, which includes a choice of vegetarian meals. Outside is a large, well-equipped play area for children and ample facilities for parking.

*The Davenport Arms*

On the A34, close to Marton Church, Wendy and Alan Shufflebotham run a beautiful farm shop called **Church Farm Produce.** Bread, cakes, pies and all manner of tempting treats are made and baked daily on the premises. In addition to this beautifully presented and delicious food, the shop also stocks all types of farm produce. An added attraction is the wonderful assortment of local crafts on display. The shop was converted from an old stable block, and at the time of our visit, a further conversion was well underway to turn more of the stables into an afternoon tea shop. Downstairs, seating is planned for 60 - 70 people and upstairs will be devoted to further displays of local crafts.

Right next door to the farm shop is a furniture shop and workshop, owned and run by Andrew Kidd. All the furniture is handmade to order by Andrew in traditional English Oak and after completion all items are stained, french polished and bees waxed. After you have viewed the showroom - where Andrew has also installed a beautiful 1840 fireplace - you can pop next door and watch the craftsmen at work. This is a fascinating place and well worth a visit after you have replenished your supplies at Church Farm Produce next door!

*Church Farm Produce*

To the west, two large radio telescopes dominate the skyline at Jodrell Bank Science Centre and Tree Park, creating a major Cheshire landmark. The largest has a bowl of 250 feet in diameter and is used for tracking satellites and space probes. The telescopes were completed in 1957 and are involved in a wide range of research programmes. A superb exhibition and planetarium excite visitors both young and old. There are various exhibitions and 'hands-on' working models to see and enjoy, including a 25 foot telescope to help explain some of the mysteries of Outer Space. There is also an extensive aboretum, containing thousands of rare trees and shrubs in extensive parkland.

Further west in a network of quiet lanes is Peover Hall - pronounced 'peever' - a three storey brick mansion with mullioned windows, built in 1585 for the Mainwaring family. It is set in a beautiful landscaped park and period gardens with topiary hedges. The Hall was used as a base for General Patton and the American Third Army in World War II, and there an American flag is hung in the Church to commemorate this Anglo-American link. Also in the Church are Civil War armour and monuments to the Mainwaring family, one of which dates from 1410 and is the oldest effigy in Cheshire depicting John and Margaret Mainwaring.

The neighbouring village of **Lower Peover,** with its thatched, half-timbered cottages, has one of the few surviving timber framed churches in England, St Oswald's, which dates from the 14th century. Its 16th century sandstone tower replaced an earlier tower, but the nave and chancel still keep their older black and white patterns. Inside is a vast oak chest hewn out of a single trunk, which is believed to have been there since the Church was founded. Access to the village is off the B5081 and a short walk down

213

either The Cobbles or Church Walk. The village inn has the evocative name, The Bells of Peover.

Undoubtedly the most apt way of describing **The Oak Cottage Motel** would be to quote the proverb by Bert Dobson which states, 'They that travel the Inca way, Have undoubtedly found the gourmet way, For food and beverage are a delight, and can be taken both day and night.' The motel is situated on the A50 near **Allostock,** halfway between Knutsford and Holmes Chapel. A warm and friendly welcome is always extended to guests by Ian and Barbara Jenkinson, who run this charming hostelry. The motel is tastefully furnished to a very high standard and has 12 comfortable and spacious bedrooms. The four double and eight twin bedded rooms all have en-suite bathrooms, and the views of the surrounding Cheshire countryside are quite exceptional. All the bedrooms are afforded the usual facilities of colour television, telephone, tea and coffee making equipment, hair dryer and also a trouser press.

As well as providing excellent accommodation, the standards set by the restaurant are also highly recommended. The restaurant is open to non-residents and has a wide and varied menu. In addition to the a la carte menu, guests can also take advantage of morning coffee, light lunches, or afternoon tea. And to accompany your choice of meal, the bar provides an excellent selection of wines. The chef supplements the menu daily with special dishes of poultry, steak and fish. Due to the personal supervision of the kitchen by Ian and Barbara, diners are sure to enjoy their meal for both the quality of produce used and the presentation. If you decide to stop off and visit The Oak Cottage Motel, we are sure you will enjoy your stay.

*The Oak Cottage Motel*

**The Laurels** in Brick Bank Lane, Allostock, is set within three acres of land amidst the rolling Cheshire countryside. The views from this charming guest house are superb, as is the setting and accommodation offered.

214

Norma Pagdin started her Bed and Breakfast business just two years ago, and so far she has done very well. This is probably because she is such a friendly, warm and amenable lady. The accommodation comprises a suite with twin bedded room, a fully fitted bathroom, and a private sitting cum dining room with television. A small kitchen area is set aside for making tea, coffee and snacks, and this is complete with fridge. A folding bed is readily available to accommodate a child. There is also a single room situated in the main house, complete with a tea and coffee hospitality tray. As well as plenty of off the road parking, there is a large, well-kept garden for guests to enjoy. Norma keeps and shows ponies, and there is always a spare stable and paddock available if guests wish to bring their own pony or horse along with them.

*The Laurels*

**The Crown Inn** at **Goostrey** was once a large detached farmhouse. It is now an inn of considerable repute, and Peter and Pat McGrath have been successfully running it for the past 14 years.

*The Crown Inn*

215

Built originally in the 15th century, the interior is typical of an English country inn, with lots of brass ornaments, beamed ceilings and lovely open coal fires. As well as full restaurant facilities, bar snacks are also available. All of the food served in the first floor restaurant is freshly prepared using prime local produce, and the menu is varied and caters for most tastes. The restaurant is also available for private parties and meetings, and can adequately seat up to 40 people. For those wishing to stay overnight, bed and breakfast accommodation is available in either a double or twin room. The Crown Inn is open all year round and there is ample parking for visitors.

Moreen and Reg Lascelles have been providing bed and breakfast facilities at a super little guest house in **Cranage** for the past six seasons. Called 'Tiree', the house is spotlessly clean and exudes the warmth and friendliness typical of a home from home guest house. The views from Tiree are truly superb and the double, twin and single rooms available are comfortable, light and spacious. Every attention to detail is paid, even down to the bubble bath, toiletries and cotton wool provided in the bathroom. The bedrooms have the added facility of tea, coffee and colour television. Easy to find, Tiree is set back from the main Middlewich to Goostrey road.

*Tiree*

East of Cranage on the A535, the picturesque village of **Twemlow Green** is perfectly positioned to satisfy the needs of business people and tourists alike. It is geographically situated in the heart of the United Kingdom in the peaceful countryside of mid-Cheshire, and yet it is so very close to major cities, towns and motorways.

**The Yellow Broom** in Twemlow Green is famous as one of Cheshire's finest restaurants. This prestigious building has been in the same ownership for many years, and it is so professionally run by the Proprietor and her Manager that it maintains a relaxed atmosphere and the kind of ambience that other establishments have long forgotten.

The kitchens are in the care of a French head chef and his highly skilled team, who prepare and cook traditional French cuisine with foods brought fresh from the markets to a standard that is second to none. When your dishes are served by well trained and friendly dining room staff, you experience good food at its best.

Select parties, weddings, functions and business meetings are catered for, and arrangements for these are individually tailored with each client so that every detail is settled beforehand.

The beautifully appointed en-suite bedrooms and suite at The Yellow Broom are a credit to their designer, who has used the finest range of wall coverings and fabrics to achieve a charming effect in the individual rooms.

The brochure and tariff will be sent to you upon request, and frankly we can think of nothing more fitting for that special evening out than dining in this superb restaurant and later retiring to the luxury of the guest rooms above.

*The Yellow Broom Restaurant*

217

*Quarry Bank Mill, Styal Country Park*

# South Cheshire

## CHAPTER EIGHT

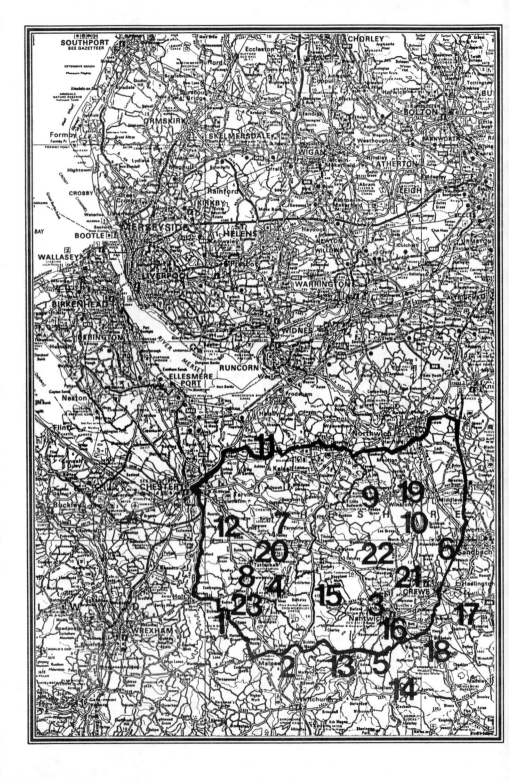

# Chapter Eight
# Map Reference Guide

| Name | Map Ref No |
|------|:----------:|
| Black Lion | 3 |
| Brighton Belle | 19 |
| Cheshire Farm Ice Cream | 8 |
| Cheshire Herbs | 9 |
| Cheshire Workshops | 4 |
| Cotman Gallery | 3 |
| Dusty Miller | 13 |
| Eddisbury Fruit Farm | 11 |
| Firs Pottery | 5 |
| The Folly | 21 |
| Forge Mill Farm. | 10 |
| Frog & Ferret | 3 |
| Godfrey C Williams & Sons | 6 |
| Goldbourne Manor | 12 |
| Green Farm | 17 |
| Jardinerie | 7 |
| Laburnum House Farm | 15 |
| La Casa Vecchia | 6 |
| Lea Farm | 18 |
| Little Heath Farm | 14 |
| Magpie Crafts | 3 |
| Morris Dancer Inn & Restaurant | 11 |
| Old Cottage Gardens. | 20 |
| Old Hall Hotel | 6 |
| Red Cow | 3 |
| Red Lion | 2 |
| Royal Oak | 22 |
| Snugburys Ice Cream Farm | 16 |
| Stokegrange Farm | 3 |
| Stretton Mill | 1 |
| Sproston Hill Farm | 13 |
| Warmingham Craft Workshops | 10 |
| Willington Hall Hotel | 7 |

*Sandback, Saxon Crosses*

CHAPTER 8

# South Cheshire

South Cheshire is a part of the county which is particularly rich in heritage interest, and often has some real surprises.

It's a rich, fertile countryside, famous for its dairy farming and for the production of that familiar white crumbly Cheshire Cheese which is still produced in the traditional way at a few farmhouses in the county.

It's also notable for its waterways, a canal network which includes the Trent and Mersey Canal from the Potteries, the Shropshire Union Canal which crosses the county from Audlem Locks by the Shropshire border to Chester, going past Nantwich, and with a branch to the Trent and Mersey at Middlewich, and the Llangollen Canal which joins the Shropshire Union north of Nantwich.

These canals no longer carry commercial traffic, but are still open and busy for leisure cruising, and boats can be hired from a number of points for a waterways holiday. But the towpaths are also open to walkers, and make delightful, almost level routes rich in historic and architecural interest, with fascinating bridges, locks, wharves, canalside pubs and marinas, as well as being havens for wildlife. The really keen canal walker can, in fact, walk the towpaths of the entire 97 mile 'Cheshire Ring', down the Trent and Mersey to Kidsgrove, up the Macclesfield to Marple and Ashton, and back along the Bridgewater to Preston Brook. A series of booklets from Cheshire County Council describes the walk in convenient stages, which is mostly well served by public transport. The route is, of course, also open to boats and is extremely popular in the summer months.

**Sandbach** would be as good a starting point as any on the Cheshire Ring, lying as it does on the Trent and Mersey Canal. It also lies barely a mile from the busy M6 motorway, and the roar and stress of modern life, but you'll find in its Market Place a link with Cheshire's pre-Conquest history - two richly carved Anglo-Saxon sandstone crosses, dating from between the 8th and 9th centuries and making a focal point in this attractive town.

One theory about the origin of the crosses is that they were set up when

Peada, son of the heathen warrior King Penda, married the daughter of the King of Northumbria. The Princess agreed to the wedding only on condition that she should become the Queen of a Christian country. She must have been a persuasive lady, for Peada duly accepted her requirements and St Chad and other holy missionaries came down from Northumbria to convert the ancient pagan kingdom of Mercia, which included what later became Cheshire, to Christianity.

The crosses were damaged by the Puritans but restored by a local historian, George Ormerod, in the last century, and placed there in their present position.

Sandbach has some interesting half-timbered buildings, including the fine old 17th century Black Bear Inn with its thatched roof.

The town has a famous and popular market every Thursday which brings people in from all over the area. It is held on Scot's Common - so called because it is the place where some of the followers of Bonny Prince Charlie were killed and buried after the battle of Worcester. Sandbach is also celebrated as the place where Edwin Foden established his world famous Foden Motor Company - when he died in 1964, his coffin was carried to its final resting place in the little church at nearby Elsworth on a steam lorry known as Pride of Edwin, which had been made in his factory in Sandbach in 1916.

Sandbach is the home of one of Cheshire's finest purveyors of good food. **Godfrey C Williams and Son** was established in 1875 and since this time has gained an enviable reputation for the produce which they sell. To wander into the shop is an experience in itself, as it is reminiscent of stepping back in time to the wonderful ambience and atmosphere of a high class grocers. This speciality grocers cum delicatessen has been operating from Corner House, The Square, in Sandbach for the last 35 years. Originally, the building was a coaching house, subsequently it became a tobacconist, and it now serves the local population as one of the finest grocers of quality and distinction in Cheshire.

Godfrey C Williams has seen four generations since its time of opening, and the present family consists of Mr Williams and his son. Throughout the four generations, their motto has been 'Quality always remembered when price is forgotten'. The present Mr Williams has a special affinity with both cheeses and coffees, particularly Cheshire Farmhouse Cheese. This is evident from the displays in the shop. He also imports raw coffee, and is one of the few remaining grocers who roasts and blends coffee on the premises. As you can imagine, the smell wafting around in the shop is delightful. As well as cheeses and coffees, Mr Williams cooks all his own hams, and goods such as sides of smoked salmon, caviar, truffles and tinned pheasant can be purchased. It is a real pleasure to visit this remarkable shop, and like us, we are quite sure you will not be able to resist leaving without first purchasing something from the impressive range of continental and British foods on display.

*Godfrey C Williams & Son*

We also found a marvellous restaurant in The Square. **La Casa Vecchia Pizzeria and Ristorante** is owned and run by Hazel and Graham Bacon. How much they enjoy their work is reflected in the warm welcome extended to all their customers. Diners are able to enjoy first class cuisine in a relaxed and informal atmosphere. This 18th century Grade II listed building was formerly a sweet shop. Catering for diners who enjoy eating out, the menu is reasonably priced and within easy reach of couples with limited spending power or those who like to push the boat out.

*La Casa Vecchia*

225

The menu is so comprehensive that most diners return time and time again in order to work their way through the entire menu. The choice of dishes ranges from reasonably priced Pasta, Pizzas, Chicken, Veal, Steaks and Fish. The chef and waiters are Italian and take particular care to ensure that the meals served are of the highest quality. The speciality of the house is fish, and ranges from Smoked Salmon to Monkfish. The wine list is extensive and complements the menu extremely well.

When entering Sandbach from the Newcastle Road, keep a look out on the left for **The Old Hall Hotel.** It is a splendid black and white half-timbered building which has been converted into a charming hotel. The Old Hall was originally built in 1656 on the site of the Ancient Manor, and much of the original building and structure has been restored and maintained. The timber used in its construction is thought to have come from Saxe Mondron Forest near Nantwich, which is said to be one of the best Oak Forests in England. If you decide to call in be sure to look out for the fireplaces and panelling - they are also original and of particular interest. As well as a priests' hole and an underground passage to the Parish Church, there is also a fine example of a left-handed spiral staircase. We were informed that the idea of a such a staircase was in order for the defending sword hand to be kept free. It really is a superb hotel with every modern convenience, and the furnishings, furniture and decoration are all to a very high standard. The restaurant facility is superb and well supported by guests staying at the hotel and locals alike. With a wealth of atmosphere, charming staff and first rate facilities, we are sure that you will not be disappointed should you choose to dine or stay overnight at The Old Hall Hotel.

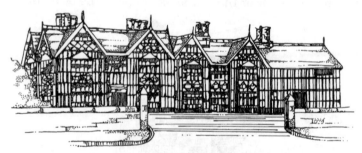

*The Old Hall Hotel*

**Forge Mill Farmhouse** is a spacious Victorian Country House, set in one acre of mature gardens overlooking the beautiful Cheshire countryside. Close to the village of **Warmingham,** it can easily be found by following the instructions given by Mrs Moss, the owner. Leave the M6 at junction 17 and travel into Sandbach, then take the A533 for approximately one and a quarter miles. Turn left after The Fox Inn into Mill Lane, then turn right on Canal Bridge. This will lead you directly towards the house. Mrs Moss aims to make her guests' stay as comfortable as possible. Her breakfast menu is varied to suit individual tastes, and the dining room is delightful.

Forge Mill Farm is the ideal place to stay if you wish to totally unwind. You can relax in the visitors' sitting room after a hard days' work or sightseeing trip. The accommodation is tastefully furnished, spotlessly clean and decorated to a very high standard. A good indication of the standards set by Mrs Moss is the fact that the English Tourist Board have awarded her establishment two crowns. Good pub food is available locally, but an evening meal can be arranged at Forge Mill if you inform Mrs Moss in advance. She also ensures that supper drinks and biscuits are always available for her guests.

*Forge Mill Farmhouse*

**Warmingham Craft Workshops and Gallery** occupy a converted water mill on the River Wheelock. Parts of the present building date back to 1780 when the mill was rebuilt, and records show the existence of a mill in Warmingham as far back as 1289. Visitors to this Aladdin's Cave of craft workshops and studios are invited to browse at their leisure and appreciate the fine selection of crafts on display. There is a wide variety of unusual and original handmade gifts, including pottery, wood, and walking and shooting sticks. In addition, there are also studios displaying leather goods and handmade wooden furniture, and a wood turner and blacksmith. One of the internal rooms is particularly interesting, with a wonderful display of carved walking sticks.

To the rear of the property, a superb museum of aircraft is open to visitors. It has a growing collection of aircraft and engines, most of which are in varying stages of restoration. There is also a helicopter, a Piel Emeraude, an Auster J1, an Addyman Glider and a Weedhopper Microlight. The engines on show include an early rotary of 1916, piston engines like the 'Merlin', and sectioned Twin Wasp radial to Jet engines from the early days, as well as a modern H.S. Viper. The collection on show is entirely run by volunteers, and the continuing restoration and preservation of these aircraft depends entirely on the generosity of public support.

Opposite the Craft Workshops and Gallery is a short-stay camping and caravan park. Situated by the river, it can accommodate up to 10 caravans and is ideal for visitors to the area who are touring. Light refreshments are available within the craft complex and opening hours vary. On Saturdays and Sundays, the complex is open from 11 am until 5 pm, and we would suggest that you telephone 027 077 366 for more information.

*Warmingham Craft Workshops & Gallery*

**Middlewich** lies further along the canal from Sandbach. As its name implies, it was another salt town, and was also the site of two Civil War battles. It also lies on King Street, a Roman Road which is now the A530. In the church, dedicated to St Michael, there are some old carvings and the coat of arms of the Kinderton family of nearby Kinderton Hall. The crest shows a dragon eating a child, and this somewhat gruesome emblem related to a legend of how a member of the family, Baron Kinderton, killed a local dragon as it was devouring a child - presumably too late to save the unfortunate youngster. A lane at **Moston** near Sanbach where the incident is supposed to have taken place is still called Dragon Lane.

**Winsford** has grown in recent years with housing development, but features of historic interest remain, including some timber framed pubs in the centre, and an unusual timber framed church built for bargees on the

River Weaver. It is actually formed from two older townships, Over and Wharton on either side of the River Weaver. Winford Bottom Flash is a popular area for angling, canoeing and pleasure boating.

Railway enthusiasts will be delighted with the restaurant attached to the **Brighton Belle** public house. Novel as it may seem, the dining facility is actually housed in the famous Brighton Belle carriage. The pub itself is particularly attractive and the addition of the Pullman coach makes it an even more interesting place to stop for a drink or bite to eat. During the 1930s this carriage ran the 51 miles between London and Brighton. We are led to believe that the Queen Mother travelled in this carriage on 26th March 1964. Situated just outside Winsford on the Middlewich road, the Brighton Belle has become very much a family type pub. Although the landlords have not been resident here for long, they have already established a friendly, welcoming atmosphere.

The dining car seats 36 and has been fitted out to the highest of pullman standards. The fixtures and fittings are superb Art Deco, a full a la carte menu is available, and 'light bites', grills and snacks are on offer for the less hungry. The house specials include Chicken Kiev, Alabama Chilli and Chicken Madras. Vegetarian dishes are available and a special menu for children has proved to be very popular. The atmosphere in the dining car is reminiscent of a first class train journey with the added attraction of a bygone era. Definitely recommended, this is an ideal opportunity to experience the luxury of first class train travel.

*The Brighton Belle*

To the north of Winsford lies the site of the Abbey of Vale Royal, founded by Edward I in 1277, who, according to the story, did so in fulfilment of a vow he made as Earl of Chester when crossing the Dee in a storm. As he came ashore the ship sank, but the future king was safe. It was a Cistercian

229

monastery and once had the longest Cistercian Abbey Church in England, and after the Dissolution in the 16th century it became a country house. It is now a special school.

Another legend of Vale Royal concerns a nun of St Mary's convent in Chester who nursed a sick Abbot of Vale Royal back to health. They could not marry, but vowed to be united in death and were buried before the high altar at the abbey. The spot is today marked by a cairn placed there in 1814 with a column and medieval cross, still known as the Nune's Grave. Vale Royal has given its name to the modern District of Cheshire in which it lies. The old lodge to the house still survives at Sandiway, whilst the Whitegate Way, from Winsford to Cuddington, is a footpath that uses the old railway line that carried salt from the Winsford Mines. There is a picnic site and car park at the old Whitegate Station.

**Little Budworth,** east of Winsford, is an attractive village with views over the Budworth Pool which gives the village its name - 'bode worth', or dwelling by the water. Close by is Little Budworth Country Park, consisting mainly of ancient heathland, with a mixture of heather, gorse, bracken and silver birch trees growing on sandy soil - much as they did thousands of years ago, though oaks and rowan trees are now appearing. This is an attractive area to sit or stroll in, with car parking and picnic areas. Close by is Oulton Park Picnic Area, whilst motor racing enthusiasts are not far from the celebrated Oulton Park racing circuit.

The revival of the use of herbs in this country has increased considerably during the last few years, and more and more of our supermarkets and specialist shops have recognised the important role that herbs have to play in our lives. The re-introduction of herbs is due to people such as Libby and Ted Riddell, who own and run a specialist herb nursery called **Cheshire Herbs** in Forest Road, Little Budworth. The main thrust of the company is the growing and selling of retail and wholesale herb pot plants, producing over 180 different varieties. The nursery boasts a herb garden where customers can see the plants in situ so as to be able to appreciate the individual stature of the plant they wish to buy. There is also a small yet comprehensive shop selling herb-related products. In the time since Cheshire Herbs have been operating, they have won gold medals for exhibiting at the Horticultural Society, the Cheshire Show, the Leicester Flower Show, the Stoke Garden Festival, the Lakeland Rose Show and the Shrewsbury Flower Show. A gold medal and diamond award was also presented to them at the Southport Flower Show. Libby is often requested to give talks on the subject of herbs, and both Libby and Ted run a series of courses during the summer months. The topics of the courses are quite far ranging and cover subjects such as 'Planning a Herb Garden'. This is a one-day course and relates the history of herbs, hints on planning a herb garden, the diversity of herbs and their use in borders. The price of £24.50 also includes lunch.

Other courses are entitled 'Uses of Herbs', 'Growing Herbs', 'Herbs in the Stillroom', 'Hooked on Herbs' and 'Midsummer Night at Cheshire Herbs'. Libby and Ted have a wealth of literature on the subject and would be delighted to forward information to any of our readers. Whilst reading through one of their handouts, we discovered a lovely poem by Walter De La Mare which we have chosen to include in our book. It goes like this:

THE SUNKEN GARDEN

Speak not - whisper not;
Here bloweth thyme and bergamot;
Softly on the evening hour,
Secret herbs their spices shower.
Dark spiked rosemary and myrrh,
Lean stalked purple lavender;
hides within bosom, too,
All her sorrows, bitter rue.

Breathe not - trespass not;
Of this green and darkling spot,
Latticed from the moon's beams,
Perchance a distant dreamer dreams;
Perchance upon its darkening air,
The unseen ghosts of children fare,
Faintly swinging, sway and sweep,
Like lovely sea - flowers of the deep;
While, unmoved, to watch and ward,
Amid its gloomed and daisied sward,
Stands with bowed and dewy head,
That one little leaden Lad.

If you choose to visit Cheshire Herbs, be sure to allow at least a couple of hours in order to enjoy the fascinating world of herbs that Libby and Ted have created. For more information, telephone (0829) 760578.

The town of **Crewe** might not at first glance seem a tourist destination, but for anyone interested in railway history it has much to offer. The town was created by the Railway Age after 1837, when the first main line from London Euston towards Scotland was built. The station was actually constructed on the edge of the original village, as Lord Crewe didn't want his estate being disturbed by smoky trains. Many of the houses in Crewe were built by the London and North Western Railway Company for their workers, and the town has a fine Edwardian Theatre. Crewe Railway Heritage Centre was opened in 1987 to commemorate 150 years of railways in the town, and it includes an exhibition area, an outdoor arena, a massive working signal box and, during the season, steam train rides often with famous main line steam locomotives in action.

*Cheshire Herbs*

**The Folly** is set back off the main A530 Middlewich to Nantwich road near Crewe. The house and gardens stand on what was initially an old Roman road. Built in 1847, it is a large imposing house set in its own magnificent secluded gardens, where croquet is occasionally played on the lawn.

*The Folly*

232

Guests are greeted warmly by Mr and Mrs Broad, who are retired art teachers. The house is superbly decorated and very comfortably furnished, and there is ample car parking space. The accommodation is light, airy and spacious, and consists of one single room on the ground floor with a toilet and shower room located next to it, and one double and one twin room with a shared bathroom. The bathroom is much larger than average, with a lovely double sized bath. The breakfast menu differs from the usual run of the mill and includes choices such as potato cakes, cheese oatcakes and kippers.

The village of **Haslington** to the east of Crewe has some interesting old cottages and a small 19th century church. The old timber Hall in the village was originally built by Admiral Sir Francis Vernon, one of Drake's Admirals who helped defeat the Spanish Armada in 1588.

**Wybunbury** has the misfortune to be a sinking village, due to the natural seepage of water dissolving the saltbeds deep underground, causing the whole area to subside. The church, famous for its leaning tower and medieval monuments, has had to be entirely rebuilt nearby on firmer terrain.

**Lea Farm** is situated in an area of natural beauty in the heart of the Cheshire countryside. It comprises a 150 acre dairy farm and a charming farmhouse, set in landscaped gardens where peacocks roam. Nearby is the leaning tower of Wybunbury, standing proudly overlooking the pretty village. Allen and Jean Callwood are the proprietors and they happily extend a very warm and friendly welcome to guests staying in their charming home. The facilities are exceptional, and include a full English breakfast and an evening meal if required. The dining room has a picture window overlooking the well tended gardens and surrounding countryside.

*Lea Farm*

233

A luxurious drawing room is available for guests' use, with a colour television and pool or snooker table. The bedrooms are fully equipped with vanity units and one of them has en-suite facilities. All are equipped with tea and coffee making facilities and colour television. Situated in beautiful surroundings, there is trout fishing, bird watching and a well-stocked fishing pool close to the farm. The farmhouse has two crowns and is AA recommended.

The little village of **Barthomley,** east of Crewe and close to the M6 motorway, has a unique church dedicated to St Bertoline. Bertoline was an 8th century Saxon prince who became a hermit on an island in the little River Sow in Staffordshire. But it was here that a terrible massacre took place in 1643 during the Civil War, when a band of Royalist soldiers arrived in the village. The villagers took refuge in the church tower, but the soldiers smoked them out with fire from burning the pews and rush mats. When the villagers surrendered, they were stripped and brutally murdered.

At **Englesea Brook,** about a mile and a half south-east of Barthomley, is one of the country's oldest Primitive Methodist Chapels. Built in 1828, and now turned into a small Museum (open Sunday afternoons April-September), it shows the simplicity typical of rural chapels of the period, and of the Primitive Methodist Movement itself, which started in Cheshire in 1811. The grave of Hugh Bourne, the founder of Primitive Methodism, is in the nearby burial ground, together with his memorial.

South of here is **Balterley,** where we discovered **Green Farm.** This is ideal if you are looking for a place to stay which resembles 'home from home'. As with most of the farmhouses we come across, it is a very large red brick building with terraced lawns. Chris and Geoff Hollins always extend a warm welcome to their guests and encourage them to treat their home as their own.

*Green Farm*

Geoff runs this 145 acre working dairy farm, which has been in the Hollins family for generations. The interior of the farmhouse is beautifully decorated and extremely comfortable. As well as a family room, there is also a single room available on the first floor. The ground floor has a twin bedded room which is suitable for disabled guests, with the shower and toilet situated next to it. Green Farm is easy to locate - take the B5078 off junction 16 of the M6, then take the first left to Bartholomley. Go past the White Lion on the right, and bear left until you come to Deans Lane. Turn left again and the farm is on the right opposite The Limes.

It's only a short drive south of Crewe along the A51 to Bridgmere Wildlife Park and Garden World, where there are 25 acres of gardens, plants, shops and glasshouses, and the Garden Kingdom which includes the Womens' Institute Cottage Garden.

Hilary and Bob Bennion are the proprietors of **Little Heath Farm,** which can be found just off the A529 road from Nantwich to Audlum. This charming farmhouse offers bed and breakfast accommodation, and is set in 50 acres of land. A working farm, it has been farmed since 1850 and is situated alongside the historic canalside village of **Audlem.** Upon being greeted by Mr and Mrs Bennion, guests cannot fail to be immediately delighted with the atmosphere which the farmhouse exudes. The accommodation is comfortable, spacious and well appointed. As well as a family room, it also has two double bedrooms, one of which is en-suite. This is a delightful place to stay and has been awarded a two crown rating by the tourist board authority.

*Little Heath Farm*

Situated close to the Shropshire border, Audlem is celebrated for its mainly 15th century church, which has a sundial scratched on a buttress supporting a wall, believed to be a relic of a far older church. Close to the

235

village are the famous 'staircase' locks on the Shropshire Union Canal, and to the north, also on the canal, is Moss Hall, a magnificent Elizabethan half-timbered house built in the traditional shape of a letter 'E'. There is also a popular canalside inn nearby, called The Shroppie Fly.

This is an area of quiet, narrow lanes, often winding between tall hedgerows which are sanctuaries of wildflowers in spring, and linking scattered farms, hamlets and villages of great charm.

Halfway between Nantwich and Whitchurch on the A530, at Aston crossroads, is **The Firs Pottery** where Joy and Ken Wild make a wide range of stoneware. Their specialities include oven and microwave wares, lamps, vases, castle bowls and planters. A converted barn provides a two storey shop and showroom, a large, bright and functional workshop, and a clay store and kiln room. It is possible to book in for one of Joy and Ken's 'Making Days', where you can work as one of a group of up to 10 people. During the course of the day you will be instructed in the art of making pinch pots and slabware, and in the use of the wheel. Children's half day workshops are held during the school holidays and half terms. Joy and Ken fire the pots to biscuit for you and you come back on another occasion to glaze your pot for further firing, or ask them to do it for you. There is ample parking space available and also conveniences for visitors' use. For further details, we would suggest you telephone Joy or Ken on (0270) 780345.

*The Firs Pottery*

**Wrenbury** is a typical south Cheshire village, with an old church by the village green which has a corner tower that carries stairs to the top of it. The village green was used for bear baiting, and it is recorded that on at least one occasion, the vicar stopped the service one Sunday morning when a travelling bear arrived, and went outside with the congregation to see the bear being paraded around the green.

A favourite, well-known local pub and restaurant in the Wrenbury area is **The Dusty Miller.** Mentioned in Hanson's Guide as one of the best 100 pubs in the country, it is not difficult to see why. Also referred to in the Daily Telegraph's 'On The Waterfront' article in 1990, it was one of the first pubs in the country to be awarded both a basic hygiene and a Heartbeat award. Robert Lloyd Jones, the proprietor, has been at The Dusty Miller for 10 years, and in 1987 - 1988 was named as the regional winner of the Innkeeper of the Year award. Although derelict in 1970, the pub was converted and remodernised into a licensed premises in 1977, and exudes character and charm. The resident proprietors renovated the first floor to provide a 38-seater restaurant with private bar facilities. Subsequently, the catering facilities were expanded to provide a wide range of bar meals at lunch time and evenings, as well as an a la carte restaurant menu. The Dusty Miller is easily accessible by canal or road, and is delightfully situated amongst picturesque surroundings. Holiday makers and locals alike can enjoy excellent food and superb ales, either inside the pub or in the extensive canalside rose garden.

*The Dusty Miller*

Jay and Roy Wilkinson run a superb farmhouse providing excellent bed and breakfast accommodation at nearby **Sproston Hill.** Dating back as far as 1750, **Sproston Hill Farm** was a working dairy farm until 15 years ago. Mushrooms were one of the main crops grown here, and the farmhouse is now set in eight acres of land. Bed and Breakfast facilities have been provided for the past six years, and the farmhouse has even been featured on Granada Television. Beautifully decorated and furnished, there are two double en-suite bedrooms and two twin rooms.

All the bedrooms have vanity units, central heating, colour television and tea and coffee making equipment. A spacious visitors' lounge provides comfortable and relaxing seating. The standards of the farmhouse can be judged by the three crowns awarded it by the tourist board.

*Sproston Hill Farm*

The town of **Nantwich** is the focal point of this part of Cheshire. This lovely old town was once second only in importance to Chester in the county, being used by the Romans as a supplier of salt for their garrisons at Chester and Stoke. It remained a salt producing town from Saxon times onwards, but production declined in the 18th century as other centres with better communications on the canal system such as Northwich increased in importance. However, a brine spring still supplies the town's outdoor swimming pool. Salt was used in the tanning of leather, and the town had a small but significant leather industry. It was also a centre for Cheshire cheese making, where for many years the rare Nantwich Blue Fade cheese was produced.

In 1583, Nantwich was devastated by a disastrous fire, which raged across the half-timbered and thatched buildings and lasted for 20 days, leaving only a few buildings standing. It is recorded that during the fire, the bears kept behind the Crown Hotel were let loose and the townswomen were afraid to help with fighting the fire for fear of the beasts. Four bears from Nantwich are mentioned in Shakespeare's comedy, 'The Merry Wives of Windsor'.

Fortunately, a few fine old buildings did survive the Nantwich fire, such as the moated half-timbered mansion belonging to Nantwich merchant Rychard Churche in Hospital Street, which was built in 1577. It is now open to the public as a small museum.

Much of the town was rebuilt after the fire, and many of the wonderful half-timbered buildings in the town centre, such as the Crown Hotel, date from this period.

Another important Nantwich building to escape fire damage was the fine 14th century Parish Church, sometimes called the 'Cathedral of South Cheshire'. It dates from a great period of Nantwich's prosperity as a salt town and trading centre, and is richly decorated with an unusual octagonal tower. Of exceptional interest is the magnificent chancel, and the wonderful carving in the choir. On the misericords (tip-up seats) are mermaids, foxes (some dressed as monks - an interesting social comment), pigs, and the legendary Wyvern - half-dragon, half-bird, whose name is linked with the River Weaver, 'wyvern' being an old pronunciation of Weaver.

An amusing tale about the building of the church concerns an old woman who brought ale and food each day from a local inn to the masons working on site. Unfortunately, the masons discovered that the woman was cheating them by keeping some of the money they put 'in the pot' for their refreshment. They dismissed her and sought revenge by carving her image in the church, being carried away by the Devil himself with her hand still in the pot. To this day, inhabitants of Nantwich are known as 'Dabbers'.

During the Civil War, Nantwich was the only town in Cheshire to support Cromwell's Parliamentary army. After several weeks of fierce fighting, the Royalist forces were finally defeated on 25th January 1644, and the people of Nantwich celebrated by wearing sprigs of holly in their hair and hats. As a result, the day became known as 'Holly Holy Day', and every year on the Saturday closest to 25th January, the town welcomes Cromwellian pikemen, and battle scenes are re-enacted by members of the Sealed Knot. There are records of the Civil War and exhibitions in the Nantwich Town Museum in Pillory Street, which also has material about the town and the dairy and cheese making industry.

We were amused to find that Nantwich has a veritable menagerie of inns and public houses. **The Red Cow** in Beam Street is the oldest building in Nantwich. Once a 14th century farmhouse, it became an inn during the 16th century in order to cater for the drovers travelling south en-route to market. It is renowned for its excellent Real Ales, such as Robinson's Best Bitter and Mild, Hartleys XB Bitter and, an old favourite with the locals, Old Tom. Due to the popularity of the Red Cow, visitors have come from as far afield as Japan, U.S.A., Sweden and Germany. The interior is very cosy, with a beautiful inglenook fireplace, low oak beams, wattle and daub panels on the walls, and a large collection of brass ornaments. There are several little nooks and crannies where customers can enjoy a drink or eat a meal in semi-private, and a section of the inn is specifically designated for non-smokers.

Nick and Libby Casson are the proprietors, and they are extremely efficient at their job. Both are chefs, and having been in the catering trade

239

for the last 20 years, they have plenty of expertise behind them. The menu is wide and varied, with a first class selection available. Starters include Garlic Mushrooms, Prawn Cocktail, Chef's Homemade Pate and Corn on the Cob. The main courses represent excellent value for money, with dishes such as Homemade Steak and Kidney or Mushroom Pie, Steak, Fish, Chicken, Moussaka, Chilli and Gammon. We thought the vegetarian menu particularly innovative, with choices including Broccoli and Cream Cheese Pie, Mushroom and Nut Fettucini, and Vegetable Curry, Chilli and Lasagne. Baked Potatoes with a variety of fillings, Beef Burgers and Open Sandwiches are also available if you require a light lunch. Children are welcome lunchtimes and evenings, and a special menu is available to them, also of excellent value. There is also a large beer garden with swings and a tractor where children can amuse themselves.

For visitors wishing to stay overnight, there is adequate and comfortable accommodation in the adjoining cottage. Each room has tea and coffee making facilities and colour television. All in all, The Red Cow is one of the finest inns we have had the pleasure of visiting, and we will definitely call in again when next in the area.

*The Red Cow*

**The Frog and Ferret** is a lovely detached black and white timber fronted building with leaded light windows. The building is well over 200 years old and has managed to retain its unique character, even though substantial renovations and remodernisation have taken place. During the winter months, the large feature fireplaces are lit and create a superb atmosphere.

The bars are extremely comfortable and exude warmth and friendliness. Situated in the centre of Nantwich, the pub is a popular meeting place for all age groups. Bob Butler is the proprietor and he takes great pride in keeping a good cellar and a well-stocked bar. A wide range of traditional ale is always available, at least three cask-conditioned bitters being served at all times. The food at the Frog and Ferret is varied and wide. As well as starters and main courses, there are also fish and vegetarian dishes available. The Chicken casserole and Lamb hot pot are absolutely delicious. The pub is very popular at lunchtimes and the food is renowned for being plentiful and excellent value for money. We thoroughly recommend popping in for lunch and enjoying a drink at the same time.

*The Frog & Ferret*

**The Black Lion,** once called The Black Leopard, is a cosy pub built in the classic black and white style of the period and dates from 1605. Now a free house, Mr Pike has established a welcoming atmosphere with the traditional pub downstairs and a 30-seater restaurant which was opened in the spring of 1991. Well worth stopping by on your way in or out of Nantwich, it can be found on the edge of the town on the main road to Wrexham and opposite the Cheshire Cat.

*The Black Lion*

Much of the central part of Nantwich is now pedestrianised and forms an attractive shopping centre, notable for its floral displays in the summer months and its selection of specialist shops, restaurants and coffee houses.

When you are in the town, be sure to pop into **Magpie Crafts** at 44 Hospital Street. It is a charming little shop with the exterior, attractively surrounded by hanging baskets and window boxes, all jammed full of the most colourful flowers and plants. Sue Adams is the proprietor, and she has been in business for seven years. The business has operated from the present premises for just two and a half years and is proving to be very successful. The exterior has a charming Victorian shop front, and immediately prior to Sue purchasing the building, the rooms at the front of the property were used as living accommodation. The interior of the shop is attractively decorated and has lovely low beamed ceilings which add to the atmosphere of the premises. Sue retails most types of crafts, ranging from hand painted designs on stained glass, to real flower gifts and miniatures of every type. Also on display are brass paperweights, pottery and paintings. Well worth a visit, Sue is happy for her customers to browse whilst selecting a special gift or perhaps a souvenir to take home. We spent a very enjoyable half hour admiring the many items she has for sale, and of course could not leave without buying a little momento of our visit to Nantwich.

*Magpie Crafts*

**The Cotman Gallery,** also in Hospital Street, is housed in a 17th century Grade II listed building, a short distance from the centre of Nantwich. When we called in we were delighted to see a choice collection of modern watercolours, original etchings, ceramics and woodware. All of the products on show are by British artists and craftsmen, and are part of a continually changing display. There is also a studio pottery which forms part of the gallery. Lovers of fine art will be in their element here.

**Stoke Grange Farm,** on the Chester Road outside Nantwich, is a traditional farmhouse which was built in approximately 1700. It was converted into a farmhouse in 1838 and now provides first class farmhouse accommodation. Fred and Georgina West are the proprietors, and they like their guests to enjoy the home comforts that their charming 120 acre working dairy farm has to offer. As well as providing bed and breakfast facilities, they can also offer first class accommodation in one of the recently converted outbuildings. This is in the form of self-catering cottages, and being newly modernised and renovated, the cottages are exceptionally well appointed.

As this is a working farm, guests are encouraged to wander down to all the activity and enjoy watching the cows being milked, feed the chickens and geese, and watch the lambs frolicking in the meadow. You may also take a pony ride if you wish. After a taxing day's sight-seeing, what could be nicer than to relax on the verandah and watch the passing canal boats on the Shropshire Union Canal. This runs past the farm and stretches a quarter of a mile upstream. Everything you need is provided by Mrs West, who is sure to make your stay a pleasant and relaxing one.

*Stoke Grange Farm*

Stapeley Water Gardens is just south of Nantwich on the A51. Reputedly the world's largest garden centre, there are acres of display lakes, pools, fountains, exotic gardens, tropical tanks, and a restaurant and coffee shop.

The home of **Snugburys Ice Cream** is a 250 acre working farm, consisting of 130 Friesian cows and 30 Jersey cows. Park Farm can be found just outside Nantwich on the A51, and is run by a charming couple called Mr and Mrs Sadler. The Sadlers have been making ice cream for three years now, and they told us that the quality of the product is most important to them and that their quest is to achieve perfection. Having sampled some of the delicious flavours available, we are convinced that they are close to reaching their aim. To ensure that the product maintains its quality, they go to the trouble of purchasing only top quality ingredients. For example, ginger is imported from Australia, honey comes all the way from Hungary, and the brandy used is Napoleon. As well as making superb ice cream, they also manufacture clotted cream, which can be purchased at the farm shop. In Devon, it is not unusual to see ice cream served in a cone with a large helping of clotted cream on the top, so we were delighted to learn that Snugbury's Ice Cream can also be purchased in the same way. If you haven't tried eating ice cream in this manner, we suggest you do - it really is delicious, even if it is very fattening!

*Snugburys Ice Cream*

In the twelve months since Robert and Rachel took over **The Royal Oak** at **Worleston,** they have worked hard to improve the trade and upgrade the standard of food available. The pub is situated on the B5074 Nantwich to Winsford road. It is an attractive, large detached black and white building with a profusion of flowering hanging baskets and a large car park. Outside the pub is an outdoor play area for children, and there is a games room inside for the winter months.

It is an ideal place to stay if touring with a caravan, as Robert and Rachel have facilities to cater for up to five touring caravans, with water laid on. Food is available during the hours of 12 pm to 3 pm lunchtimes, and 7 pm to 9.30 pm in the evenings. The menu is varied and includes dishes such as Chicken a la Creme, Lasagne, Gammon, Plaice, Salmon and Steaks ranging from a standard size up to an enormous 32 ounce T-Bone Steak. Sandwiches, salads and light lunches range in price and provide excellent value for money. Private parties can be catered for, as can other functions for up to 65 people.

*The Royal Oak*

The name **Acton,** a village some two miles west of Nantwich, means 'township among the oak woods' - a reference to Delamere Forest, which once stretched this far. The church, with its large tower, was restored after the Civil War, but a Norman font survives from the earlier church, as well as an impressive tomb of William Mainwaring, a local nobleman, dating from 1399.

Dorfold Hall close by is said to stand on the site of a hunting lodge and deer park used by Leofric, Earl of Mercia, and his wife, who is better known as Lady Godiva. The present Hall is a magnificent Jacobean country house, built in mature brick with a beautiful cobbled courtyard, with richly decorated plaster ceilings and panelling. One of the upstairs rooms has been described as one of the finest in England, whilst another room prepared for a visit by James I has coat-of-arms in plasterwork and a secret cupboard for his personal possessions. Sadly, the visit of the King never took place and the expense was in vain. The gardens have lawns, woodlands and a fine avenue of old limes. An ancient oak tree in the grounds is reputed to have been the southern-most point of Delamere Forest.

If a country retreat is your idea of a relaxing break away, then we can thoroughly recommend a visit to **Laburnum House Farm,** at Hearns Lane, Larden Green, **Faddiley.** Sheila and Eddie Metcalfe are the proud owners of this beautiful country farmhouse and dairy farm. Eddie works the 60 acre farm and looks after 35 cows and one bull. As well as managing the farm, Eddie is also a capable builder, and this is very much in evidence from the magnificent job he has done with the remodernisation of the farmhouse and accommodation.

A three roomed suite is available, and it is superbly furnished. It consists of a lovely light and spacious double bedroom, a well-furnished sitting room, and a bathroom. There is a private balcony, fully equipped with patio furniture and sun lounger. Full central heating, colour television, and washing and drying facilities are available. The price of bed and full English breakfast is very reasonable, and visitors wishing to stay may request a brochure prior to booking. We were certainly impressed, and we know you will not be disappointed if you decide to stay at Laburnum House Farm. Sheila and Eddie's aim is to please, so if there is anything you require do not be afraid to ask.

*Laburnam House Farm*

The western side of Cheshire approaching the Welsh border begins to have the feel of border country, where ancient tribal feuds and wars between Saxon and Celt have their memory in the great castles of the Warlords of the Marches, which were designed to defend disputed territory.

Such a feature is Beeston Castle, which, positioned on a craggy cliff towering over the Cheshire Plain, makes a major landmark. The castle lies on a site once occupied by neolithic tribesmen and Iron Age warriors. The present fortress goes back to 1220, when it was built by Earl Randle, Seventh Earl of Chester, as protection against the army of the Welsh Prince, Llewllyn the Great. Its design was based on castles that the Earl had seen on Crusade in the Holy Land, with a massive outer bailey which could contain a whole battalion of soldiers.

The castle continued to play a role in Anglo-Welsh politics over the centuries, and Richard II stayed here before leaving for Ireland and being forced to abdicate. Legend has it that the King stored his treasure here before leaving England, but it has never been found. Beeston Castle last saw action in the Civil War, when it was captured for the King by Captain Sandford in a daring attack. Damage caused by cannon balls can still be seen. It is now in the care of English Heritage and is open to the public, being one of the finest viewpoints in the whole of the North West.

Peckforton Castle, visible from Beeston, has a very different history, its purposes being far from military. It is a grand Victorian mansion, occupying a three and a half acre hilltop site. It was built between 1844 and 1851 in exact Norman style, to the designs of the architect Anthony Salvin for Lord Tollemarch, Member of Parliament for Cheshire between 1841 and 1872.

Described by the Victorian architect Sir George Gilbert Scott as 'the largest and most carefully and learnedly executed Gothic mansion of the present', Peckforton Castle with its 60 foot high towers is a fantasy in stone. It has been superbly restored and is now open to the public with guided tours, refreshments and a speciality shop.

Peckforton Castle lies at the end of a range of beautiful wooded hills, the Peckforton Hills, crossed by footpaths, including the Sandstone Trail. Paths continue to Bickerton Hill, where the remains of a hill fort can be seen.

**Burwardsley** (pronounced 'Boosly'), at the western edge of the Peckforton Hills, is said to have been the home of the Bear Warden in the days of bear-baiting, but it could be simply the name of its founder, probably a Saxon by the name of Burward.

The **Cheshire Candle Workshops** in Burwardsley is easy to find, and provides a very enjoyable and interesting day out for both adults and youngsters alike. The owner of this thriving craft centre is Mr James, and he has succeeded in creating a flourishing business of no small means. The buildings have been on the site since 1830, and are situated right in the heart of the Cheshire countryside in a setting surrounded by medieval castles. The popularity of the place will be evident by our telling you that during the last year, over 2,000 coach parties visited the premises. A visit here is a unique experience steeped in history, and proves to be exciting for all the family. If the children's attention should stray a little while Mum and Dad are watching the candles being made, there is a large play area for them to amuse themselves in.

Jacqueline is responsible for making the candles, and she told us that she is capable of producing up to 60 ornamental candles per day. Depending upon the style, she is quite happy to make candles for special occasions to the client's specification. We thought this was a super idea for personal presents, birthdays, anniversaries and weddings. As well as the art of

Candlemaking, there is also a Glass Studio. Rod Beckhurst runs this craft shop, and he has been making glass ornaments of every description for the past 37 years. Like Jacqueline, Rod will also happily accept private commissions for special gifts, and when you are buying a gift for someone special, it is always rather a nice touch to actually watch the article being made. Exquisitely made jewellery can also be purchased, and although we were unable to meet Beverley Edwards who makes it, we were delighted with what we saw set out on her stall.

*Cheshire Candle Workshop*

As well as much to see, there is also a restaurant which serves a variety of delicious meals. Called The Hayloft, it is furnished in the traditional 'olde worlde' style. Originally, it served its purpose as an old Granary and Coach House. Now it is possible to enjoy a simple cup of tea or coffee, a light snack, or a full a la carte meal. It is reasonably priced, and there is also a special childrens' menu available. Of the two dining rooms, the upper floor will seat as many as 50 or 60 people, and has a side room which can cater for as many as 60 more. It is possible to book the lower dining area for coach parties with prior notice, and a further 100 seats are available here. The workshops are attractively laid out and enable visitors to browse at leisure whilst watching the individual crafts being made. There is so much to see and do here that we know you will enjoy this hidden place with its many attractions.

At **Bunbury,** east of Peckforton, there is a 19th century watermill originally built to grind corn for the Peckforton estate. It has been carefully rebuilt by North West Water and is open to the public most weekends. Information panels explain the working of the mill, and stone-ground flour is for sale.

248

Bunbury itself is a particularly attractive village, with narrow, twisting streets and a fine church. Sir Hugh Calverley added a College for priests to the church in the 14th century, and the tower was made higher in the 16th century. It was restored in Victorian times and again after World War II, when the roof was damaged by a German bomb.

The village has several lovely timber-framed Tudor cottages and elegant Georgian houses. On the Whitchurch road is the Image House, on the walls of which are some curious carvings. They were supposedly made by a poacher who, returning from deportation to Australia, claimed a common right to build on the Heath by having a chimney built and smoking between sunset and sunrise. He took revenge on the Squire and the Sheriff and his men who arrested him by carving their likenesses in sandstone reliefs and cursing them. All are supposed to have died before the poacher, and all are still to be seen, as well as the Devil waiting to take their souls.

Cholmondley Castle, to the south, is a beautiful 19th century castle. The Castle is not open to the public, but the grounds are, and visitors can enjoy superb ornamental gardens, a lakeside area, a home farm with animals and an ancient private chapel. The grounds are open on Sunday afternoons in the summer months and refreshments are available.

**Tarporley** to the north of Peckforton was an old forest town, and the Swan Inn is still the meeting place of the Cheshire Hunt. The ancient Foresters or Forest Wardens lived here, and in **Utkington,** north of the village, is an old farmhouse and a Hall, which has a column formed by an ancient forest tree, its roots still in the ground. The Hunting Horn of Delamere was once hung on this column as a symbol of authority for the Foresters. It is now kept in the Grosvenor Museum in Chester.

**Willington Hall Hotel** dates back to the 17th century, and stands in 17 acres of beautiful tranquil parkland near Tarporley. The Hall was originally built by one Col. Tomkinson, who made his fortune during the Peninsular War. Thirteen years ago, one of his descendants, Richard Tomkinson, decided to go into partnership and convert this beautiful house into a hotel. His partner, Ross Pigot, is responsible for managing the hotel.

The hotel has 10 beautifully furnished bedrooms, all with bathrooms en-suite, colour television, radio, tea and coffee making facilities and a telephone. A la carte lunches and dinners are served in the licensed restaurant every day, and the wine list accompanying the menu is extensive, with as many as 56 different wines to chooses from. A variety of delicious bar snacks are also served for those not wishing to over-indulge. Willington Hall Hotel is not only highly recommended by the AA and the RAC, but also by Ashley Courtenay.

*Willington Hall Hotel*

Set in the heart of the Cheshire countryside, on the road between Sandiway and Tarporley, is the **Jardinerie Garden Centre.** Visitors can spend many an hour wandering through the superb displays of items relevant to gardening and the art of landscaping. There is something of interest for every level of gardening enthusiast, whether it be for the amateur or the professional. Specialist talks are often arranged for group bookings, and subjects are wide and varied. It is ideal for groups such as the Chamber of Commerce, The Rotary Club and the Womens' Institute, and professional associations and gardening clubs are frequent visitors.

The information centre on the premises will arrange for their gardening expert to visit individual premises to discuss your garden needs. Exhibits to be seen at the Centre include Aquatics, Bonsai, Shrub Galleries, Olive Tree Terracotta and Garden and Building requisites. There is also a Cafe on the site, which sells beverages, salads, sandwiches and hot specials daily.

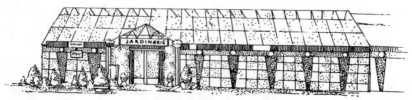

*Jardinerie Garden Centre*

**Eaton,** to the north of Tarporley, has a lovely little village green, half-timbered cottages and an old smithy. A tree now grows out of the steps of its ancient cross.

Immediately upon meeting the owner of **Haworth's Eddisbury Fruit Farm,** we could tell that he receives a tremendous amount of job satisfaction from the long, hard hours of work he puts into his fruit farm and shop. Located at **Kelsall,** we left the new bypass at the top junction and entered the village. Turning right opposite Th'ouse at Top, we continued along Yeld Lane (signposted Mouldsworth three miles) and the farm is approximately a mile further on. Situated on a 50 acre site, the farm has magnificent views of the rolling Cheshire countryside. Of all the varieties of fruit that are grown here, Mr Haworth's favourite crop is apples - he has as many as 16 different varieties for sale. How many of us are aware of varieties such as Howgate Cooker (available from September to February), Chivers Delight (October to January), and Kidd's Orange Red (November to March). These are just a few of the lesser known apples, and obviously the more familiar varieties such as Cox, Gala, Crispin, Golden Delicious, Russet Sunset, Spartan and Jonagold may be purchased too.

As well as apples, Mr Haworth also grows a selection of pears, strawberries, gooseberries, rhubarb, raspberries, black and red currants, tayberries, plums and loganberries. We can easily see why this man is kept so busy, tending to such an impressive array of fruit trees and bushes. As well as selling to wholesalers, Mr Haworth has a farm shop for visitors. The shop stocks a variety of farm produce, including fruit, vegetables, ice cream, honey, fruit juices, potatoes and home made jams. The idea of 'pick your own' fruit has become increasingly popular over the last few years, and is encouraged at the farm. Special leaflets are available in the shop, giving visitors instructions on how to pick professionally and store for a maximum length of time. The leaflet advises on the apples that may be picked well in advance of Christmas and stored until required.

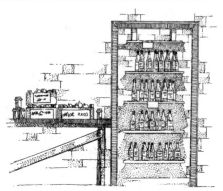

*Haworth's Eddisbury Fruit Farm*

**The Morris Dancer Inn and Chikito's Restaurant** is a large, detached building of Spanish appearance, situated on the Old Chester Road in Kelsall. The inn is over 150 years old, and has a very warm and cosy atmosphere. The interior is furnished in keeping with the character of the premises, and an unusual collection of keys and stirrup pumps are displayed in the bar. The pub is renowned for its excellent choice of ales, and a selection of bar snacks may be puchased across the bar. Chikito's Restaurant is situated within the same complex, split into three different sections. The Tapa's bar is beautifully furnished and has a distinctly Spanish theme to it.

*Morris Dancer Inn & Chikito's Restaurant*

As well as enjoying the food, customers may also just pop in for a quiet drink. As one would expect, there is a wide variety of Tapas to choose from to accompany your chosen drink. The restaurant is superbly furnished and seats up to 70 people. The menu is excellent and varied, and features English, continental and vegetarian dishes. Prices are very reasonable and the choice is enormous. In addition to the restaurant and bars, there is also a large function suite which caters for up to 120 people.

At Corkscrew Lane in **Hoofield** (turn off the A51 at the Bulls Head in Clotton, about three miles west of Tarporley), there is a unique nursery called **'The Old Cottage Gardens'**. Here you will find over 30 garden displays, including herbs, herbaceous, alpines, a nature trail alongside a 400-year-old hedge and a recreated meadow. The cottage itself was built between 1580 and 1620. It is timber framed, still the original size, and has walls of wattle and daub. Sadly, the thatched roof is no longer in existence and has been replaced.

'The Old Cottage Gardens' conjures up evocative pictures of bees gathering nectar from the old single Hollyhocks, and butterflies fluttering about and sipping from Honesty, Small Scabious, Buddleia, and the Autumn flowering Sedums. Dragonflies dart around with birds of different coloured hues in hot pursuit. The rich, lingering perfume of Valerian, Old Dianthus and Lavender chases and pervades, enticing you to stay and enjoy these delights a while longer.

*The Old Cottage Gardens*

As the sun sets and dusk descends over the Garden, the heavy scent of our favourite Honeysuckle, Lonicera Periclynum 'G.S. Thomas', becomes evident. Night scented Stocks, Sweet Rocket (Hesperis Matrionalis), night flowering Campion (Silene Nocturna) and 'Maiden's Bower' (Clematis Flammula) - all of these fill the air with their own uniquely fragrant cocktail for visitors to savour and remember during the bleak winter days and nights. Even winter can provide a breath of fresh air in 'The Old Cottage Gardens', as this is when the tiny Golden Winter Aconites are followed by the shy Snowdrops, who tend to hide their innermost beauty. The yellow heads of Helleborus Foetidus droop down as if to point to the Dwarf Iris in full flower. Later, the Globe Flower with its large, solid looking Yellow Buttercup flowers glows, and suddenly that corner with a dark foreboding shade becomes warmed and welcoming. Whenever you decide to visit, Carol and Ray Bailey will delight in sharing with you the insight which has recreated this wonderful world of flowers.

South of here, on the other side of the Shropshire Union Canal, is **Tattenhall.** The village has a fine church that was mainly rebuilt last century, but it has kept its old tower. The village high street has some particularly handsome houses, including a Jacobean Hall.

**Cheshire Farm Dairy Ice Cream** is truly a family day out with a difference, and even if you are not a lover of ice cream it really is a fascinating place to visit. Located in the picturesque Cheshire countryside, bordering the delightful village of Tattenhall, the farm is only two miles

253

from the ancient ruins of Beeston Castle and The Castle Workshops. The production of real dairy ice cream here uses the cream and milk from their own dairy herd, with no artificial ingredients. Established over the last few years, the farm has a marvellous selection of ice cream and sorbets, with over 30 flavours to choose from. The liqueur ice creams are especially luxurious.

Typical of any working farm in the Cheshire Plain, the cows are milked daily and can be viewed through the gallery window between 1.30 and 3.30 pm. Added to the attraction of seeing where the ice cream is produced, the public can see the new calves in their pens, and the fortunate few can witness a calf being born. Rabbits delight the younger visitors, and the planned play area will provide welcome exercise.

*Cheshire Farm Ice Cream*

Also on the site is Caroline's Pantry. Set in cosy surroundings and reminiscent of a farmhouse kitchen, the Pantry provides a tempting selection of home-made sandwiches, cakes and lunches, all freshly prepared. Open seven days a week, the afternoon teas are always a firm favourite, consisting of home-made scones with real clotted cream and strawberry jam.

The pantry also sells preserves and dairy produce, and of course, it is impossible to leave without one of the handy three quarter litres of superb ice cream. It is also possible to obtain a price list prior to visiting - just telephone (0829) 700995 for details.

To find **Goldbourne Manor,** we travelled four miles south of Chester on the A41 Whitchurch road, and just after Demon Tweeks Garage, we turned right into the driveway. We were delighted with our first impressions of the house. Anne and Robert Ikin are renowned for running a high class bed and breakfast facility here. The house is a fully modernised Victorian Country residence of great character, and once belonged to the Duke of Westminster. The quality of the accommodation is excellent, and the house itself has been renovated to a very high standard. It is situated in a delightful rural setting, which has an almost tangible air of peace and tranquility. Children are welcome, and there are swings and a slide for them to play on in the grounds.

*Goldbourne Manor*

**Eccleston,** close to Chester, was originally an estate village belonging to the Dukes of Westminster, though the original Eaton Hall, a glorious piece of Victorian neo-Gothic extravaganza, has been demolished, and a new hall has been built in modern style in the grounds.

Eccleston lies on the River Dee and is a popular destination for trip boats from Chester. The Victorian church was built by the first Duke of Westminster and his effigy is to be seen inside, together with that of his son, killed at Ypres in 1914. The son's memorial is an effigy in bronze standing by his horse. Lovely riverside footpaths lead from Eccleston into the centre of Chester, or up-river past the Eaton Hall estate.

**Aldford** has a beautiful iron bridge over the Dee, built by Thomas Telford. The remains of a Norman motte and bailey castle can be seen behind the church.

**Farndon** is another lovely border village on the Dee, overlooking the village of Holt in North Wales from its rocky outcrop. Farndon has lovely half-timbered houses and an attractive church which was used as a garrison in the Civil War, and one of its painted windows shows the Royalists of Cheshire, including pikemen and musketeers. John Speed, the famous Elizabethan map maker, was born in Farndon.

The two villages and two countries are linked by a beautiful medieval bridge, dating from the 14th century, with recesses above its buttresses to allow pedestrians to dodge the traffic. At the bottom of the hill by the bridge, there is now a picnic site with access to pleasant riverside walks along the banks of the Dee.

At **Stretton,** situated just south of the A534 between Farndon and Broxton, we were delighted to discover **Stretton Mill.** Set in glorious, peaceful countryside, this beautiful little water mill has been carefully restored and is now open to the public. The wooden mill machinery dates back to the 18th century and is the oldest in Cheshire. Visitors can enjoy guided tours of the mill where they will be given demonstrations of how grain is ground, and in the nearby stable block, fascinating displays and models reveal the mill's history and workings.

*Stretton Mill*

Stretton Mill is open Tuesdays to Sundays from 2 pm till 6 pm, from 1st March to 31st October. There is a shop and picnic area, and group visits are most welcome if booked in advance.

If you are within travelling distance of **Broxton** and feel the need for a drink, a bite to eat or somewhere to stay, we can thoroughly recommend a visit to **The Egerton Arms.** We are sure you will not be disappointed, as the pub, restaurant and accommodation is ideal for visitors wishing to relax and get away from it all. The Egerton Arms is closely situated to Stapely Water Gardens, Candle Workshops and miles of meandering canal walks, and it is within 15 minutes drive of the Historic City of Chester. It is ideally affordable for families with young children, and there are excellent facilities for young ones to play.

Whether you are staying at The Egerton for business or pleasure, you will be greeted by warm, friendly staff who do their best to please. Completely refurbished, the accommodation and restaurant facilities are superb. The bar, restaurant and bedrooms have been tastefully furnished, and no expense has been spared in recreating an atmosphere full of ambience and elegant Victorian charm.

The dining room can cater for up to 85 diners, and the menu is wide and varied and caters for the most discerning of tastes. The choice of starter can range from Smoked Salmon Cornets, Baked Mushrooms and Mexican Tortilla to Spicey Ribs and Wings. Black Pudding is a favourite starter - sliced, served on Basmati rice and coated with a pepper sauce, it is an unusual and imaginative way to begin a meal. Main courses range from Tandoori Chicken and Oriental Pork to the more familiar, such as Chicken Chasseur, Tournedos Rossini, Duckling and Peppered Steak. Fish dishes are also available and include Salmon in Herb Sauce, Dover Sole, Queen Scallops and Fillet of Plaice. Sandwiches, salads and a special childrens' menu are also on offer.

*The Egerton Arms*

The accommodation consists of two singles, one twin, two doubles and two family rooms. Every effort is made to accommodate the disabled, who are always welcome. The bedrooms are light and spacious, and complete with the usual modern conveniences. The Egerton Arms is located on the A41 Chester to Whitchurch road, centrally positioned between Chester, Nantwich and Wrexham.

**Malpas** is one of the most delightful old villages in Cheshire, though its Norman French name implies that it once lay in difficult border terrain - 'mal passage'. There was once a castle in the town, the seat of one of the Norman barons, the site of which can be seen behind the red sandstone church as a grassy green mound. There is an ancient village cross on steps, and some charming black and white cottages as well as elegant Georgian houses. In the 18th century, the village belonged to the Cholmondleys, who built the town's almshouses.

Visitors to this part of Cheshire and nearby Shropshire will appreciate the comfort and hospitality that the **Red Lion** at Malpas has to offer. Originally an old coaching inn, King James I was once a guest when it was a house in 1624. Malpas was considered to be a major stopping off place for traffic between London, Wales and Liverpool. Today's visitor will find nine bedrooms, which all have en-suite facilities. A relic to King James's visit remains in the bar. According to local tradition, customers must pay a penny to sit in 'The King's Chair', or else they must buy drinks for everybody who is in the bar. The impressive chair, made unusually of yew wood, was large enough to accommodate the fashionable doublets worn in the 17th century.

*The Red Lion*

The Red Lion is probably the oldest hostelry in the South of Cheshire, and is thought to date from the 13th century. At one time, the speedy Albion stage coach travelling from London to Liverpool made frequent visits, enabling travellers to stop and enjoy the friendly welcome and a much needed break. Today, The Red Lion is a pub full of character and charm, with a wealth of old panelling and low beams. Licensee Shelagh Lever and husband Bill offer a warm and friendly welcome to weary travellers and locals alike. A fine selection of bar food is served both at lunchtimes and in the evenings in the lounge bar. Just across the car park, there is a superb cottage which has excellent accommodation. It is full of character, and provides guests with every modern amenity.

*Cholmondeley Castle, Malpas*

# Reference Guide

to

Hotels, Guest Houses, Inns, Public Houses,

Self-catering Accommodation, Farm Accommodation,

Caravan and Camping Parks, Restaurants,

Riding Schools and Places of Interest

Details in this section are for guidance only.
For more information please contact the individual establishments
who will be only to pleased to help.

# Chapter 1 : Cottonopolis

## Inns & Public Houses

| MAP REF | NAME & ADDRESS | TEL. NO | PAGE NO |
|---------|----------------|---------|---------|
| 10 | Waggon & Horses<br>West Houghton | 0942<br>812273 | 12 |

## Hotels & Guest Houses

| MAP REF | NAME & ADDRESS | TEL. NO | PAGE NO |
|---------|----------------|---------|---------|
| 8 | Imperial Hotel<br>157 Hathersage Road<br>Manchester | 061<br>2256500 | 10 |
| 6 | Lennox Lea Hotel<br>Irlam Road<br>Sale | 061<br>9731764 | 23 |
| 1 | Morden Grange Guest House<br>15 Chadwick Street<br>Bolton | 0204<br>22000 | 14 |
| 7 | Springfield Hotel<br>Station Road<br>Marple | 061<br>4490721 | 19 |

## Restaurants

| MAP REF | NAME & ADDRESS | TEL. NO | PAGE NO |
|---------|----------------|---------|---------|
| 4 | Gallaghers Restaurant<br>Little Scotland<br>Blackrod | 0942<br>833101 | 15 |
| 8 | Ganders Go South<br>Barton Square<br>Manchester | 061 832<br>8360 | 8 |
| 9 | Harrisons<br>191 Woodsend Road<br>Flixton | 061 755<br>3008 | 24 |

## *Restaurants*

| MAP REF | NAME & ADDRESS | TEL. NO | PAGE NO |
|---------|----------------|---------|---------|
| 2 | New Langtrees Restaurant<br>Preston Road<br>Standish | 0257<br>423025 | 13 |

## *Farmhouse Accommodation*

| MAP REF | NAME & ADDRESS | TEL. NO | PAGE NO |
|---------|----------------|---------|---------|
| 3 | Needhams Farm<br>Werneth Low, Gee Cross<br>Nr Hyde | 061 368<br>4610 | 18 |

## *Places of Interest*

| MAP REF | NAME & ADDRESS | TEL. NO | PAGE NO |
|---------|----------------|---------|---------|
| 5 | Bramall Hall<br>Bramall Park<br>Bramall | 061 485<br>3708 | 20 |
| 11 | Dunham Massey Hall<br>Altrincham<br>Cheshire | 061 941<br>1025 | 22 |

# Chapter 2 : East Lancashire

## Inns & Public Houses

| MAP REF | NAME & ADDRESS | TEL. NO | PAGE NO |
|---------|----------------|---------|---------|
| 1 | Cavendish Arms<br>Brindle<br>Nr Chorley | 0254<br>852912 | 44 |
| 11 | Herders Inn<br>Lancashire Moor Road<br>Nr Colne | 0282<br>863443 | 36 |
| 4 | Hole In The Wall Inn<br>Foulridge<br>Colne | 0282<br>863568 | 33 |
| 7 | Old Rosin's Inn<br>Pick Up Bank<br>Hoddlesden | 0254<br>771264 | 45 |

## Hotels & Guest Houses

| MAP REF | NAME & ADDRESS | TEL. NO | PAGE NO |
|---------|----------------|---------|---------|
| 11 | Crown Hotel<br>Albert Road<br>Colne | 0282<br>863580 | 36 |
| 8 | Fernbank Guest House<br>Bolton Road, Anderton<br>Chorley | 0257<br>483441 | 48 |
| 12 | Gaghills House Hotel<br>Waterfoot<br>Rossendale | 0706<br>830359 | 39 |
| 2 | Malt Shovel Hotel<br>Clifton Farm Estate<br>Burnley | 0282<br>30920 | 37 |
| 10 | Monks House<br>5 Manchester Road<br>Barnoldswick | 0282<br>814423 | 34 |
| 6 | Mytton Fold Farm Hotel<br>Langho<br>Blackburn | 0254<br>240662 | 32 |

## Hotels & Guest Houses

| MAP REF | NAME & ADDRESS | TEL. NO | PAGE NO |
|---------|----------------|---------|---------|
| 14 | Wytha Farm<br>Rimmington<br>Clitheroe | 0200<br>445295 | 35 |

## Restaurants

| MAP REF | NAME & ADDRESS | TEL. NO | PAGE NO |
|---------|----------------|---------|---------|
| 10 | Genevieve<br>7 Station Road<br>Barnoldswick | 0282<br>813572 | 35 |
| 3 | May House Restaurant<br>208 Preston New Road<br>Blackburn | 0254<br>53160 | 42 |

## Places Of Interest

| MAP REF | NAME & ADDRESS | TEL. NO | PAGE NO |
|---------|----------------|---------|---------|
| 8 | Astley Hall<br>Astley Park<br>Chorley | 02572<br>62166 | 47 |
| 10 | Doug Moore (Boatbuilders)<br>Kelbrook Road<br>Barnoldswick | 0282<br>815883 | 34 |
| 9 | Moons Mill<br>47 Cann Bridge Street<br>Higher Walton | 0772<br>628036 | 43 |
| 5 | Valley Aquatics<br>Flip Road<br>Haslingden | 0706<br>228960 | 40 |
| 13 | Weavers Cottage<br>Rawtenstall<br>Rossendale | 0706<br>229937 | 39 |

# Chapter 3 : Lancaster & The Forest Of Bowland

## Inns & Public Houses

| MAP REF | NAME & ADDRESS | TEL. NO | PAGE NO |
|---------|----------------|---------|---------|
| 2 | Corporation Arms<br>Longridge<br>Nr Preston | 0772<br>782644 | 73 |
| 6 | The Royal Kings Arms<br>Market Street<br>Lancaster | 0524<br>32451 | 56 |

## Hotels & Guest Houses

| MAP REF | NAME & ADDRESS | TEL. NO | PAGE NO |
|---------|----------------|---------|---------|
| 9 | Brickhouse Hotel<br>Chipping<br>Nr Preston | 0995<br>61316 | 72 |
| 1 | Brooklyn Guest House<br>32 Pimlico Road<br>Clitheroe | 0200<br>28268 | 65 |
| 6 | Farmers Arms Hotel<br>Penny Street<br>Lancaster | 0524<br>36368 | 58 |
| 12 | Hodder Bridge Hotel<br>Chaigley<br>Nr Clitheroe | 0254<br>86216 | 70 |
| 5 | Harrop Fold Country Hotel<br>Bolton By Boland<br>Clitheroe | 02007<br>600 | 63 |
| 13 | Meadow Side<br>Knowle Green<br>Nr Longridge | 0254<br>878325 | 74 |
| 11 | Moorcock Inn<br>Titterington Brow<br>Waddington | 0200<br>22333 | 69 |
| 14 | Brown Leaves Hotel<br>Copster Green<br>Longridge<br>Preston | 0254<br>249523 | 75 |

# Hotels & Guest Houses

| MAP REF | NAME & ADDRESS | TEL. NO | PAGE NO |
|---------|----------------|---------|---------|
| 1 | Old Post House<br>King Street<br>Clitheroe | 0200<br>22025 | 65 |
| 10 | Parrock Head Hotel<br>Woodhouse Lane<br>Slaidburn | 0200<br>6614 | 62 |
| 8 | Scarthwaite Country Hotel<br>The Crook 'O' Lune<br>Caton | 0524<br>770267 | 61 |

# Restaurants

| MAP REF | NAME & ADDRESS | TEL. NO | PAGE NO |
|---------|----------------|---------|---------|
| 6 | Elliots<br>64 Market Street<br>Lancaster | 0524<br>36092 | 57 |
| 3 | Mitton Hall<br>Bilsborrow<br>Nr Preston | 0995<br>40010 | 67 |

# Self Catering Accommodation

| MAP REF | NAME & ADDRESS | TEL. NO | PAGE NO |
|---------|----------------|---------|---------|
| 1 | Red Rose Cottages<br>1a Newmarket Street<br>Clitheroe | 0200<br>27310 | 66 |

# Farmhouse Accommodation

| MAP REF | NAME & ADDRESS | TEL. NO | PAGE NO |
|---------|----------------|---------|---------|
| 5 | Baygate Farm<br>Holden<br>Bolton By Bowland | 02007<br>643 | 63 |
| 7 | Charnley House<br>Preston Road<br>Longridge | 0772<br>782800 | 75 |
| 4 | Greenbank Farmhouse<br>Over Wyresdale<br>Dolphinholme | 0524<br>792063 | 59 |

# *Farmhouse Accommodation*

| MAP REF | NAME & ADDRESS | TEL. NO | PAGE NO |
|---------|----------------|---------|---------|
| 9 | Hough Clough Farmhouse<br>Houghclough Lane<br>Chipping | 09956<br>272 | 73 |
| 3 | Mitton Green Barn<br>Great Mitton<br>Whalley | 0254<br>86673 | 68 |
| 10 | Pages Farm<br>Woodhouse Lane<br>Slaidburn | 02006<br>205 | 61 |

# Chapter 4 : North Lancashire

## Hotels & Guest Houses

| MAP REF | NAME & ADDRESS | TEL. NO | PAGE NO |
|---------|----------------|---------|---------|
| 6 | The Bower<br>Yealand Conyers<br>Carnforth | 0524<br>734585 | 87 |
| 4 | Castle Hotel<br>Main Street<br>Hornby | 0524<br>21204 | 84 |
| 7 | Globe Hotel<br>Overton<br>Nr Moreeambe | 0524<br>71228 | 92 |
| 8 | Grosvenor Hotel<br>Sandylands Promenade<br>Morecambe | 0524<br>412606 | 90 |
| 1 | Middle Holly Cottage<br>Forton<br>Nr Preston | 0772<br>749383 | 93 |
| 3 | Pine Lake Motel<br>Carnforth<br>Lancs | 0524<br>736191 | 86 |
| 5 | Stonegate Guest House<br>The Promenade<br>Arnside | 0524<br>761171 | 89 |

## Farmhouse Accommodation

| MAP REF | NAME & ADDRESS | TEL. NO | PAGE NO |
|---------|----------------|---------|---------|
| 7 | Trailholme Farmhouse<br>Overton<br>Nr Lancaster | 0524<br>71258 | 92 |

## Places Of Interest

| MAP REF | NAME & ADDRESS | TEL. NO | PAGE NO |
|---------|----------------|---------|---------|
| 2 | Wood 'n' Wool Miniatures<br>Silverdale<br>Nr Carnforth | 0524<br>701532 | 88 |

# Chapter 5 : Lancashire Coast & The Wirral

## Inns & Public Houses

| MAP REF | NAME & ADDRESS | TEL. NO | PAGE NO |
|---------|----------------|---------|---------|
| 8 | The Martin Inn<br>Martin Lane<br>Burscough | 0704<br>895788 | 120 |
| 3 | Rigbye Arms<br>High Moor<br>Wrightington | 02576<br>2354 | 116 |
| 6 | Robin Hood Inn<br>Mawdesley<br>Nr Ormskirk | 0704<br>822275 | 118 |

## Hotels & Guest Houses

| MAP REF | NAME & ADDRESS | TEL. NO | PAGE NO |
|---------|----------------|---------|---------|
| 8 | Brandreth Barn<br>Burscough<br>Nr Ormskirk | 0704<br>893510 | 119 |
| 19 | Chester Court Hotel<br>48 Hoole Road<br>Chester | 0244<br>320779 | 134 |
| 1 | Olde Duncombe House<br>Bilsborrow<br>Preston | 0995<br>40336 | 107 |
| 17 | Phoenix Hotel<br>Sefton Park<br>Liverpool | 051 727<br>4754 | 127 |
| 20 | Rake Hall<br>Little Stanney<br>Cheshire | | 132 |
| 2 | Smithy Guest House<br>Leyland<br>Preston | 0772<br>455832 | 113 |

# Hotels & Guest Houses

| MAP REF | NAME & ADDRESS | TEL. NO | PAGE NO |
|---------|----------------|---------|---------|
| 9 | Springfield House Hotel<br>Pilling<br>Nr Preston | 0253<br>790301 | 105 |

# Restaurants

| MAP REF | NAME & ADDRESS | TEL. NO | PAGE NO |
|---------|----------------|---------|---------|
| 16 | The Cottage<br>Marton<br>Blackpool | 0253<br>64081 | 102 |
| 11 | The Italian Orchard<br>Broughton<br>Nr Preston | 0772<br>861240 | 109 |
| 16 | L'Alouette<br>Aigburth<br>Liverpool | | 128 |
| 9 | The Old Ship<br>Pilling<br>Preston | 0253<br>790216 | 106 |
| 13 | Pegotty's<br>Churchtown<br>Southport | 0704<br>26676 | 124 |
| 7 | Smugglers Cove<br>Cleveleys<br>Nr Blackpool | 0253<br>867222 | 103 |
| 10 | Wesley House<br>Lostock Hall<br>Preston | 0772<br>627557 | 111 |

# Farmhouse Accommodation

| MAP REF | NAME & ADDRESS | TEL. NO | PAGE NO |
|---------|----------------|---------|---------|
| 2 | Calverts Farm<br>Ulnes Walton<br>Leyland | 0772<br>433116 | 114 |
| 4 | Swarbrick Hall Farm<br>Weeton<br>Nr Kirkham | 0253<br>836465 | 102 |

## Caravan & Camping Sites

| MAP REF | NAME & ADDRESS | TEL. NO | PAGE NO |
|---------|----------------|---------|---------|
| 6 | Abbey Farm Caravan Park<br>Abbey Lane, Off Dark Lane<br>Ormskirk | 0695<br>572686 | 123 |

## Places Of Interest

| MAP REF | NAME & ADDRESS | TEL. NO | PAGE NO |
|---------|----------------|---------|---------|
| 12 | Bygone Times<br>Times House, The Green<br>Eccleston | 0257<br>453780 | 115 |
| 18 | National Museums<br>& Galleries<br>Liverpool | 051<br>207 0001 | 131 |
| 10 | Turbary House<br>Whitestake<br>Preston | 0772<br>36664 | 111 |
| 5 | West Lancs. Council<br>52 Derby Street<br>Ormskirk | 0695<br>577177 | 123 |
| 2 | Worden Arts & Craft Centre<br>Worden Park<br>Leyland | 0772<br>455908 | 112 |

# Chapter 6 : North Cheshire

## *Inns & Public Houses*

| MAP REF | NAME & ADDRESS | TEL. NO | PAGE NO |
|---|---|---|---|
| 2 | Forest View Inn<br>Gallowsclough Lane<br>Oakmere | 0606<br>882860 | 174 |
| 6 | George & Dragon<br>High Street<br>Great Budworth | 0606<br>891317 | 158 |
| 1 | Old Broken Cross<br>Rudheath<br>Northwich | 0606<br>42420 | 168 |
| 16 | Red Bull<br>The Brow<br>Kingsley | 0928<br>88097 | 175 |
| 20 | Railway Hotel<br>Heatley<br>Lymm | 0925<br>752742 | 150 |
| 13 | Salt Barge<br>Ollershaw Lane<br>Marston | 0606<br>43064 | 170 |
| 8 | The Smoker<br>Plumley<br>Nr Knutsford | 0565<br>722338 | 160 |
| 12 | Turners Arms Hotel<br>Ingersley Road<br>Bollington | 0625<br>573864 | 151 |
| 4 | Waterside Tavern<br>Wincham Wharf<br>Lostock Gralam | 0606<br>48354/<br>48581 | 163 |
| 22 | White Lion<br>Manley Road<br>Alvanley | 0928<br>722949 | 178 |

## *Hotels & Guest Houses*

| MAP REF | NAME & ADDRESS | TEL. NO | PAGE NO |
|---------|----------------|---------|---------|
| 1 | Ayreshire Guest House<br>Winnington Lane<br>Northwich | 0606<br>74871 | 168 |
| 21 | Barratwich<br>Cuddington<br>Northwich | 0606<br>882412 | 172 |
| 19 | Beechwood House<br>206 Wallerscote Road<br>Weaverham | 0606<br>852123 | 172 |
| 1 | Friendly Floatel<br>London Road<br>Northwich | 0606<br>44443 | 167 |
| 10 | Hartford Hall Hotel<br>School Lane<br>Hartford | 0606<br>75711 | 171 |
| 24 | Nunsmere Hall Hotel<br>Tarporley Road<br>Sandiway | 0606<br>889100 | 173 |
| 15 | Old Hall Hotel<br>Main Street<br>Frodsham | 0928<br>32052 | 177 |
| 3 | Pickmere House Hotel<br>Pickmere<br>Knutsford | 0565<br>893433 | 160 |
| 25 | Springfield Guest House<br>Chester Road<br>Oakmere | 0606<br>882538 | 181 |
| 14 | Victoria Hotel<br>Stockton Heath<br>Warrington | 0925<br>63060 | 145 |

# Restaurants

| MAP REF | NAME & ADDRESS | TEL. NO | PAGE NO |
|---|---|---|---|
| 7 | Lymm Bistro<br>16 Bridgewater Street<br>Lymm | 0925 75<br>4852 | 146 |
| 15 | Rowlands<br>31 Church Street<br>Frodsham | 0928<br>33361 | 177 |
| 7 | Statham Lodge Hotel<br>Warrington Road<br>Statham | 0925<br>752204 | 149 |

# Caravan & Camping Parks

| MAP REF | NAME & ADDRESS | TEL. NO | PAGE NO |
|---|---|---|---|
| 2 | Forest View Inn<br>Gallowsclough Lane<br>Oakmere | 0606<br>882860 | 174 |

# Farmhouse Accomodation

| MAP REF | NAME & ADDRESS | TEL. NO | PAGE NO |
|---|---|---|---|
| 23 | Tattondale Farm<br>Ashley Road<br>Knutsford | 0565<br>54692 | 155 |

# Places Of Interest

| MAP REF | NAME & ADDRESS | TEL. NO | PAGE NO |
|---|---|---|---|
| 7 | Actons Of Lymm<br>231 Higher Lane<br>Lymm | 0925<br>756370 | 148 |
| 1 | Arley Hall & Gardens<br>Nr Northwich<br>Cheshire | 0565<br>777353 | 156 |
| 8 | Ascol Drive Nursery<br>Ascol Drive<br>Plumley | 0606<br>47694 | 163 |
| 7 | Casa Maria<br>1 Church Road<br>Lymm | 0925<br>757838 | 146 |

# Places Of Interest

| MAP REF | NAME & ADDRESS | TEL. NO | PAGE NO |
|---------|----------------|---------|---------|
| 8 | Coppelia Antiques<br>Plumley<br>Knutsford | 0565<br>812197 | 162 |
| 13 | Groundwork Discovery<br>Lion Salt Works<br>Ollershaw Lane, Marston | 0606<br>40555 | 169 |
| 18 | High Legh Garden Centre<br>High Legh<br>Knutsford | 092575<br>6991 | 152 |
| 17 | Hill Top Equestrian Centre<br>Newton-by-Frodsham<br>Cheshire | 0928<br>88235 | 176 |
| 15 | Kingsley Mills<br>Nr Frodsham<br>Cheshire | 0928<br>88210 | 178 |
| 11 | Norton Priory Museum<br>Tudor Manor Park<br>Runcorn | 0928<br>569895 | 143 |
| 1 | Salt Museum<br>162 London Road<br>Northwich | 0606<br>41331 | 166 |
| 23 | Tattondale Carriages<br>Ashley Road<br>Knutsford | 0565<br>650618 | 154 |
| 23 | Tatton Park<br>Knutsford<br>Cheshire | 0565<br>654822 | 153 |

## *Places Of Interest*

| MAP REF | NAME & ADDRESS | TEL. NO | PAGE NO |
|---------|----------------|---------|---------|
| 7 | The Wharfage Boat Co<br>Warrington Lane<br>Lymm | 092575<br>4900 | 147 |
| 9 | Yew Tree Farm Equestrian<br>Centre, Budworth Road<br>Aston by Budworth | 0565<br>894100 | 159 |

# Chapter 7: Cheshire Peak & Plains

## Inns & Public Houses

| MAP REF | NAME & ADDRESS | TEL. NO | PAGE NO |
|---------|----------------|---------|---------|
| 2 | Chapel House Inn<br>Broad Oak Lane<br>Mobberley | 0565<br>872391 | 193 |
| 9 | Davenport Arms<br>Manchester Road<br>Marton | 0260<br>224269 | 211 |
| 2 | Railway Hotel<br>Station Road<br>Mobberley | 0565<br>873155 | 194 |

## Hotels & Guest Houses

| MAP REF | NAME & ADDRESS | TEL. NO | PAGE NO |
|---------|----------------|---------|---------|
| 1 | Fernbank Guest House<br>Handforth<br>Wilmslow | 0625<br>523729 | 198 |
| 4 | Heatherfield Hotel<br>Tabley Road<br>Knutsford | 0565<br>633428 | 191 |
| 2 | Laburnum Cottage<br>Knutsford Road<br>Mobberley | 0565<br>872464 | 195 |
| 3 | The Laurels<br>Brick Bank Lane<br>Allostock | 0477<br>33151 | 214 |
| 4 | Longview Hotel<br>Manchester Road<br>Knutsford | 0565<br>632119 | 190 |
| 3 | Oak Cottage Motel<br>Vale Royal<br>Allostock | 0565<br>722470 | 214 |
| 11 | Tiree<br>5 Middlewich Road<br>Cranage | 0477<br>33716 | 216 |

# Hotels & Guest Houses

| MAP REF | NAME & ADDRESS | TEL. NO | PAGE NO |
|---|---|---|---|
| 7 | Prospect House Hotel<br>Knutsford Road<br>Alderley | 0565<br>872034 | 196 |

# Restaurants

| MAP REF | NAME & ADDRESS | TEL. NO | PAGE NO |
|---|---|---|---|
| 14 | The Crown Inn<br>111 Main Road<br>Goostrey | 0477<br>32128 | 215 |
| 12 | Yellow Broom Restaurant<br>Twemlow Green<br>Nr Holmes Chapel | 0477<br>33289 | 216 |

# Farmhouse Accomodation

| MAP REF | NAME & ADDRESS | TEL. NO | PAGE NO |
|---|---|---|---|
| 10 | Rough Hey Farm<br>Gawsworth<br>Macclesfield | 02605<br>2296 | 209 |
| 13 | Sandhole Farm<br>Hulme Walfield<br>Congleton | 0260<br>224419 | 206 |
| 9 | Sandpit Farm<br>Messuage Lane<br>Marton | 0260<br>224254 | 210 |

# Places Of Interest

| MAP REF | NAME & ADDRESS | TEL. NO | PAGE NO |
|---|---|---|---|
| 2 | Barnshaw Smithy<br>Pepper Street<br>Mobberley | 056587<br>3743 | 191 |
| 9 | Church Farm Produce<br>A34, Marton<br>Nr Macclesfield | 0260<br>2243441 | 212 |

# *Places Of Interest*

| MAP REF | NAME & ADDRESS | TEL. NO | PAGE NO |
|---|---|---|---|
| 4 | Fiddly Bits<br>24 King Street<br>Knutsford | 0565<br>51119 | 189 |
| 2 | Hillside Ornamental Fowl<br>Damson Lane<br>Mobberley | 0565<br>873282 | 192 |
| 23 | Knutsford Heritage Centre<br>Tatton Street<br>Knutsford | 0565<br>653650 | 188 |
| 8 | Longden Workshop<br>2 Shaw Street<br>Macclesfield | 0625<br>433953 | 192 |
| 6 | Lyme View Marina<br>Four Lane Ends Farm<br>Wood Lane East, Adlington | 0625<br>874638 | 199 |
| 9 | Marton Heath Trout Pool<br>Pikelow Farm, School Lane<br>Marton | 0260<br>224231 | 210 |
| 5 | Prince Studio<br>Prince Road<br>Higher Poynton | 0625<br>876476 | 200 |

# Chapter 8 : South Cheshire

## Inns & Public Houses

| MAP REF | NAME & ADDRESS | TEL. NO | PAGE NO |
|---------|----------------|---------|---------|
| 3 | Black Lion<br>29 Welsh Row<br>Nantwich | 0270<br>629700 | 241 |
| 13 | The Dusty Miller<br>Wrenbury<br>Nr Nantwich | 0270<br>780537 | 237 |
| 23 | Egerton Arms<br>Whitchurch Road<br>Broxton | 0829<br>782241 | 256 |
| 3 | Frog & Ferret<br>4 Oat Market<br>Nantwich | 0270<br>629324 | 240 |
| 11 | Morris Dancer Inn<br>Chester Road<br>Kelsall, Nr Tarporley | 0829<br>51291 | 252 |
| 3 | The Red Cow<br>Beam Street<br>Nantwich | 0270<br>628581 | 239 |
| 22 | The Royal Oak<br>Mair Road<br>Worleston | 0270<br>624138 | 244 |

## Hotels & Guest Houses

| MAP REF | NAME & ADDRESS | TEL. NO | PAGE NO |
|---------|----------------|---------|---------|
| 21 | The Folly<br>Middlewich Road<br>Minshull Vernon | 0270<br>71244 | 232 |
| 6 | Old Hall Hotel<br>Newcastle Road<br>Sandbach | 0270<br>761221 | 226 |
| 2 | The Red Lion<br>Old Hall Street<br>Malpas | 0948<br>860368 | 258 |

# Hotels & Guest Houses

| MAP REF | NAME & ADDRESS | TEL. NO | PAGE NO |
|---------|----------------|---------|---------|
| 7 | Willington Hall Hotel<br>Willington<br>Tarporley | 0829<br>52321 | 249 |
| 12 | Goldbounre Manor<br>Platts Lane<br>Hatton Heath | 0829<br>70310 | 254 |

# Farmhouse Accomodation

| MAP REF | NAME & ADDRESS | TEL. NO | PAGE NO |
|---------|----------------|---------|---------|
| 17 | Green Farm<br>Deans Lane<br>Balterley | 0270<br>820214 | 234 |
| 10 | Forge Mill Farm<br>Warmingham<br>Middlewich | 0270<br>77204 | 226 |
| 15 | Laburnum House Farm<br>Hearns Lane, Faddiley<br>Nantwich | 0270<br>74378 | 245 |
| 18 | Lea Farm<br>Wrinehill Road<br>Wybunbury, Nantwich | 0270<br>841429 | 233 |
| 14 | Little Heath Farm<br>Audlem<br>Nr Crewe | 0270<br>811324 | 235 |
| 13 | Sproston Hill Farm<br>Wrenbury<br>Nr Nantwich | 0270<br>780241 | 237 |
| 3 | Stoke Grange Farm<br>Chester Road<br>Nantwich | 0270<br>625525 | 243 |

# Restaurants

| MAP REF | NAME & ADDRESS | TEL. NO | PAGE NO |
|---------|----------------|---------|---------|
| 19 | Brighton Belle<br>Middlewich Road<br>Winsford | 0606<br>593292 | 229 |
| 11 | Chikito Restaurant<br>Kelsall<br>Nr Tarporley | 0829<br>51291 | 252 |
| 6 | La Casa Vecchia<br>4 Old Market Square<br>Sandbach | 0270<br>761077 | 225 |
| 23 | Egerton Arms<br>Whitchurch Road<br>Broxton | 0829<br>782241 | 256 |

# Places Of Interest

| MAP REF | NAME & ADDRESS | TEL. NO | PAGE NO |
|---------|----------------|---------|---------|
| 8 | Cheshire Farm Ice Cream<br>Newton Lane<br>Tattenhalll | 0829<br>70995 | 253 |
| 9 | Cheshire Herbs<br>Little Budworth<br>Nr Tarporley | 0829<br>760578 | 230 |
| 4 | Cheshire Workshops<br>Burwardsley<br>Nr Chester | 0829<br>70401 | 247 |
| 3 | Cotman Gallery<br>126 Hospital Street<br>Nantwich | 0270<br>624567 | 242 |
| 11 | Eddisbury Fruit Farm<br>Yeld Lane<br>Kelsall, Tarporley | 0829<br>51300 | 251 |
| 5 | The Firs Pottery<br>Sheppenhall Lane<br>Aston, Nantwich | 0270<br>780345 | 236 |

# *Places Of Interest*

| MAP REF | NAME & ADDRESS | TEL. NO | PAGE NO |
|---------|----------------|---------|---------|
| 6 | Godfrey C Williams & Son<br>Corner House<br>The Square, Sandbach | 0270<br>762817 | 224 |
| 7 | Jardinerie Garden Centre<br>Forest Road<br>Tarporley | 0829<br>760433 | 250 |
| 3 | Magpie Crafts<br>44 Hospital Street<br>Nantwich | 0270<br>629808 | 242 |
| 20 | Old Cottage Gardens<br>Corkscrew Lane<br>Hoofield, Tattenhall | 0829<br>24596 | 252 |
| 16 | Snugburys Icecream Farm<br>Park Farm<br>Hurleston, Nantwich | 0270<br>624830 | 243 |
| 10 | Warmington Craft Workshops<br>The Mill<br>Warmingham, Nr Sandbach | 0270<br>77366 | 227 |
| 17 | Green Farm<br>Deans Lane<br>Balterley | 0270<br>820214 | 234 |
| 10 | Forge Mill Farm<br>Warmingham<br>Middlewich | 0270<br>77204 | 226 |
| 15 | Laburnum House Farm<br>Hearns Lane, Faddiley<br>Nantwich | 0270<br>74378 | 245 |
| 18 | Lea Farm<br>Wrinehill Road<br>Wybunbury, Nantwich | 0270<br>841429 | 233 |
| 14 | Little Heath Farm<br>Audlem<br>Nr Crewe | 0270<br>811324 | 235 |
| 13 | Sproston Hill Farm<br>Wrenbury<br>Nr Nantwich | 0270<br>780241 | 237 |

## Places Of Interest

| MAP REF | NAME & ADDRESS | TEL. NO | PAGE NO |
|---------|----------------|---------|---------|
| 3 | Stoke Grange Farm<br>Chester Road<br>Nantwich | 0270<br>625525 | 243 |
| 1 | Stretton Mill<br>162 London Road<br>Northwich | 0606<br>41331 | 256 |

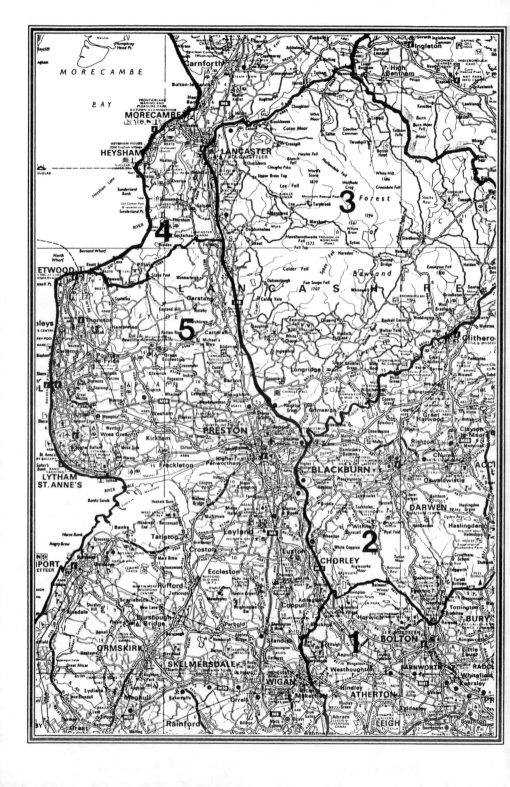

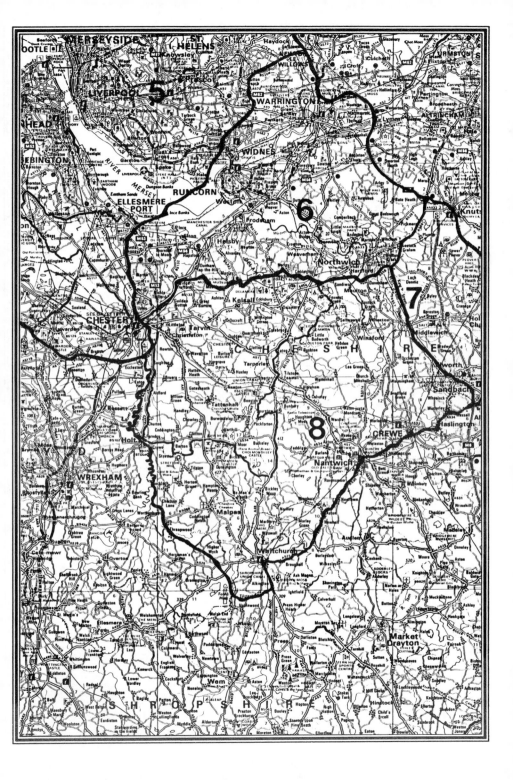

# Notes

You may like to use this page to make your own notes.

# Notes

You may like to use this page to make your own notes.

# Notes

You may like to use this page to make your own notes.

# *Notes*

You may like to use this page to make your own notes.

# Notes

You may like to use this page to make your own notes.

# THE
# HIDDEN PLACES

If you would like to have any of the titles currently available in this series, please complete this coupon and send to:

M & M Publishing Ltd
Tryfan House, Warwick Drive
Hale, Altrincham
Cheshire, WA15 9EA

| | |
|---|---|
| Somerset, Avon and Dorset | £ 5.90 inc. p&p |
| Norfolk and Suffolk | £ 5.90 inc. p&p |
| Yorkshire South, East andWest | £ 5.90 inc. p&p |
| Devon and Cornwall | £ 5.90 inc. p&p |
| North Yorkshire | £ 5.90 inc. p&p |
| Cumbria | £ 5.90 inc. p&p |
| Southern and Central Scotland | £ 5.90 inc. p&p |
| Sussex | £ 5.90 inc. p&p |
| Hampshire and the Isle of Wight | £ 5.90 inc. p&p |
| Gloucestershire & Wiltshire | £ 5.90 inc. p&p |
| Nottinghamshire, Derbyshire & Lincolnshire | £ 5.90 inc. p&p |
| Oxfordshire, Buckinghamshire & Bedfordshire | £ 5.90 inc. p&p |
| Lancashire & Cheshire | £ 5.90 inc. p&p |
| Set of any Five | £ 25.90 inc. p&p |

*Please tick to receive further information about future titles*

NAME..................................................................................................

ADDRESS............................................................................................

............................................................................................................

TEL. No. (Daytime)............................................................................

Please make cheques/postal orders payable to: M & M Publishing Ltd
Access/Visa/Barclaycard (please delete)
Card No.

Expiry date.................................. Signature...................................